# The Colorado State Capitol

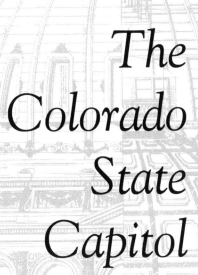

# The Colorado State Capitol

## History, Politics, Preservation

## Derek R. Everett

UNIVERSITY PRESS OF COLORADO

© 2005 by the University Press of Colorado

Published by the University Press of Colorado
245 Century Circle, Suite 202
Louisville, Colorado 80027

The University Press of Colorado is a proud member of
the Association of University Presses.

The University Press of Colorado is a cooperative publishing enterprise supported, in part,
by Adams State University, Colorado State University, Fort Lewis College, Metropolitan
State University of Denver, Regis University, University of Colorado, University of Northern
Colorado, Utah State University, and Western State Colorado University.

∞ This paper meets the requirements of the ANSI/NISO Z39.48-1992 (Permanence of Paper)

ISBN: 978-0-87081-790-8 (cloth)
ISBN: 978-1-60732-905-3 (pbk)

Library of Congress Cataloging-in-Publication Data

Everett, Derek R.
  The Colorado State Capitol : history, politics, preservation / Derek R. Everett.
     p. cm.
  Includes bibliographical references and index.
   ISBN 0-87081-790-6 (hardcover : alk. paper) — ISBN: 978-1-60732-905-3 (pbk : alk. paper)
   1. Colorado State Capitol (Denver, Colo.)—History. 2. Denver (Colo.)—Buildings,
structures, etc. 3. Historic buildings—Conservation and restoration—Colorado—Denver. 4.
Colorado—Politics and government. I. Title.
  F784.D48C375 2005
  978.8'83—dc22
                                                              2004029433

Let's to the Capitol,
And carry with us ears and eyes for th'time,
But hearts for the event.

—Junius Brutus, from Shakespeare's<br>
*Coriolanus,* Act II, Scene I

In our advanced American civilization there need be no apprehension that the Capitol building of Colorado will not stand, a handsome and stately structure, the admiration of future ages.

—Elijah E. Myers, 1886

# Contents

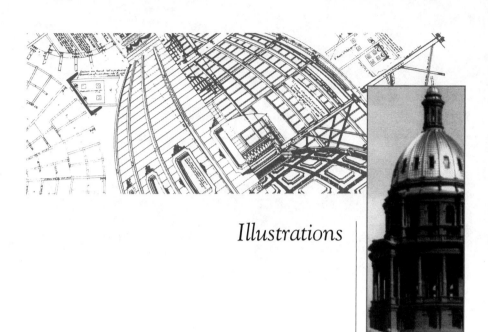

# Illustrations

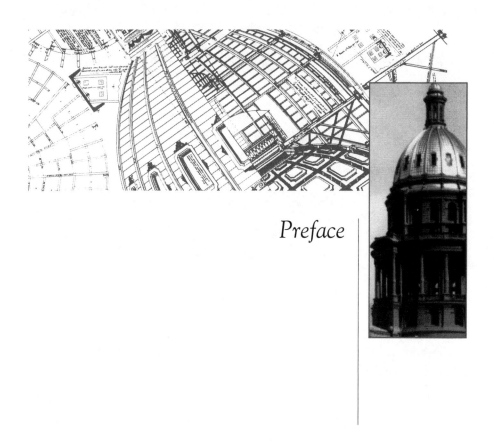

# Preface

I SUPPOSE THAT IN MANY WAYS THIS BOOK BEGAN during spring break in 1989 when my parents and I played tourists in our own backyard, visiting places like the Denver Zoo, the Forney Museum, and the Colorado State Capitol. Only a few elements of that first trip to the statehouse stick out in my mind, but like most children who tour the building I remember best the seemingly endless climb up the ninety-three stairs to the dome observation deck. Gaping in amazement at Denver and the mountains and plains beyond from the opulent capitol, I fell in love with the building. Little did that third grader know where his first visit to the statehouse would eventually take him.

In the spring of 1997, as I finished my junior year in high school, my parents encouraged me to find a respectable summer job, and I got the idea of serving as a tour guide at the capitol. After an interview with coordinator Edna Pelzmann, conducted in the office she still promises me she'll clean up one of these days, the good folks at Legislative Council signed me on as a guide. For the next five summers I spent five days a week giving tours and researching the statehouse for myself and my colleagues. Over the years I gathered reams of information about the building, inspiring my good friend and fellow guide Lew Hopkins to nickname me "the Great and Wise Historian of the Colorado State Capitol." I wanted to provide a more complete narrative of the statehouse's history than any I could find, and I used college opportunities to collect more tidbits about the edifice and compile them into a sensible story. Two works of scholarship emerged from that effort, a paper written for the Honors Program at Western State College in 2001 and my master's thesis at Colorado State University in 2003. After I passed my final M.A. examinations, my committee enthusiastically recommended I explore the possibility of publishing the hefty tome. Almost a year and several substantial edits later, the University Press of Colorado graciously approved my manuscript, and this book marks the culmination, but not the end, of my relationship with the capitol.

Just as the story that follows often revolves around personalities, I must thank a number of individuals for their help and encouragement. From my collegiate experience: Beth Avery, Francene Czillinger, Barry Daniel, Paul Edwards, Nancy Gauss, Wally Lewis, Lavonne Maness, Patrick Muckleroy, Jim Stewart, Heather Thiessen-Reily, and Duane Vandenbusche at Western State College; John Albright, Kelly Barlow, Heather Craig, Mark Fiege, Cynthia Rand, John Straayer, Frank Towers, Stephen Webb, and my exceptional friends in the Office of Conference Services and ACCED-International at Colorado State University; and Elliott West, Jeannie Whayne, my fellow disciples Julie Courtwright and Jason Pierce, the Department of History, the Fulbright College of Arts and Sciences, and the Graduate School at the University of Arkansas. From my research stages: Laura Amman at the Beulah quarry; Martha Campbell at the Colorado State Supreme Court library; Jim Cappa of the Colorado Geological Survey; Lance Christensen, Elena Cline, and George Orlowski at the Colorado State Archives; Barbara Dey, Caryl Klein, Rebecca Lintz, and Meg Van Ness at the Colorado Historical Society; Gus Grosland at the Gunnison Pioneer Museum; Rheba Massey at the Fort Collins Public Library; Elinor Packard at the Golden Pioneer Museum; Terri Ross at the Indiana State Supreme Court Law Library; and Coi Drummond-Gehrig and Phil Panum at the Denver Public Library. I am unable to adequately express my appreciation to Sandy Crooms, Laura Furney, Michelle McIrvin, Dan Pratt, and Darrin Pratt, the enthusiastic staff of the University Press of Colorado who guided this project to fruition, as well as my reviewers Charles Goodsell and Ron James and copyeditor Cheryl Carnahan.

Many individuals at the capitol merit special recognition. Edna Pelzmann, the manager of visitor services who first hired me in 1997, stopped being my boss years ago but will always remain my good friend. I also greatly appreciate the wisdom and assistance of Barb Espinoza and Mike Garcia of the Colorado State Patrol. Members of the tour staff with whom I worked also deserve my thanks, including Olga Elena Bashbush, Bessie Boyd, Dave Dean, Linda Dean, Pat Dutton, Debra Faulkner, Michelle Garcia, K. J. Green, Bill Handley, B. G. Harris, Lew Hopkins, Luverne Jorgensen, Carol Keller, the Kronewitters (Colin and Scott), Pat La Moe, Lois Lana, Dennis and Mary Ann Larsen, Vera Lundquist, Eva Mackintosh, Marilyn Miller, Doris Noack, the O'Melvenys (Erin, Kathy, and Sean), Ted Polito Jr., Jane Swanson, Sara Varney, and Emory Walker.

None of this would have been possible without the unending support and love of my family, especially my parents, Dave and Sandy Everett, and my grandparents, Claire Everett and Don and Glenita Emarine.

Finally, I express my gratitude to the hundreds, probably thousands, of people who have listened to my seemingly limitless stories about the capitol over the years. Tourists, fellow guides, bosses, co-workers, academic peers, professors, students, family, friends, enemies, complete strangers I'd stop on the street when a particularly remarkable insight struck me—thanks to you all for your understanding smiles and words of encouragement. The support of all these people helped keep me on track and helped make this project a wonderful experience.

This book, like the statehouse it describes, is dedicated to my fellow Coloradoans in the hope that we will one day ensure that the capitol receives the preservation and restoration it so richly deserves. It's our building, and it's up to us to pass it along, strong and proud, to the future citizens of the Centennial State.

Enough of the opening act; it's time for the main event. Let's to the Capitol.

DEREK R. EVERETT
UNIVERSITY OF ARKANSAS, FAYETTEVILLE
NOVEMBER 2004

# The Colorado State Capitol

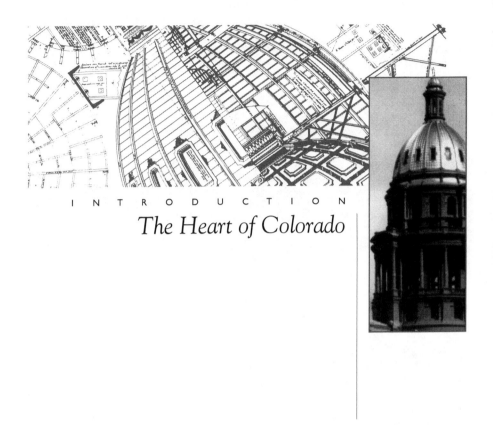

# The Heart of Colorado

G EOGRAPHICALLY, THERE IS NO SENSIBLE REASON for the state of Colorado to exist. Four arbitrary lines drawn by national politicians hundreds of miles away bound together environments with little in common. Plains of sandhills and grasslands, vast plateaus dotted with sagebrush, shallow rivers that swell with spring runoff, shadowy chasms, towering snowcapped mountains, isolated basins, all of which endure violent weather, from relentless winds to blinding snowstorms to searing heat to freezing cold—these elements and more make up Colorado. Aridity affects practically all parts of the state, as well as much of the western United States, but the simple rectangle that demarcates Colorado's boundaries affords practically nothing else capable of bringing this disparate region into a single political entity.

Many states in the Union suffer the same difficulty as Colorado, constricted by indiscreet boundaries that offer perhaps the most obvious modern legacy of European colonial policies. Shortly after the Revolution the federal republic adopted similar measures as a relatively straightforward way to manage newly acquired lands in the West. In Colorado's case, sectional U.S. politics in the 1860s inspired much debate over drawing these four simple divisions, but eventually compromise resulted in a territory and later a state that lacked a common cultural or physical landscape. Settlers from the United States at the base of the mountains and in mining camps, Hispanics along the southern border, American Indians to the east and west, and many other ethnicities merged, however unwillingly, into this federally imposed community. As the inhabitants of this new region gathered together into a political society, they needed something to unify them as a people, a symbol that transcended the hodgepodge of geography and cultures. In the decades that followed, they came together to erect and utilize a physical representation of their collective identity, the Colorado State Capitol.[1]

Crowning the summit of Brown's Bluff with granite and gold, the capitol symbolizes the political community created by all the citizens of the Centennial State. It provides a stage for the dramas of a society, celebrations and protests alike, a great gray temple of popular sovereignty surveying the capital city. By housing the democratically elected representative government, the statehouse brings together the needs and interests of every Coloradoan, from Four Corners to Julesburg, from Brown's Park to the Cimarron River. Although the capitol stands in the state's largest city and events in Denver by necessity impact the structure most directly, it belongs to every citizen equally as the seat of civil authority. The governor does not dominate the building by holding that office, nor does a legislator simply by serving in the General Assembly. All Coloradoans own the capitol by virtue of its purpose and its history. As he gazed up at the dome in 1950, *Denver Post* reporter Bert Hanna glowingly remarked: "You look at this fine old building and you think of all the tremendous work and pride that went into it. It is the heart of Colorado." The capitol pulses in accordance with the interests of the people, and its condition reflects the ways they interpret the needs of their political community. The statehouse's history is Colorado's history, changing with the times to meet contemporary needs while always hearkening back to the vibrant past of the state. Nothing else better exemplifies this region made up of disparate landscapes and peoples.[2]

All Coloradoans, consciously or not, understand the significance of their capitol. The evolution of the statehouse's condition structurally and within the public consciousness reflected broader trends in the region and the nation. The story of the state capitol is the story of the issues, motives, and beliefs important to Coloradoans for a century and a half. As Jay M. Price astutely observed: "Adaptation to change is a natural part of any building's lifespan. But for capitol buildings, it occurs in a very public way that often

West front of the Colorado State Capitol, the state's greatest backdrop for momentous events, on September 14, 1899, when thousands assembled to welcome troops back from the Spanish-American War. Courtesy, Colorado Historical Society, Harry Buckwalter, CHSB869

reflects a shift in how residents of the state see themselves. The history of a state capitol, therefore, can provide insight into changes in the larger community." Although today Denver's skyscrapers tower over the building that once pierced the brilliant blue sky higher than any other, the structure still embodies the collective emotion of pride in popular accomplishment. Efforts to preserve the edifice, however, have failed to adequately capture this innate sense of distinction possessed by the symbol of representative authority. John A. Straayer dedicated the 2000 edition of his book *The Colorado General Assembly* "to the dream of a safe, beautiful, historic, fully restored State Capitol Building, a fitting monument to a civil society." Even after recent difficulties in gaining support for such a project, the hope that the statehouse might eventually receive the physical and emotional attention it so richly deserves remains high for those who watch with frustration its decay. This optimism, as is often the case, shines through particularly brightly in the hearts and minds of many younger Coloradoans. Not too many years ago, after a visit to the statehouse, a fourth grader from Steamboat Springs wrote a note of thanks to his tour guide, stating simply: "I love the Capitule."[3]

Several works dominate the limited academic historiography of state capitols. Henry-Russell Hitchcock and William Seale coauthored *Temples of Democracy: The State Capitols of the U.S.A.* in 1976, perhaps the most comprehensive work on the building type. It presented factual information about the structures in a chronological format and offered a useful and readable starting point for many public architecture scholars. In 2001 Charles T. Goodsell picked up where Hitchcock and Seale left off with *The American Statehouse: Interpreting Democracy's Temples*. He honored his predecessors' work in the title, but far more expertly than had previous scholars, Goodsell successfully accepted the challenge of deciphering the social and political meaning behind capitol buildings. Goodsell also wrote a masterful article in 1988 entitled "The Architecture of Parliaments: Legislative Houses and Political Culture," an insightful study into methods of interpreting public architecture in representative political traditions. In the generation after Hitchcock and Seale, Goodsell dominated the understanding of statehouses with his thoughtful works.[4]

The works of Hitchcock and Seale and Goodsell covered the building type in general, and therefore the Colorado State Capitol only received one-fiftieth of the statehouse histories, if that. Three recent encyclopedic books about state capitols have the same limitation. Of the three, Don Severin's *The Encyclopedia of State Capitols and Capitals* (1999) is better researched and illustrated than Thomas G. Aylesworth's *State Capitals* (1990) or Eldon Hauck's *American Capitols* (1991). Few academic historians have written about the Centennial State's chief building. The two most notable works were both master's theses written by graduate students at the University of Denver. Clarice Eleanore Moffett composed a "History of Colorado's Capitals and Capitols" in 1936, tracing the evolution of cities and buildings that served territorial and state government. William R. Pyle completed his "History of the Colorado State Capitol Complex" in 1962, paying closer attention to the current statehouse than Moffett had, as well as to its surrounding structures built in the twentieth century to house an expanding bureaucracy. Both scholars incorporated comprehensive and useful factual information but offered little interpretation into the capitol's meaning. Tourist booklets sold to visitors over the years also included similar details, although they were not always as accurate. Of the visitors guides, two provide the best narrative story: the 1985 work *Under the Golden Dome: Colorado's State Capitol* by Margaret Coel, Gladys Doty, and Karen Gilleland; and Coel's solo 1992 piece *The Pride of Our People: The Colorado State Capitol*. Although most earlier capitol histories tell the story well, none adequately investigates the impact on the building of broader trends in the state, the nation, and the world.[5]

I decided to write *The Colorado State Capitol: History, Politics, Preservation* to interpret and analyze the statehouse's story through the narrative structure. Although I focused on the building itself, I could not fully tell the tale without delving into state and national history, economic and political developments, and, most important, the human aspect of the building. This book is organized into roughly chronological chapters. The first two cover the period from settlement to 1886, overlapping each other as their subject matter demands: the selection of a capital city, acquiring the capitol site, and architectural planning. Chapters 3 and 4 tell the story of the building's construction, which lasted from 1886 to 1901. The growth of state government and the use and abuse of the capitol in the twentieth century provide a structure for Chapters 5 through 7. The final chapter deals with the most recent years, including the thorny issues of preserving the statehouse and security in the modern world.

Standing proudly on Brown's Bluff, the capitol tells a story simply by virtue of its existence. As the home to a democratically elected representative government, it embodies the desires, concerns, and hopes of all Coloradoans. The building's changing position as the symbol of collective identity parallels the evolutionary nature of a civil authority. Nothing else more fully and accurately reflects the state's vibrant political and social community. The story of the Colorado State Capitol is the story of the people of the Centennial State.

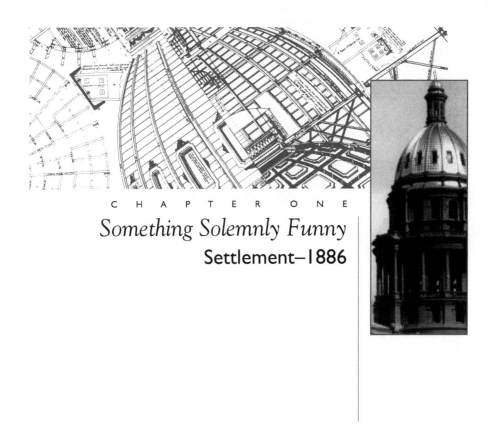

*Something Solemnly Funny*

## Settlement—1886

OR CENTURIES, SOLITUDE HAD REIGNED at the crest of a dusty, windswept ridge rising over two shallow traces of water, a quiet interrupted only occasionally by passersby. The ridge marked the edge of the high plains, where the flatlands dipped before climbing up toward towering peaks. Many generations of Amerindian hunters traversed this gradual rise on the edge of the prairie as they followed herds of mammoths and bison. European explorers and their descendants followed ancient trails nearby, but almost without exception they considered the region someplace to get across, not to remain. To the west, towering peaks stood as barriers against both thought and action. Stretching the horizon, they formed a picturesque but forbidding wall. To the east, the brown, dry plains extended as far as the eye could see. The tranquil region promised a difficult life for anyone who contemplated remaining in the ridge's shadow. But with the arrival of a group intoxicated by dreams of wealth hidden in the rugged surroundings, a process began that would change the landscape forever.

In the mid-nineteenth century, the isolated area around this ridge experienced an almost immediate alteration, the legacies of which impact twenty-first-century people in innumerable ways. The creation of a political society that geographically bound mountain, plain, and plateau, summed up with the romantic title "Colorado," resulted in both opportunities and challenges for all who lived there. Arbitrarily drawn boundaries inspired sectional conflicts that threatened to tear the region asunder. Battles between towns for the seat of government reflected a desperate desire for recognition from the older states east of the Mississippi River. For thirty years after the gold rush of the late 1850s, Colorado attempted to prove itself every bit as respectable as more senior parts of the country. The national government had established a policy in the 1780s of admitting new states to the Union on an equal basis with earlier members, but these later states still felt the need to establish their worthiness through dedicated and oftentimes unintentionally amusing means. Mark Twain once described the early years of a western territory as "something solemnly funny," and his comment suitably illustrates Colorado's struggle to prove its significance to itself and others by building a proper capitol. During the period 1858 to 1886, Colorado's seat of government shifted several times among three primary contenders: Denver, Golden, and Colorado City. Although Denver captured the prize in 1867 and began the long, bitter process of building a structure to centralize a nomadic government, various regions of the state continued to battle over the capital designation. Several legal contests over the statehouse grounds only exacerbated the uncertainty. But by 1886, after almost thirty years, with both the capital city and the capitol site secure, Coloradoans could erect a proper edifice for a democratic people.

By the late 1850s, members of many cultures had crossed the plains of the North American continent: American Indians on the hunt, Spanish searching for the mythic wealth of Quivira, military expeditions investigating continental crossings, settlers bound for Oregon, Mormons seeking a religious asylum, argonauts desperate for riches in California. The first of these groups often camped along the streams at the edge of the high plains, using the region as a jumping-off place for pursuing game. Their presence extended the story of human settlement along the Front Range of the Rocky Mountains back many centuries before the descendants of Europeans arrived. Emigrants from the United States crossed the plains as quickly as possible with little intention of remaining there. The warnings of early American expeditions, which titled the plains the "Great American Desert," resonated with many settlers who feared the dry land and native peoples. But with the discovery of promising gold deposits in the central Rocky Mountains, the landscape along the windward side of the peaks became a destination unto itself. In the lingering atmosphere of an economic downturn that started in 1857, the promise of free gold in the Rockies appealed to many people. In 1858 and 1859 waves of fortune hunters headed to the mountains. The heady years of the Pikes Peak Gold Rush brought thousands of people to the streambeds of what was then far western Kansas Territory.

In the booming atmosphere of the gold rush, many towns seemed to emerge overnight. Camps in the mountains served as bases of operation for miners, and supply towns rose downstream to outfit the burgeoning population. Shortly after their rapid establishment, these towns began competing for dominance in the region. The distance and ineffectiveness of Kansas territorial officials, and to a lesser extent those of Nebraska and New Mexico, added to the unrest. Local settlers needed the recognition of the federal government to separate themselves from the faraway rule of law and create a system of their own. But national politics of the era, particularly the controversy of slavery spreading into the region, prevented significant federal response. When the United States House of Representatives failed to enact legislation for a proposed Territory of Colona in January 1859 to give the region its own government, settlers took matters into their own hands. A Denver newspaper rallied its readers:

> Government of some kind we must have, and the question narrows itself down to this point: Shall it be the government of the knife and the revolver, or shall we unite in forming here in our golden country, among the gulches and ravines of the Rocky Mountains, and the fertile valleys of the Arkansas and the Plattes, a new and independent state?

When the federal government failed to answer their call, 167 delegates met in Denver in late summer of 1859. They declared the creation of Jefferson Territory, which stretched from the 37th to the 43rd parallel, from the northern boundary of New Mexico Territory to just beyond the northernmost point of the North Platte River. From east to west, Jefferson Territory commenced at the 102nd meridian, presently the Colorado/Kansas boundary, to the 110th meridian, extending somewhat into modern Utah.[1]

In the new territory, which federal officials declined to recognize, selecting the seat of government took precedence over other issues. Denver, a town at the confluence of Cherry Creek and the South Platte River near that dusty and isolated ridge, seemed a sensible choice. A party from Kansas Territory including Edward Wynkoop and William H. Larimer had established the town in November 1858, and clapboard hovels rose quickly as more gold seekers arrived in the region. With the capital question for the moment settled, the citizens of Jefferson Territory organized governmental structures. They elected Robert W. Steele governor in a rather corrupt election on October 24, 1859.

Voters also approved a constitution that called for the first territorial legislature to meet in Denver. In early November the assembly convened and felt confident in its ability to justly govern. Even the *Rocky Mountain News* proudly changed its masthead from "Kansas Territory" to "Jefferson Territory." But regardless of how much local support the territory enjoyed, the federal government paid it little heed. The conflict over slavery's future in the United States overwhelmed almost all other concerns. With John Brown attempting insurrection in Virginia and relations with the southern states worsening daily, the activities of a few disgruntled western settlers seemed inconsequential.[2]

As the eastern situation grew progressively worse, however, more northern leaders in Washington, D.C., acknowledged the need for legal institutions in this far-flung region, hundreds of miles from any territorial capital. In February 1860 President James Buchanan received eight memorials from the new inhabitants of the rapidly growing plains and mountain communities. They reported that "this region has not and cannot have peaceful political affinities" with its distant territorial authorities. Only the federal government could authorize the local government they desired. In the meantime, sectional controversies intensified between slave and free states, so reigning in the western region and ensuring its loyalty to the Union was a must. Southern congressmen regularly tabled bills for a local government, fearing the free soil movement would prevent slavery's spread into the region. With the secession of several southern states in late 1860 and early 1861 and the departure of their representatives from Washington, D.C., however, congressional opposition to the creation of a new Unionist territory dwindled.[3]

Exacerbating the need for local government in the Rocky Mountain region, Kansas became a state in January 1861, with new borders that did not include its far western environs. Jefferson Territory leaders sent Beverly D. Williams to Washington, D.C., to represent local interests. He worked with several members of Congress to draft legislation for what would be a recognized political entity, and, responding to requests from many settlers in the gold camps and supply towns, they amended the new territory's proposed name from Idaho to Colorado. Indeed, naming debates played a substantial role in the development of many western territories. Some of the names suggested at one time or another for Colorado included Arapahoe, Cibola, Columbus, Franklin, Lafayette, Lula, Montana, Nemara, Osage, Pikes Peak, Platte, San Juan, Shoshone, Tahosa, and Weapollao. Colorado, more than any other name, conjured in many minds a romantic vision of the region. Choosing the Spanish name for the great river of the American Southwest also helped to ease tensions between Anglo settlers of the northern part of the territory and Hispanics in the south, who were upset by political separation from Santa Fe without their consent.

On February 28, 1861, President Buchanan signed legislation establishing Colorado Territory. Within weeks, similar laws were approved to grant local control to Nevada and Dakota. Preexisting territories supplied the land for Colorado: the eastern plains from Kansas, the south-central mountains and valleys from New Mexico, the western slope from Utah, and the northeastern plains and mountains from Nebraska. Smaller than the extralegal Jefferson Territory, Colorado began roughly at the 102nd meridian and stretched west to the 109th and from south to north from the 37th to the 41st parallel. The borders isolated Hispanics in the upper Rio Grande and Arkansas valleys from their ancestral homes in New Mexico Territory, setting the stage for ethnic tension in the years to come. Howard R. Lamar has argued that Colorado's borders purposely isolated the region from transcontinental railroad routes, slavery, and Mormon control. Although the boundaries limited some potential development and regional cultures, they finally provided the local authority greatly desired by argonauts in northeastern and central Colorado. Politicians in Washington, D.C., recognizing the impending conflict between slave and free states, knew the importance of securing the loyalty of the expanding population of the central Rockies, as well as the natural resources contained therein. With a new territory and legal recognition at last, the placated citizens began organizing a government dominated by Anglo interests and centered on the Front Range.[4]

The act creating Colorado granted the selection of the capital to the first territorial chief executive, Governor William Gilpin. He arrived on May 27, 1861, two months after his appointment in March, and descended from a dust-covered stagecoach to great applause in the streets of Denver. Governor Gilpin had expected some opposition from Jefferson Territory governor Robert Steele, but the latter welcomed Gilpin amicably, encouraged allegiance to Colorado, and proclaimed Jefferson Territory defunct. As Mark Twain commented, "There is something solemnly funny about the struggles of a newborn Territorial government to get a start in this world."[5]

Shortly after Governor Gilpin's arrival, he declared Denver the capital and called for election of a territorial legislature. That body first met in Denver on September 11, 1861. The *Rocky Mountain News*, owned by local booster William N. Byers, doubted "if there was ever a more respectable and well informed body of men assembled as a first Legislature, than is the first assembly of Colorado." During its session in the fall of 1861, the small group divided Colorado Territory into seventeen counties and focused much attention on formalizing mining law. In the words of Colorado judge and historian Wilbur F. Stone: "Great praise is due to this legislative body for the laws they enacted, and though some have been found faulty and others repealed, yet they effectually served the needs of the Territory." Certain members of the body, however, found little reason to praise the first assembly's meeting. Hispanic representatives from southern Colorado sat in bewildered silence while their counterparts discussed territorial matters until someone realized they did not understand English and begrudgingly provided an interpreter.[6]

Although the assembled officials found their simple quarters comfortable enough, they recognized the need for an official capital. The earliest territorial statutes authorized the legislature to select, and the executive to confirm, a seat of government. Representative M. S. Beach, who served El Paso and Pueblo counties, negotiated with his peers to establish Colorado City as the territorial capital, at the foot of Pikes Peak. The choice emerged as a geographic compromise between supporters of Denver and Pueblo. The *Rocky Mountain News* weighed in on the issue, claiming that "Denver is the *only* place to be thought of for the Capitol" and that Colorado City could never hope to have similar economic influence or political power. Regardless, the legislature agreed to move all territorial offices to Colorado City, and Governor Gilpin approved the choice on November 5, 1861.[7]

In the meantime, the Civil War had been raging for several months to the east of Colorado. The federal government pulled troops from frontier posts, and many Coloradoans felt threatened by the lack of protection. Governor Gilpin issued federal treasury warrants to equip a regiment of Colorado infantry to aid in the defense of the new territory. In late March 1862 these troops took part in the most significant battle of the war in the far West, at Glorieta Pass in New Mexico Territory. Two days of battle, during which Colorado troops served with distinction, resulted in an emphatic Union victory. The Colorado goldfields, the target of the invading army to relieve the financially strapped Southern Confederacy, remained in Northern hands.

With the immediate danger of invasion thwarted, the legislature felt comfortable moving the capital to the foot of Pikes Peak. Few executive officials approved of Colorado City as a territorial capital, however, including the new territorial governor, John Evans. Governor Gilpin had been removed from office in May 1862 by President Abraham Lincoln, who had never authorized the funds Gilpin spent to defend Colorado. Set up in a comfortable home in Denver, Governor Evans wanted the capital to be permanently located there. He considered Denver "really the only tolerable place" and, defying territorial law, refused to move the executive offices to Colorado City. Nonetheless, legislators and the territorial supreme court arrived at the base of Pikes Peak for work in early July 1862 "in wagons, ambulances, [on] horseback, and on foot." They found preparations for their work abysmal. The only hotel in Colorado City could not find accommodations for them, and some legislators and justices slept outdoors in tents with their families. The House of Representatives met in a small log room with a pine table and stool for the speaker and boards laid across boxes as benches for the members. Representatives slept in their meeting hall and prepared communal meals at the fireplace. Meanwhile, the territorial council assembled in a tavern kitchen as well as in the nearby home of Colonel John M. Francisco, a member of the council who, along with Representative Beach, had adeptly lobbied to make his hometown the capital. Although the life of the territorial government in Colorado City seemed at first amusingly rustic, the appeal soon wore off, and legislators began to consider moving the capital.[8]

The men who had encouraged the selection of Colorado City as the capital would not give up without a fight. The House of Representatives passed a joint resolution to move back to Denver, but members from the southern districts of the territory blocked it in the council. Leading the opposition was Robert B. Willis of El Paso County, who owned stock in the Colorado City town company. Councilman Willis and his followers fled Colorado City to his ranch on Fountain Creek but returned after some members, waving a flag of truce, coaxed them back to the meeting. When the party reached Colorado City, however, legislators barred the doors, and the territorial assembly forced Willis and his followers to move the capital. Some expressed sympathy for Representative Beach "and the other nice fellows who had laid out the town originally," since "the legislature had 'laid it out' completely." Not twenty minutes after the vote, "teams were hitched up, mules saddled," and territorial officials commenced the trek back to Denver. Legislators and justices returned to Cherry Creek five days after the bizarre session at Pikes Peak concluded. There they resumed their work and remained for the next month.[9]

Back in spacious rented quarters in Denver, Governor Evans addressed the assembly members, feeling vindicated by their return. He did not celebrate for long. The territorial legislature refused to choose Denver as the permanent seat of government. Instead, the members voted to relocate to Golden, several miles west of Denver in the foothills of the Rocky Mountains, on August 14, 1862. The territorial supreme court, content to conduct its affairs out of the limelight, moved into relatively humble accommodations in Denver. Unlike the legislative and executive branches, which occupied many different buildings in Denver over the years, the justices preferred to remain in their small but comfortable quarters and leave the arguments to their fellow territorial leaders. That territorial leaders accomplished any government work was a miracle.[10]

Like Colorado City, Golden owed its brief existence to supplying mining towns, serving the camps along Clear Creek. Now, with the territorial legislature moving in, Golden residents conveyed a destined sense of superiority and expected to supplant Denver, something Colorado City had failed to do. Denver and Golden began a tight battle for territorial dominance, in part

The Old Capitol

LEGISLATURE
MEETS HERE.

Artist's rendering of the territorial legislature's spartan conditions at Colorado City during its brief session there in July 1862. Author's collection

because of their proximity to each other. During the five years Golden held the title of capital, the legislature alternated between both towns for its meetings without any sense of permanency. The first such meeting convened in early February 1864 in Golden. Locals, worried about repeating the unpleasantness of Colorado City, attempted to ensure the legislators' comfort. Hotels provided cheap accommodations, and many businessmen donated provisions and supplies. Perhaps most important, Golden's *Weekly Commonwealth* reported that a local saloon keeper prepared for the session by "putting up more ice and importing more whiskey." Legislators anticipated a comfortable session in Golden. The territorial government found its duties unexpectedly difficult, however. Many other towns hoped to take advantage of the battle for capital designation and win favor in the legislature. Central City, deep in the heart of a key mining district, pushed for territorial capital status, which the council rejected. Wishing to be rid of the problem, which retarded the execution of more serious business, the legislature simply decided to return to Denver. Coaches made several trips along Clear Creek to bring the legislators back to Denver, and several exasperated members decided to walk, setting out in the morning and reaching Cherry Creek by nightfall.[11]

Times were tough for Colorado, as they were all over the West during the Civil War era. A natural disaster struck Denver on May 19, 1864, when heavy rains caused Cherry Creek to swell its banks. The previous year a fire had damaged much of Denver, and the city's first flood added to the woes. Water wiped out Governor Evans's offices, and other structures, including the *Rocky Mountain News* building, were lost altogether. Additionally, conflicts between white settlers and Indian populations on the eastern plains spread fear and warfare across the countryside. A series of attacks along the Platte River in the Nebraska and Colorado territories followed the massacre of a family of Colorado settlers in June 1864. As fall approached, tensions eased between the settlers and the Indians, but the peace was shattered by some Coloradoans focused on revenge. On Governor Evans's orders, Colonel John M. Chivington led Colorado volunteers on an early morning attack of a peaceful village of Arapahoes and Cheyennes—mostly women, children, and elderly tribesmen— along Sand Creek on the eastern plains on November 29, 1864. Awakening to the sounds of death and butchery, some Indians attempted to mount a defense, whereas others fled up the streambed. The Colorado troops killed well over 100 individuals and defiled many victims' bodies. They scalped the dead and wounded and used their knives to remove the genitalia of Indian women, which the white troops wore around their necks as trophies of war. Denverites, with minds clouded by bloodlust and paranoia, welcomed back the "Bloody Third" regiment and gathered in theaters to gape at the body parts soldiers brought back from the massacre.[12]

The horrific atrocities committed by Coloradoans at Sand Creek incensed the native peoples of the plains. Most of Colorado was isolated from the rest of the country in the following weeks as outraged Indians cut telegraph lines and attacked stagecoaches. In this atmosphere of constant fear, the Fourth Legislative Assembly convened in Golden on January 2, 1865. Golden residents orchestrated numerous social events during the session to raise spirits during those trying times. Tucked into the foothills, Golden seemed like a refuge, a good place to hide. Meanwhile, in part as a response to Governor Evans's role in the Sand Creek Massacre, Alexander Cummings replaced him as the territorial chief executive in 1865. The third territorial governor, who agreed with President Andrew Johnson's opposition to Colorado statehood, arrived in Denver to little fanfare on October 17. On New Year's Day 1866, the Fifth Legislative Assembly convened in Golden, on the second floor of a new building built by William Loveland on the northwest corner of Second (now Twelfth) Street and Washington Avenue. Both houses met in this building, still standing today in downtown Golden. The handsome quarters apparently did not impress the legislature, however. The same day they convened, both houses voted to return to Denver.[13]

Governor Cummings enjoyed a brief period of cooperative government, but the next territorial political crisis was instigated by the executive himself. The lukewarm reception he received upon his arrival turned into outright hostility in 1866. Cummings deeply resented the power of territorial secretary Samuel H. Elbert, son-in-law of former governor Evans, both of whom strongly supported Colorado statehood. Cummings claimed that Elbert hoarded the territory's executive records without providing proper access for politicians, a claim Elbert angrily dismissed. The situation grew increasingly hostile when the governor confiscated the territorial seal, the symbol of the secretary's office, in January 1866. The House of Representatives backed Cummings, whereas the council refused to choose a side. To reaffirm his position as chief territorial officer, Cummings moved the executive offices from Denver to Golden in October 1866. Gradually throughout the next two months, executive officers begrudgingly moved from Denver into rooms in Cummings's large new Golden home. The legislature moved around by its own resolution, a confusing tactic now adopted by the executive branch.[14]

Much of the political division in Colorado originated from a difference of opinion on the question of statehood. Denverites more often than not supported the change and were represented by former governor John Evans and Jerome B. Chaffee. Golden residents, led by Henry M. Teller, opposed statehood and anything else that might detract from their tenuous hold on the capital. The constant shuttling of government between the two cities caused great consternation to territorial secretary Elbert, who commented that "the

The Old Capitol Grill in Golden, built in 1865 by William A.H. Loveland, the oldest surviving statehouse in Colorado and currently a popular restaurant. Author's collection

first railroad needed in Colorado was the most direct line between its two capitals."[15]

Shortly after his surprising move to Golden, Governor Cummings grew disillusioned with the town, a feeling shared by many territorial politicians. The Sixth Legislative Assembly convened in early December 1866, while executive officials argued over moving from Denver. Again, representatives from mining districts attempted to change the capital, this time to Idaho Springs, but after a heated debate the capital remained at Golden. Bowing to public opinion against his actions, Governor Cummings returned to Denver with other executive leaders in the winter of 1866–1867, and many Denverites called for the capital to return permanently to the banks of Cherry Creek. The *Rocky Mountain News* observed on December 7, 1866: "Nearly all the members [of the legislature] are in Denver, and they without exception, testify that the same time spent in prison would be equally pleasant as at Golden City. 'Tis a good place for Cummings to force the honorable body to accede to his plans." The governor's popular image spiraled downward, and some locals petitioned President Johnson to send a new territorial chief executive. In May 1867 he acquiesced and replaced Cummings with Alexander C. Hunt, a Republican who supported statehood. Most of Denver's inhabitants eagerly welcomed Governor Hunt, who could help them achieve their dreams of ending the tumultuous territorial experience.[16]

Political controversies calmed somewhat in December 1867, when the Seventh Legislative Assembly met in the Loveland building in Golden. Five days after the start of the session, both houses voted to make Denver the capital of Colorado Territory. Governor Hunt quickly signed the measure, hoping to make wandering capitals a thing of the past. Citizens of Golden, meanwhile, did everything they could to retain the capital, including offering cheaper accommodations than Denver's and even more ice and whiskey, but to no avail. As one scholar observed, Golden's "early selection as [the capital] seems to have occasioned but little jubilation, its abandonment but little mourning. Probably the average legislature of those days brought but little profit and less distinction." "The peregrinations of the capital," as historian Robert G. Athearn remarked, "were suggestive of the turmoil, the uncertainty, the transitory nature of the newly created government at the foot of the Rockies." Finally, after six years of wandering, the statutory capital had been reestablished at Denver—the capital of Jefferson Territory, the first capital of Colorado Territory, and, as it turned out, the permanent seat of authority from then on.[17]

In many ways, Denver's selection as the capital in 1867 was a Pyrrhic victory; it was a town apparently destined to serve as the seat of government for a backwater region. Most of the placer gold had been panned out of streams, and the rich veins lay deep inside mountain peaks, inaccessible and useless without improved technology and transportation. Little else existed to draw settlers to the dry landscape. When the Pacific Railroad Act was passed in 1862, several surveys had already studied Colorado in search of a transcontinental route. Most of these teams agreed that such a line could be built through the central Rockies only after extensive tunneling. By the time Denver captured the capital on December 7, 1867, the Union Pacific had already laid track north of the territorial border in what later became Wyoming. The "hell-on-wheels" town of Cheyenne pronounced Denver "too dead to bury," and many considered the Colorado capital inconsequential to the rest of the country. But many Coloradoans refused to surrender their optimism. Local businessmen and boosters worked with the Kansas Pacific Railroad, a branch of the Union Pacific, to link Denver to the east. When the line ran short of funds and construction stopped in western Kansas, Denverites spent more money to build a line north to Cheyenne, later called the Denver Pacific Railroad and linked with the Union Pacific's main line there. By the summer of 1870 Denver found itself connected to the rest of the country by rail. Since Golden's attempts to build competing lines had temporarily stalled, Denver's dominance in the territory seemed assured with the help of the iron horse.

A drawing of Denver in the mid-1860s as viewed from the ridge southeast of town, near the future site of the capitol. Courtesy, Colorado Historical Society, WPA1L91

But if Denverites wanted to end the capital squabbling once and for all, they needed to erect a capitol building, a permanent seat of government in an uncertain time. To that end, one of the most important and colorful characters in the story of the Colorado State Capitol appeared: Henry Cordes Brown.[18]

Born in Ohio in 1820, Brown spent his first decades farming and wandering the West. He crossed the continent to California with an ox team in 1852, visited Oregon and Washington territories, and sailed to Peru and around Cape Horn in 1858. Returning to the states he met Jane C. Thompson, a schoolteacher in Hannibal, Missouri. They married, and after the birth of their first child, James Henry Brown, the couple set off westward with hopes of striking it rich in the Colorado goldfields. After forty-five days of crossing the plains, Brown and his wife arrived at Denver on June 9, 1860. Legend records that the pair stood on that dusty ridge about a mile south of town, watching a multicolored sunset over the Rocky Mountains, and decided to settle down in the supply town instead. Brown soon established himself as a reputable contractor and builder. But the couple's memories clung to the image of that view from the windswept ridge south of town, and after losing their first home in the flood of 1864 they decided to move to higher ground. In December 1865 Brown purchased a strip of land southeast of town, one-quarter mile wide and one mile long, following the windswept ridge. He built a new home at roughly the present intersection of Twelfth Avenue and Sherman Street and started a farm. His solitary home sat almost a mile from Denver, on the ridge locals started calling "Brown's Bluff." The owner of the

Henry Cordes Brown, the Denver entrepreneur who donated the capitol grounds, in an 1886 portrait. Courtesy, Denver Public Library Western History Collection, Rose & Hopkins, H-15

isolated farm achieved immediate notoriety in 1867 when he offered ten acres in the center of his property as a site for a capitol building to help his adopted hometown.[19]

With prominent views of the Rocky Mountains to the west and its dominating elevation over the fledgling capital, Brown considered his land an ideal spot for a statehouse. But others, even many fellow Denverites, expressed concern that their statehouse would sit about a mile from the town, which at that point still focused around Larimer Street. To ensure Denver's hold on the seat of government, though, Colorado leaders accepted Brown's gift. In January 1868 many territorial officials breathed a sigh of relief when he signed the deed transfer paperwork. In return, Brown asked Denver officials to realign new streets to follow a compass axis instead of paralleling Cherry Creek and the South Platte River, since the former system would better conform to his property and make it easier to sell plots of land to developers. The city leaders agreed and started laying out new streets that stretched toward the capitol site, named for heroes of the recent war including Lincoln, Sherman, Grant, and Logan. Securing Brown's donated land, however, marked only the first step in a long and difficult path toward establishing the permanency of government. The thorny matter of building a capitol occupied the attention of territorial and state politicians for the rest of the century.

Many of Colorado's elite found the idea of a home near the capitol site an appealing prospect. Fourteenth Street, the first neighborhood of Denver millionaires, waned as the rich and powerful rushed to live in the next fashionable area, appropriately christened Capitol Hill. This exodus of the rich and powerful began almost immediately after Brown's donation, as the shrewd landowner started selling off chunks of his farm at tidy profits. In 1868 Samuel Bowles remarked that "Denverites all wear a fixed fact sort of air, and most of them are able to tell you, in a low and confidential chuckle, calling for envy rather than sympathy, that they own a quarter section just out there on the bluff, to which the town is rapidly spreading, and where the capitol buildings and the fine residences will all be located." Businessman and philanthropist Charles Boettcher, smelting magnate Nathaniel P. Hill, United States senator Charles J. Hughes Jr., newspaperman William N. Byers, mine owners James J. and Margaret Tobin Brown and Horace and Augusta Tabor, Governor Job A. Cooper—they and dozens more of Denver's rich and powerful in the late nineteenth century lived in homes built on land purchased from Henry Brown. The gradual rise of churches and hotels, such as Brown's Palace and Trinity Methodist and Central Presbyterian, added to the area's newfound popularity and respectability. Expressing themselves through fanciful architecture, Denver residents built personal representations of a deep and abiding faith in their city's destiny.[20]

To make the swiftest possible use of Brown's donation, Governor Hunt organized a committee to raise funds for the construction and maintenance of a statehouse and its grounds. Over a dozen citizens, including Hunt and former governor Evans, also donated land either for a capitol site or to sell for construction. Within five years, the government of Colorado collected over 200 lots in Denver to use for statehouse funds, with a total value of $50,000. With such strong support, territorial officials considered themselves ready to begin work. Hunt's committee consisted of Allen A. Bradford of Pueblo, Joseph M. Marshal of Boulder, and William M. Roworth of Central City. However, each believed his hometown could one day lay claim to the seat of government and expressed little interest in his duties. Meanwhile, the federal government recognized the need for capitols in all the western territories, not just Colorado. Although members of the U.S. House of Representatives expressed displeasure that so much money each year went to renting quarters for territorial officials, they could not agree on a proper appropriation for building projects. The Colorado legislature passed a law in 1872 authorizing a fund for capitol construction, directing a triumvirate of the governor, secretary, and chief justice to award a contract "to the lowest and best bidder." But the territory could not raise enough money and sent memorials to the U.S. Congress asking for $100,000 to solve the increasingly desperate problem.[21]

As Coloradoans approached statehood, interest again grew in constructing a capitol. In 1874 the territorial legislature created a new organization, the Board of Capitol Commissioners, to direct the building project. With members of the board from Denver, Trinidad, and Evans, the group was still an eastern slope affair but held more dedication to Denver than Hunt's committee had. However, the forces of territorial sectionalism almost thwarted the board before it could take action. In February 1874 the House of Representatives passed a bill transferring the seat of government to Pueblo. Only the dedicated efforts of many Denverites defeated this legislation in the upper house. The *Rocky Mountain News* expressed itself: "Capital removal would appear to be an act which can be defended on no grounds of justice, right, or even good policy."[22]

The fact that strong objections to Anglo Denver as the seat of government came from the southern, predominantly Hispanic reaches of the territory demonstrated an important division within Colorado. With western borders drawn by politicians in Washington, D.C., that more often than not ignored geographical and ethnic concerns, such opposition seemed inevitable. In 1877 the southern portion of the state considered secession; its model was West Virginia, which separated from Virginia during the Civil War. The supporters of the measure were led by delegates from Del Norte who advocated that all southern Coloradoans should unite in opposition to Denver's domination and form the state of San Juan. With its Hispanic population, this proposal appealed to many in the south. When Pueblo citizens opposed designating Del Norte as the new state's capital, however, regional unity splintered. Eventually, the embarrassed activists acquiesced, and Colorado remained whole. But sectional and ethnic tensions would play an important role in the state's history for decades to come.[23]

Debate in Denver kept the capitol proposal alive. The legislature called for a territorial government building to be erected on Brown's land by New Year's Day 1876. Meanwhile, the Board of Capitol Commissioners accepted donations of money and land for a building fund and asked Denver officials to grade the land and enclose it with a fence. The *Rocky Mountain News* expressed disappointment that "strangers come from the east and look upon an unimproved piece of ground as the future site of the capitol building." The commissioners had little success with any of their efforts toward construction, however, particularly considering the pronounced sectional opposition in the territorial legislature. In the meantime, locals used Brown's land as an unofficial public park, most notably as the site of a popular annual fireworks show on Independence Day.[24]

When the Board of Capitol Commissioners faltered in its progress, a group of Denverites met on May 5, 1875, to push for a capitol. The assembled citizens agreed that a statehouse might improve Colorado's chances for admission to the Union, and they decided to erect such a building without the legislature's help. They asked their fellow Denverites to donate $30,000 to a capitol fund and requested $5,000 from the commissioners of Arapahoe County, of which Denver was the seat. William Byers of the *Rocky Mountain News* supported the effort but expressed concern at the amount of funding suggested: "If in a score of years a million people are gathered within our border, [a capitol] costing a half million dollars will be little enough to meet the demands of the state." The general lack of action infuriated Henry Brown. He built a new house on Sherman Street and spent a great deal of time there brooding on the situation.[25]

Even with the donation of land on Brown's Bluff, Denver enjoyed only a tenuous hold on the territorial capital. With the prospect of statehood looming, controversy about the location of the seat of government became a central focus for Coloradoans in the mid-1870s. Even though Colorado had achieved sufficient population for statehood years earlier, problems such as the Sand Creek Massacre and several controversial territorial governors had stifled the process. An enabling act passed by the federal Congress in March 1875 finally gave Coloradoans the chance to write their own state constitution. After the third convention assembled for that purpose in the territory's history, Colorado presented federal officials with the key document. A brief but important provision in the 1876 constitution mandated that all territorial property would belong to the state, including Brown's donated land. To ensure a smooth transition to the Union, territorial governor Edward McCook, who had been removed once before in favor of Samuel Elbert, stepped aside. Ending the carousel of executive leadership, John L. Routt replaced McCook, and statehood for Colorado at last seemed a certainty. On August 1, 1876, President Ulysses S. Grant signed legislation establishing the state of Colorado, ending fifteen years of tumultuous frontier territorial government.

According to the Northwest Ordinance of 1787, which had established the procedure for territories to become states equal with others in the Union, Colorado now enjoyed every benefit and shouldered every responsibility expected of other states. In reality, however, Coloradoans still sought to prove their suitability to stand among the older parts of the nation, and a dignified statehouse seemed the best way to achieve this goal. But even after the dream of statehood had been realized, the capitol situation grew more problematic. The 1875 citizen effort failed, and without action from the legislature, no concerted effort to erect a capitol building developed as the state's first years passed. In the Enabling Act, the federal government had granted Coloradoans fifty sections of public land to sell for funds to build a capitol, but the new state constitution prevented any immediate action on the situation. Until a referendum scheduled for 1881 was taken, the permanent seat of government remained in question, precluding any immediate plans for a statehouse. The foundational document also stated in Article VIII that no legislative appropriation for such an edifice could be made prior to the vote to locate the capital. Since Denver might lose such an election, Brown grew increasingly perturbed.[26]

Worried that his "Capitol Hill" land deals would fall through and that his fortune would be lost, Brown instigated a lawsuit in 1879 to reclaim the ten acres for himself. Some sources valued the parcel at $50,000, twice as much as the entire state treasury. After filing a deed of revocation on May 9, Brown set to work building a fence around the site, inspiring the *Denver Tribune* to report that "lot jumping fever had broken out in Denver in its worst form." Attorney General Charles W. Wright promptly countered with a suit of ejectment. Henry Brown's legal firm claimed that since eleven years had passed without capitol construction, he could justifiably reclaim the site. State officials countered that the deed which transferred the land to Colorado Territory in 1868 was flawless, and Brown had no further claim to it. Frank Hall, the territorial secretary who oversaw the land transfer, clearly stated his opinion:

> It is a mistake to assume that such property was a donation. . . . Even were the conveyancing not such as to clearly and fully vest the title in the State, it would be an act of baseness on the part of the original owners of this property to undertake now to pick a flaw in the title. But fortunately no such defect exists. This title to the State is absolute and unconditional, and the property can never revert unless the capital should be removed from

Denver, or other location for capitol buildings should be accepted and
used. . . . If there are any flaws in that deed it will take a smart lawyer to
find [them].

The lines were drawn, instigating seven years of legal battles over the capitol
site.[27]

Brown's revocation made many in Denver nervous. Newspapers encouraged support for the state in the lawsuit against him and called Brown an
"Indian-giver." The Denver Tribune worried that other cities in Colorado could
use the fracas as a way to wrest away the capital. Accusing Brown of display-
ing "Punic faith as a citizen," the Tribune shamed him for endangering Denver by going back on his donation, which had seemed so agreeable in 1868.
Unshaken, Brown attempted to reclaim the land in two separate cases in
Arapahoe County courts. He pointed out that the state had not yet made
improvements to his land and succeeded in convincing the second court to
support his right to reclaim the land, the first and only time a court sided with
Brown. Attorney General Wright claimed the Denver courts had been bi-
ased, and a new trial took place in Jefferson County, with the state victorious
this time. The part of Brown's Bluff donated for a capitol all the while sat
vacant, filled with grass and weeds instead of architectural magnificence.[28]

The need for a suitable statehouse increased with each passing day, as the
young government desperately sought to convey a permanence of state authority to Coloradoans and the rest of the nation. On a practical level, the
state needed suitable quarters for official institutions and safe storage space
for important records. Colorado politicians grew increasingly desperate, and
Brown's courtroom shenanigans made an already difficult situation even worse.
After losing two of three minor court battles in Jefferson and Arapahoe counties, Brown filed a writ of error with the Colorado Supreme Court in early
1881. He argued that the transfer of the deed implied construction of a capitol in a timely fashion, but the state court did not agree:

> Capitol buildings are usually large structures, requiring large sums for their
> construction, and involving increase of the public indebtedness. . . .
> Rented government buildings served the purpose of the Territorial
> government, as they have and do serve the purpose of our present State
> government, and who shall say that both Territorial and State legislatures
> have not acted wisely and prudently in this postponement of an undertak-
> ing which would largely increase the public burthens? Who shall say that
> there has been a delay for an unreasonable time, having reference to our
> sparse population, slender revenues, and other prudential considerations
> which control legislation in the public interest?

Since no technical requirements for a capitol building existed in the deed he
had signed in 1868, Brown's argument failed. The Colorado Supreme Court

The view south down Sherman Street along Brown's Bluff in 1882, with the new homes of Denver's millionaires rising around the land donated for the capitol (*top center*). Author's collection

ruled against him in April 1881, granting the state full legal right to the donated land.[29]

The first five years of Colorado statehood were nervous ones for Denver, made no easier by Henry Brown. Every year Denver endured demands from other cities to move the capital. Following a constitutional directive, the legislature placed a question on the 1881 ballot for all voters to write their choice for the permanent capital of Colorado. Several cities officially entered the competition, whereas others opted to stay out of the debacle. Those who remained in the running provided ample fodder for Denver newspapers. Colorado Springs, founded in 1871 by the Denver & Rio Grande Railroad to succeed nearby former capital Colorado City, seemed the strongest challenger. The *Rocky Mountain News* charged Colorado Springs and Pueblo, both vying for the capital, of bad faith. Denver politicians had promised the deaf and mute asylum to the former and the insane asylum to the latter in exchange for supporting Denver as the capital, which settled the matter as far as the *News* was concerned. The *Denver Tribune* also targeted Cañon City, since it had received the state penitentiary under a similar agreement but still tried to become the capital. Boulder, Fort Collins, and Golden had all received educational institutions—the university, the agricultural college, and the school of mines, respectively—and politely decided not to challenge Denver.[30]

Support for Denver as the capital came from some surprising sources. Golden could easily have lobbied for the seat of government again but had come to befriend Denver in the years since 1867. Newspapers in the San Luis Valley and South Park also championed Denver as the right choice. Although sectionalism remained a substantial force within the state, many saw Denver's designation as the capital the best choice for the common good. It was the center of industry and transportation in the state, and most people in the eastern part of the nation considered the city important—points that encouraged Coloradoans to support Denver. The vote in November 1881 took place in a somewhat hostile atmosphere, but in the end Denver's victory surprised few in Colorado. Of all major competitors, Denver received approximately five times as many votes as the runner-up, Pueblo. Colorado Springs, Cañon City, and Salida, in that order, rounded out the top five, with many other towns getting a vote or two. Apparently, the victory did not cause long-lasting animosity with at least one competitor—a January 2004 article in the *Pueblo Chieftain* observed that its hometown "was designated home of the Colorado State Fair in 1888 and Denver got stuck with the State Capitol building (talk about a money-losing operation)."[31]

With Denver's claim to the capital legally secure, the *Denver Tribune* called for construction on a statehouse to begin as soon as possible. "No attempt will be made to plunge the State deeply into a bonded debt in order to realize any fanciful idea in a monument of folly," the paper claimed. The *Tribune* saw no reason for delay, "but for some unexplained reason the State authorities have done nothing. It is time to begin." The 1881 legislature appropriated money for improvements to the capitol grounds donated by Henry Brown, but with an important clause. The legislation passed Colorado's Third General Assembly with the provision that the money would be spent only if the state won the court battle working its way through the judicial process. It also called for a small frame house to be built on the property for a permanent guard and for tools for the guard's use to improve the grounds. As often happened with capitol affairs in Colorado, executive staff members interpreted the legislature's specific mandates to fit the situation, which means they were not followed at all.[32]

In the meantime, after the embarrassing loss in the Colorado Supreme Court, Brown again filed a writ of error and made the ultimate appeal—to the United States Supreme Court. *Brown v. Colorado*, spiraling in expense and public ridicule, moved to the nation's capital in the fall of 1882. In the high court debates, Brown's primary claim differed from those he had used in the state courts. He argued that Colorado Territory had no jurisdiction to accept his land in 1868. The highest court in the land disagreed, believing the territory had broken no federal law. The state's new attorney general, Charles H. Toll, filed a motion to dismiss the case "for want of jurisdiction." The United States Supreme Court listened to arguments and granted the motion to dismiss in November 1882. Chief Justice Morrison R. Waite explained the decision:

> The question is not, whether the constitutional provisions and the statutes in question are valid, but whether, by the adoption of the Constitution by the people, and the passage of the statutes by the legislature, any condition attached to the conveyance has been broken which authorized [Brown] to revoke his deed and take possession of the property he conveyed. . . . All the obligations of the original contract remain, and the State has not attempted to impair them. If the contract is all that he claims it to be, and the Constitution and statutes are just what he says they are, the most that can be contended for is that the State has refused to do what the Territory agreed should be done.

Back in Colorado, the *Denver Tribune* expressed surprise at the ruling, although "only in the promptness in which it was rendered." No federal issue existed for the high court to involve itself, and the justices decided to let Coloradoans hash it out for themselves.[33]

Many in Colorado expressed profound relief that the Supreme Court had ended the land debate in favor of the state. But Henry Brown would not give up that easily. With his son, James, leading the legal team, the former landowner decided to try again. In early 1884 they took the case to the United States Circuit Court of Appeals, under the direction of Judge Moses Hallett. The Browns brought charges against a slew of defendants, including the current governor, James B. Grant, who had refused to call a special session of the legislature to deal with capitol construction the year before. Attorney General David F. Urmy argued for the state, and James Brown made the case for his father. Judge Hallett decided that his federal court had no jurisdiction to hear a case between Coloradoans, which pleased Henry Brown, who wanted another chance to argue before the United States Supreme Court. He remained defiant and sure of his position: "I have right on my side, and must win in time. I can afford to wait. I have lots of money and am not suffering in the meantime."[34]

The Browns packed their bags, heading east again to Washington, D.C. Following close behind was Theodore H. Thomas, the fourth state attorney general to argue the capitol site case. State leaders increasingly viewed the situation as ridiculous and pointlessly aggravating. Governor Benjamin H. Eaton sent a telegram to U.S. senator Henry Teller, asking him to urge the Supreme Court to act quickly on the case, as there could be no construction "till [the] State has clear title." But the court did not hear arguments until the middle of December 1885 and rendered its judgment in *Brown v. Grant, et. al.* on January 4, 1886. Associate Justice John M. Harlan drew the task of delivering the high court's opinion for the second time in the statehouse grounds case. He observed that unless the federal Congress made specific regulations, any property belonging to a territory belonged to the state once statehood was achieved, a position supported by Colorado's constitution. Justice Harlan indicated that Brown's financial desires unfairly motivated his case, and the high court would not judge such matters. Harlan also pointed out that voters had maintained the seat of government at Denver in 1881, and the court could find little reason to side with Brown. The Supreme Court belittled Brown for trying to reclaim the grounds, since in recent sessions of the General Assembly Colorado lawmakers had approved legislation to build a capitol on Brown's Bluff. Justice Harlan and the other members of the court decided that Brown did not deserve any money for the land or any more of the court's time. In the first days of 1886, Henry Brown lost his ten acres once and for all.[35]

Coloradoans reacted to Brown's second high court defeat with immediate jubilation. Attorney General Thomas wrote home: "The decision is final and I take great pleasure in now certifying that the title to the ten acres of land donated to the Territory of Colorado . . . by Henry C. Brown for the purpose of building a Capitol . . . thereon is now vested in the State of Colorado in fee simple and beyond controversy." Never again did Henry Brown and the state of Colorado face each other in court over the capitol matter. What he lacked in judicial victories, Brown made up for in notoriety as a stubborn, profiteering man who never knew when to acknowledge defeat.[36]

Like any adolescent, Coloradoans during this period desperately wanted both freedom to act independently and respect from their peers. After fifteen years of raucous and often unscrupulous territorial leadership, with the seat of power moving from town to town and building to building, Coloradoans anxiously awaited the day when they could find a permanent home for their representative government. Legal battles over the donated parcel on Brown's Bluff delayed even longer the relief territorial and state citizens so eagerly sought. But by 1886, with the donated land firmly in state hands and plans for a capitol under way, construction could begin on a structure that was to unify Coloradoans divided by region and politics. After a string of events best described as "something solemnly funny," the Centennial State began to stand on its own, proud and dignified, an equal member of the Union.

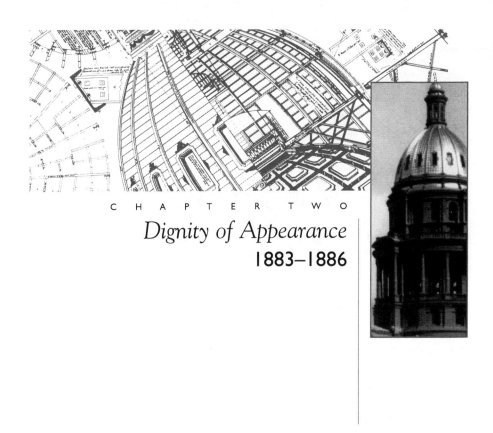

C  H  A  P  T  E  R    T  W  O

# Dignity of Appearance
## 1883–1886

O N THE DUSTY RIDGE SOUTHEAST OF DENVER, a ten-acre plot of ground teeming with prairie grass and tumbleweeds sat vacant while lawyers and politicians wrangled over its fate. But in the early 1880s the combined elements of economic prosperity, dedicated executive and legislative officials, and the perennial need to solidify the authority of representative government inspired many Coloradoans to prepare for the construction of a statehouse. Within three years state leaders selected a plan to erect a building fulfilling the needs of a respectable republican authority and boasting "dignity of appearance" inside and out. From 1883 to 1886, Coloradoans took the first steps toward creating for themselves and their posterity a capitol to house their government and provide a focus for popular accomplishment.

The three years immediately preceding statehouse construction merit careful examination. Territorial and state officials had muddled along with simple, unadorned accommodations long enough. In 1776 Thomas Paine, describing the representative bodies of such young societies, commented: "Some convenient tree will afford them a State-House, under the branches of which, the whole colony may assemble to deliberate on public matters." But Colorado officials wanted to prove their authority and the potential of the new state's citizens through grand architecture. The design of the building, connected to both ancient civilizations and American traditions, emulated other states and the federal government as Coloradoans asserted a common heritage with the older members of the Union. A flood of mineral wealth allowed for a building that blended the traditional reserve of representative institutions with the showiness desired by a proud people. To lead the project, the General Assembly created the Board of Capitol Managers in 1883, and over the next three years the board selected architectural designs and assigned construction contracts. By 1886, with court battles concluded and plans in hand, laborers commenced the long-awaited prospect of building the state-house. As a result of the efforts of many Coloradoans of this era, the capitol remains the most significant building in the state and represents all citizens better than anything else within Colorado's borders.[1]

As with any large undertaking, the design and construction of the state capitol demanded the appropriation of substantial funds. The state's wealth of natural resources provided the needed money, as agricultural production on the plains increased exponentially while millions of dollars a year flowed down from the mountains. Improved mining technology had resulted in an incredible amount of gold and silver ore, among other minerals, culled from rich and previously inaccessible veins. At the same time, the smelting and refining industry changed the landscape of Colorado towns, piercing the sky with smokestacks of factories that processed the raw ore. The state's population doubled as workers flooded the area looking for jobs in the rapidly expanding economy. This boom in extractive industries meant that while some citizens grew remarkably wealthy, the state could also invest in and tax these new sources of capital. Bond issues passed in the years that followed also helped put the providentially delivered bounty to good use. In simple terms, Colorado in the 1880s was filthy rich and ready to show off its wealth.

As the seat of government and the largest city in the state, Denver witnessed a burst of grandiose architecture during this period. With wealth cascading down from the mountains like so much spring snowmelt, the city of wood and locally fired brick slowly evolved into a metropolis of iron and stone. A journalist in 1884 commented on the "general air of 'd—m the expense'" as Denverites competed with one another to transform the dusty city. Most citizens equated financial success with dignified gentility, and Denver's changing physical appearance reflected this attitude. The promise of the capitol site drew construction southeast from the core of the city. New residences rose on the regally named Capitol Hill, a fancier term that replaced Brown's Bluff in local vernacular. The first serious debates about the state capitol came about in this atmosphere of excitement, of hope for continued prosperity.[2]

As his tenure in office drew to a close, Governor Frederick W. Pitkin spoke to the General Assembly, meeting in cramped rented quarters in Denver in 1883. The state's improving economy and recent victory over Henry Brown in the United States Supreme Court encouraged Pitkin and others to consider proceeding with plans for a statehouse. He demanded a suitable structure to preserve key state records as well as house the agencies of government, and shortly thereafter the Fourth General Assembly commenced deliberations on the statehouse matter. Within a month the members passed legislation setting aside $150,000 "for the construction and erection of a wing, to what is now or may hereafter be, the Capitol building of the State of Colorado." The law also authorized the creation of a state agency, the Board of Capitol Managers, to direct the statehouse project. In the coming years, this group would evolve into one of the most powerful, respected, and at times despised boards in Colorado. James B. Grant, who succeeded Governor Pitkin, signed the measure on February 11, 1883, formally commencing the task of building a capitol. After several decades of renting office space and shuttling records, politicians finally expressed a concerted interest in building a proper home for state institutions.[3]

The seven members of the Board of Capitol Managers, including men with scientific, financial, and political backgrounds, met for the first time on February 24, 1883. They expressed some concern at the task before them, particularly since the legislature had written such specific guidelines for design and construction. According to law, the board needed to erect a wing with several committee rooms and a chamber for the House of Representatives of no less than 9,000 square feet. The legislature wanted the wing ready for occupation by December 1, 1884, at the latest, before the next meeting of the General Assembly. Not quite sure of themselves but eager to tackle their daunting task, the board members prepared to carry out the legislature's directives.[4]

The managers requested samples from sandstone and granite quarries across the state to determine Colorado sources of construction materials. They also advertised in local and national newspapers for plans for the first statehouse wing. As befitted the specificity of the 1883 legislation, the architectural notice described in excruciating detail the dozens of offices needed for state government. The managers asked for preliminary drawings no later than early May 1883. When the deadline had passed, the board debated the nine plans it had received, all of which came under noms de plume, behind closed doors for several days. Many contained complaints from architects about the short time allowed for preparing submissions. The artisans argued that the hasty deadline had forced them to rush their craft and offer designs of poorer quality. The board agreed in spirit, but the managers bestowed praise on one entitled "Tuebor," likely submitted by the most noted statehouse architect of the period, Elijah E. Myers. Myers had drawn the winning plans for the Michigan and Texas statehouses, both of which bore the title of the favored plan in Colorado. He also wrote to the Colorado board of his disappointment in the short time allotted for architectural submissions in 1883. State engineer Edward S. Nettleton, a member of the capitol board, drew up a lengthy proposal for erecting the "Tuebor" design. The managers likely would have been prejudiced toward accepting the designs of this popular architect, but they eventually rejected "Tuebor" and the eight others. After this failure, the managers awoke to the fact that they had no idea how to do what they were supposed to do.[5]

With a legislative deadline to start construction slowly but steadily approaching, the Board of Capitol Managers needed to gather as much knowledge as possible on how to build a statehouse. They therefore resolved to "visit immediately the several Capitol buildings in the Northwestern States," a historical term for the region of the upper Mississippi River. By talking with politicians, architects, and other statehouse commissions, the managers hoped to settle their doubts and increase their awareness of construction and design techniques. They also resolved to visit factories and warehouses to study available materials and methods of building. Board members including Governor Grant, former governor John Routt, and Secretary George T. Clark left Denver's Union Station on May 22, 1883, and in less than two weeks visited six state capitols. The inspection tour began in Des Moines, Iowa, and continued through Madison, Wisconsin, to Lansing, Michigan. The board then turned south to Indianapolis, Indiana, headed west to Springfield, Illinois, and finally stopped to see the progress on the rising Topeka, Kansas, statehouse before returning to Denver on June 4. Over the course of their journey, the managers visited the best new examples of state government architecture. Construction had recently finished on the buildings in Michigan and Wisconsin, and the four other structures would be completed within a few years. The board members logged 3,750 miles on their tour and spoke with dozens of officials on the perils and possibilities of capitol construction. In the managers' minds, with these six examples for inspiration, the Colorado State Capitol began to take shape.[6]

The Centennial State's chief building did not emerge from an architectural vacuum. Each statehouse the board visited shared a common design popular in government buildings of the time, inspired by the national Capitol in Washington, D.C. This building, especially its dome, rose as a symbol of perseverance, determination, and victory in the Civil War. In the years that followed, many northern and western states believed imitation to be the sincerest form of flattery. In the wealth of the Gilded Age, therefore, statehouses served as the best vehicle for this symbolism. Modernity and patriotism went hand in hand in the industrial expansion after the Civil War, as Henry-Russell Hitchcock and William Seale argued:

> The end of the war witnessed a building boom in state capitols. Old states needed more space, and wanted more grandeur, and the new Western states, in spite of their sparse populations, wanted to build proud emblems. . . . They wanted buildings on the patriotic model of the national Capitol, but they also wanted urban stylishness and grandeur befitting their booming nation; little whitewashed and marbled temples were no longer enough. They wanted their legislative chambers to blaze with gas light, and their steam-heated marble halls to be as fine as those in the grandest metropolitan hotels. All this was to be done, of course, at the lowest possible cost.

All the best modern technologies deserved a place in a state capitol, and the building's design should hearken to exalted principles of government. Colorado's wealth of natural resources allowed such grandiose dreams to become realities.[7]

Following their return to Denver the managers debated the needs of the statehouse project. Secretary Clark told the *Rocky Mountain News* that the significance of the managers' trip lay in the promise of a "vast saving of money, avoidance of the mistakes made by other states, and a better building in the matter of size and rooms, construction, and general adaptibility [sic] for the purpose than any that we saw during our whole trip." Clark relayed the board's concern about the relatively small legislative appropriation for construction, since some recent capitols had cost over $4 million. Only five days after their return to Colorado, the managers assembled in Governor Grant's office and released a statement: "From such examination, inspection, and cost of erection of said buildings, we are of the opinion that a State House for Colorado cannot be properly built under the provisions of existing law." Unable to accomplish their goals, the board members placed the blame for their failure squarely with the legislature.[8]

Explaining their lack of success, the managers called the General Assembly's excessively technical requirements "impractical." The 9,000-square-foot House of Representatives chamber would be 30 percent larger than the one in Texas then under construction, the largest in the nation, and the *News* claimed that the forty-nine members of that body would need telephones to communicate with each other in the cavernous room. Some board members, the *News* reported, "are convinced that the present statute would work a great public injury if an attempt were made to carry out its provisions, [and] will resign their positions rather than permit their names to be connected with such a costly and foolish blunder." The managers proposed that Governor Grant call a special session of the legislature to revise the statehouse law, and they expectantly awaited his decision. Eleven days later, Grant issued a reply. He told the board that he did not consider the construction of a capitol important enough to demand a special session and that rented quarters would suffice until the Fifth General Assembly could take up the matter in 1885. Grant remarked: "The occasion is certainly not an extraordinary one; none of the vital interests of the people are affected in the least. It is simply a question of whether we will begin the erection of a State Capitol in the fall of 1883 or in the spring of 1885." The board continued to request stone samples and prepared a committee to test the quarried pieces it received for strength and durability. Henry Brown inspired the managers to settle the deeds on other parcels of land donated for the statehouse, after the refusal to call a special session caused him to attempt again to reclaim his land in court. But without revised guidelines for statehouse construction, the board accomplished little else as 1883 came to a close.[9]

The Board of Capitol Managers was even less active in 1884. The few meetings held that year focused on proposing legislation for the statehouse project, and Secretary Clark presented a draft to the board in early December. Also, a committee of geologists and engineers tested the dozens of stone samples the managers received in the first months of 1884. Members of the Denver Society of Civil Engineers, along with Regis Chauvenet, president of the Colorado School of Mines, and Joseph A. Sewall, president of the University of Colorado, used the Denver and Rio Grande Railroad facilities to conduct freezing and pressure tests. The committee compared the stone samples with granite, limestone, and sandstone from around the world. The scientists issued a splendid description of Colorado's quarry industry in the 1880s that helped shape the managers' opinions when time came for construction several years later. With prospective legislation ready and logistical concerns answered, the managers finished their first two years ready to help the General Assembly create new guidelines for the statehouse project in January 1885.[10]

Eager to get the managers back to work, the state legislature followed many of the board's suggestions in drawing up new guidelines. The 1885 bill reorganized the Board of Capitol Managers into a body with great discretionary authority and again included a number of provisions for construction. The legislation detailed the executive offices and legislative and judicial chambers needed in a suitable building, as well as storage space for state records.

Construction should finish no later than New Year's Day 1890 and should "in no event exceed the sum of one million dollars." The most significant requirement stated: "The said Capitol shall be built of stone, brick and iron, as far as practicable, and all the material[s] used in the construction of the same shall be those found and procured in the State of Colorado." This dedication to Colorado building materials made construction in the years that followed truly a statewide effort. Governor Benjamin Eaton signed the new legislation on April 1, 1885, and the revised board got to work immediately. The managers submitted advertisements to Denver, Chicago, and Boston newspapers for a "Capitol building to be erected upon the summit of a plat of ground in the City of Denver, State of Colorado, known as Capitol Hill, with its principal façade to the west." The managers gave the nation's designers until mid-July 1885 to send in their best work, slightly more time than the 1883 contest had allowed.[11]

With a later deadline, the managers expected a greater number of submissions and ones of better quality than they had received two years earlier. Before any responses arrived, they received a letter from Elijah Myers, the architect who had likely submitted their favorite plan in 1883, letting them know that he would start on a new set of designs immediately. On their cross-country tour two years earlier, the board had spent a great deal of time at the Michigan statehouse he designed and even visited Myers at his Detroit home after the stop in Lansing. Many on the board considered Myers the best man for the Colorado job, giving rise to justifiable speculation that the managers were predisposed to approve his submission in the 1885 architectural competition, regardless of the merits of other plans sent in by less famous individuals.[12]

The role of Elijah Myers in the Colorado State Capitol project, as well as his domineering presence in Gilded Age public architecture, demands more than a passing glance at his career. Born in Philadelphia in 1832, Myers studied law before switching to carpentry and design. He apprenticed with Samuel Sloan, one of the most influential structural designers of the era, and before starting his own firm Myers served as an engineer in the Union Army during the Civil War. Myers created detailed plans for the Macoupin County Courthouse in Carlinville, Illinois, in 1870, his first significant commission. He went on to design many other courthouses and city halls over the course of his career. While working in Springfield, Illinois, Myers closely followed the proposals for a new statehouse there. When Michigan issued a call for architects for a new Lansing capitol, Myers decided to try his luck. Plans submitted under the pseudonym "Tuebor," a Latin phrase from the Michigan state seal meaning "I will defend," impressed the Lansing commission. Out of twenty designs, the upstart Myers won. His simple yet dignified structure rose over

Elijah E. Myers, the controversial architect of the Michigan, Texas, and Colorado statehouses, among many other buildings, in an 1880s portrait. Courtesy, Colorado Historical Society, F94

the next few years, surmounted by a dome reminiscent, but not a copy, of the national Capitol. As one historian stated, "Myers was the right man for the job: he was good, and he was cheap."[13]

After his success at Lansing, Myers moved his family to Michigan and set up an architectural office in Detroit. In 1880 he won several contracts for government buildings, including the Arapahoe County Courthouse in Denver. Construction of the building on Sixteenth Street, several blocks northwest of the statehouse grounds, lasted three years and cost a little over $311,000. Denverites Lester Fillmore and Peter Gumry directed work at the structure, built of Cañon City sandstone. In the meantime, Myers tried and failed to secure appointments to design statehouses in Connecticut, Indiana, and Georgia. Those losses faded from his attention as Myers entered another capitol competition with designs again named "Tuebor," submitting them to Texas commissioners in need of a new government building in Austin. He provided the Lone Star State with an immense structure that used the national Capitol as a guide more than any other Gilded Age statehouse had. Although conflicts with the managing board in Texas resulted in Myers's eventual dismissal from the project, crews in Austin carried out his designs and completed the majestic structure in 1888. Questions of dishonesty on Myers's part, which plagued him through his many projects across the country, adversely affected the architect but not his creation. Indeed, Myers kept a drawing of the Texas capitol on his letterhead for many years afterward.[14]

Generally, historians have given Myers a great deal of credit for creating remarkable designs, but some have rightly pointed out his substantial personal flaws. Henry-Russell Hitchcock and William Seale described the controversial Myers in glowing terms. They pointed out that he always thought of himself as an amateur architect, never having received professional training in the craft. Rhapsodizing on his ability, Hitchcock and Seale commented that appreciating "one of Elijah Myers's capitols from across the open land was to feel the immensity of its scale and the vigor of its decoration; to push through its doors even today is to vanish from the world outside into fantasies of vines and maidens and state flowers in glass and bronze." But perhaps Paul Goeldner provided the most accurate description of the mercurial architect when he called Myers "a talented, dishonest, hard-working, spiteful, clever, unbalanced, self-assured, self-destructive hypochondriac." Myers displayed all of these traits in substantial amounts while participating in the Colorado capitol project.[15]

In this atmosphere of success and praise, the Board of Capitol Managers held the controversial Myers in great esteem. During the early summer of 1885 the managers awaited what promised to be an architectural bonanza of Gilded Age splendor as top designers hurried to prepare their plans. The

West front of the "Corinthian" design for the capitol, drawn by Elijah Myers in 1886. Author's collection

managers assembled in Denver on July 13 to study the twenty-one submissions. After three days of deliberation, the managers chose their five favorites, named "Corinthian," "Classic," "Granite," "Simplex Munditiis," and "Nil Sine Numine." After opening the sealed envelopes that accompanied each submission, the managers invited the five selected architects to Colorado to try to convince the board to approve their designs. Not surprisingly, Myers's plans, entitled "Corinthian," were among the five selected, and board members voted it their favorite. After listening to the architects' testimony on the five plans, the managers voted on August 31 for the three most deserving designs and, most important, for the submission that would eventually crown Brown's Bluff. Two Denver architects came in second and third, Frank E. Edbrooke for "Simplex Munditiis" and H. B. Seeley for "Nil Sine Numine," respectively. Surprising practically no one, the managers awarded the top accolades to Myers's "Corinthian" design in what might easily have been a fixed contest from the start.[16]

Myers presented a detailed report to the managers in August 1885 describing various elements of his plan, but delivering designs specific enough for construction posed problems. That year Myers's firm also produced plans for a territorial capitol in Boise, Idaho, and he still held the post of supervising architect for the Texas statehouse. Consequently, Myers's attention often wandered from his responsibilities in Denver. He often overestimated his ability to manage his time wisely, but the Colorado statehouse board retained faith in the period's most famous architect of public buildings. Secretary Clark claimed that erecting Myers's statehouse would take five years and, referring to the financial cap of $1 million set by the legislature, added: "If we can't build it for that amount, we shan't build it at all." Confidence in the board members and their architect soared.[17]

To understand the significance and symbolism of Myers's plans for the state capitol, one must first examine the background of this architectural genre. The connection to classical design dominates any initial interpretation of the Colorado statehouse. The word *capitol* comes from the ancient Romans, upon whose Capitoline Hill the republican and imperial Senate often met. American culture paid homage to its classical foundations by not only using terms like *Senate* in its politics but also imitating Greek, Roman, and even Egyptian architecture. After the American Revolution, neoclassicism, a design style that reflected the ancient civilizations, grew in popularity and reflected the belief that one day the United States would achieve similar greatness. Many eighteenth- and nineteenth-century American government structures employed classical styles, most notably the national Capitol at Washington, D.C. Amateur architect William Thornton drew plans for the federal legislature's home in 1792, adopting the simplicity and dignity of these ancient forms. Although the U.S. Capitol has undergone repairs following a wartime burning in 1814, expansion to accommodate a growing country, and many renovations over the years, it reached its basic shape familiar to modern Americans by the 1860s. Although not the first building in the nation to adopt ancient styles, the home of Congress served as the example for many state buildings designed in the years to come. Political scientist Charles T. Goodsell has remarked that classical architecture directly connects a government "with antiquity, thus establishing its temporal permanence beyond doubt." In 1886 Myers proudly claimed that his use of the Corinthian order of architecture, one of the most popular of the Roman era, would place the Colorado capitol on par with buildings of the best ancient civilizations. Myers provided Coloradoans with an expectation of greatness by architecturally entrenching their future statehouse amid classical temples of authority.[18]

The idea of a state capitol indicates the need for permanency and consistency in a representative government, something Coloradoans in the 1880s sought desperately. Goodsell identified six physical characteristics that often unite such structures across the nation: a prominent site, parklike grounds, cruciform massing, a central dome, a temple front, and a grand central space. Goodsell went on to define the general purpose of a state capitol:

> In sum, the American statehouse is both an imposing and open edifice. It represents sovereign power, on the one hand, and constitutional restraint on power, on the other. It is controlled by government officials, but crowded with ordinary people. It is a building whose symbolism is rooted in remote antiquity, yet still contains symbols and history of one of the fifty American states.

It also represents the preservation of a certain set of political ideas or philosophies and replicates the basic structure of federal authority at the state level through similar executive, legislative, and judicial bodies.[19]

The home of government, a capitol becomes the automatic site for expressions of state interests, whether by politicians or citizens, used collectively as "stages for the performance of political rituals." John A. Straayer has referred to the capitol and its assembly halls as, among other things, a "comedy club," "business office," "gold leaf big top," "casino," "pure theater," "the cave of the winds," an "arena," and a "fraternity house." In ancient Athens the theater provided a physical space for the populace to gather, not only to watch a compelling scene but also to host debates about shared political concerns. The Roman arena, likewise, served as both a place of entertainment and a sphere of social interaction, where emperors, patricians, and plebeians joined together to share a common experience. Thousands of years later, thousands of miles away, the Colorado State Capitol represents many of the same ideals as those ancient sites. It stands as a stage for the great dramatic moments of its society and exists as the place where the citizens' political needs and desires find expression, where the chorus and spectacle of government both create and are created by the perceptions of the broader audience.[20]

Myers called simplicity the "grand characteristic" of ancient architecture and proudly employed that principle in his designs. He cautioned Colorado's statehouse board to avoid the excessive and fanciful decoration seen in some Gilded Age structures, which only detracted from the basic purpose of the building—governing a society. Myers designed the exterior of the Colorado capitol to appear like most other office buildings of the day, with the dome constituting the only substantial ornamentation. Explaining this reserved style, Myers stated:

> Where laws are enacted for the government of a great State, public records preserved, and accommodations provided for the executive and judiciary branches of the government, the character of the building should be such as to command respect for these high purposes; and the grotesque and fanciful styles of architecture resorted to so extensively at the present day, should be carefully shunned, as unbefitting to a structure where dignity of appearance is demanded by its uses.

For Myers, decoration should only augment the primary functions of a capitol building. He designed simple yet substantial legislative and judicial chambers, ensuring politicians and judges would focus on their statutory duties. By making the chambers primarily functional, with limited but dignified ornamentation, Myers hoped to shape the behavior of future Colorado legislators.[21]

The designs of the Colorado statehouse also expressed the American principle of favoring representation over individual authority. Like many other capitol buildings across the nation, Myers placed executive officials on the lower floors, whereas the legislature sits symbolically above the governor. For most of the building's history the executive office has blended inauspiciously with the other rooms on the first floor, deserving of no more or less attention than any other. Perhaps most important, Myers intended the capitol to house every possible agency of state government, every board and commission, every politician and civil servant. With a structure as large as Colorado's statehouse, future generations of leaders would have no need to expand beyond the building's walls.[22]

Crowded into the capitol's lower floors, Myers located what the legislature proscribed as all the offices needed to manage Colorado's interests for years to come. On the first floor the governor's office took up only part of one quadrant, close to the secretary of state. Also on that floor Myers assigned offices for the state treasurer, state auditor, attorney general, superintendent of public instruction, land and railroad commissions, and the state engineer. The rest of the executive branch occupied the ground level, including the adjutant general, the historical and horticultural societies, the state geologist and mineral board, and the mine inspector. The concerns of a western state demanded that such important issues as water and irrigation, railroads, mining, and land management deserved suitable quarters near the pulse of government. Myers divided up the offices "with especial reference to their business connections with each other, and the convenience not only of the officers who will occupy them, but of those who will have public business transactions therein." Along with the boiler room, which extended down into the subbasement, the ground floor even boasted living quarters for the janitorial staff. The new statehouse demanded perpetual care to maintain its physical condition. Under the public floors, Myers designed the labyrinthine subbasement to store records and serve the logistical needs of a working office building. To avoid the mess of coal deliveries to the capitol, the architect proposed a network of tunnels with carts to shuttle fuel from a depot south of the building under Fourteenth Avenue to the boilers. Although statehouse caretakers stopped using the carts many years ago, some of the twin rails of this ingenious system still remain in the tunnels.[23]

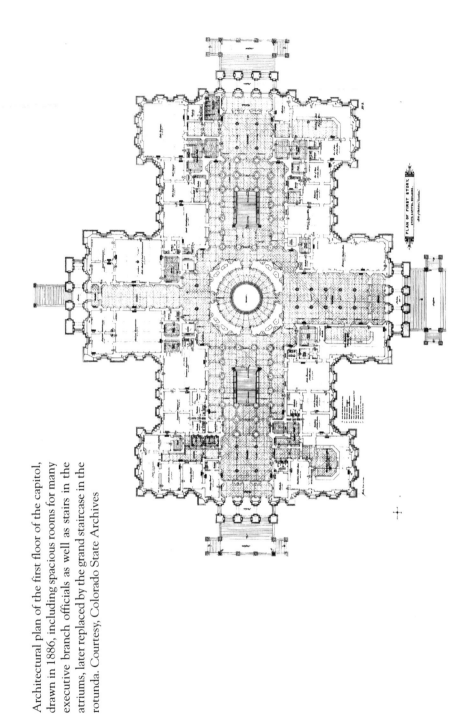

Architectural plan of the first floor of the capitol, drawn in 1886, including spacious rooms for many executive branch officials as well as stairs in the atriums, later replaced by the grand staircase in the rotunda. Courtesy, Colorado State Archives

Tunnel underneath Fourteenth Avenue with preserved rails of the coal cart system, as viewed from the subbasement of the capitol in 2002. Author's collection

Resting above this buzz of activity, Myers placed the chambers for the Senate and House of Representatives and the supreme court room on the second floor, stretching up to the third. The high court occupied the north wing, and a massive state and law library filled the east wing with sagging shelves of deerskin-bound volumes. Although many statehouses place bicameral legislative chambers at opposing ends of the structure, Myers located Colorado's on a perpendicular axis, with the Senate to the south and the House of Representatives to the west. The legislative desks would face the presiding officer's dais in a semicircular pattern, a tradition in representative bodies that dated back to the *estates-general* of revolutionary French King Louis XVI's reign. The third-floor chamber galleries, from which citizens could keep a wary eye on the assembly, filled an important democratic function. Accompanying these ringside seats, Myers provided every legislative committee with its own room on the third floor. Their chamber desks gave members of the legislature their only private space in the building. Contemporary political thought considered permanent quarters outside the chambers an abomination to the concept of citizen legislators who would hastily finish their tasks and return home.[24]

The desire to follow the national example both in governmental structure and architectural appearance influenced many states looking for a sense of belonging to the Union. Construction on the most famous aspect of the U.S. Capitol, its dome, continued through the dark days of the Civil War at the request of many leaders. President Abraham Lincoln commented in 1863, "If the people see this Capitol going on, they will know that we intend the Union shall go on." State capitols that rose in the Gilded Age almost invariably included the rounded top. Domes crowned the statehouses in California, Illinois, Indiana, Iowa, Kansas, Michigan, Texas, and Wyoming, among others built in the decades just after the war. Myers's designs for capitols and courthouses almost without exception included domes surmounting a central rotunda, and he made no exception for Colorado.[25]

In Myers's 1886 narrative architectural description submitted to the Board of Capitol Managers, he saved his greatest praise for the rotunda and dome, "a magnificent feature of the building." He credited the tower with bringing light into the building while drawing air up and out like a chimney, continually cycling fresh air through the lower floors. Just as his overall "Corinthian" design rests heavily on the architecture of the ancient world, the Colorado dome expands on work done by the Greeks and Romans many centuries ago. The Pantheon in Rome, perhaps the best-known and sturdiest dome of the ancient world, influenced construction all over the empire, and succeeding generations expanded upon its example. Additionally, Myers's design connects to the pioneering work of Filippo Brunelleschi, who designed the dome for the cathedral in Florence, Italy, in the 1400s. By designing both an inner and an outer dome, a technique relatively unused in Europe at the time, Brunelleschi introduced a method that allowed for building larger and more impressive domes. Myers used the inner/outer shell style in all his statehouse designs. The most important provision for his favorite element of the building, however, was to allow visitors to ascend to observation decks that would present "to the sight-seer an unequaled view of the surrounding country." For the benefit of future generations, Myers wanted to exploit this natural resource in Denver that Lansing and Austin lacked. He always intended the dome to serve as both decoration and a tourist attraction, providing all who came to the capitol with an opportunity to brave the climb and marvel at the breathtaking panorama.[26]

Since the 1880s, architects and historians have debated the merits and defects of Myers's plans. Henry-Russell Hitchcock and William Seale included Colorado's statehouse in their thorough work *Temples of Democracy* in 1976. At times they glorified Myers and belittled the Board of Capitol Managers for later altering such a wonderful architect's designs. A change to the rotunda that added the grand staircase from the first to the second floors, in Hitchcock and Seale's opinion, destroyed "the sense of spatial surprise that Myers provided." Perhaps the two scholars best speak for themselves: "Because of inappropriate

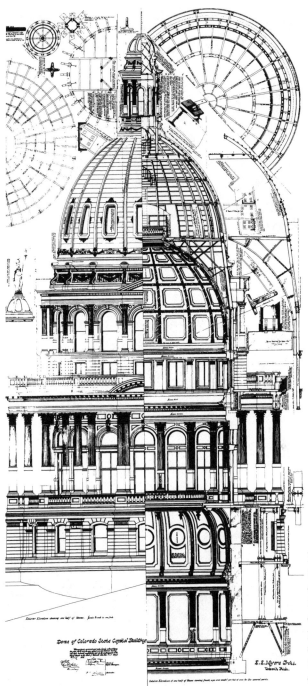

Elevation and cross section of the capitol dome, drawn in 1886, with the inner and outer domes, observation levels, and proposed model of a statue for the top. Courtesy, Colorado State Archives

changes made after Myers's departure, Colorado's Capitol has a piecemeal look not characteristic of Myers, and the interior lacks the grandeur of the architect's work at Lansing and Austin." Hitchcock and Seale's rhapsodic defense of the architect, which often ignores his many ethical transgressions, results in a description of the Colorado statehouse as a neglected, unappreciated stepchild of its brilliant father.[27]

Others over the years expressed sarcastic disapproval of the executed design. Robert L. Chase of the *Rocky Mountain News* bemoaned the structure in 1950, when a lack of adequate space demanded new structures to house state government. Chase chastised the state for such wasteful construction sixty years earlier:

> It cost $2,800,000—which would be just a fraction of what it would cost to build the same building today. Not that we would, I hope, build the same building today. I hope we wouldn't waste all that space in a dome and all the space in nooks and crannies and stairways and corridors and whatnot. I hope if we were doing it again we would put in fewer places to catch dirt and fewer places to get lost in and a whole lot more places which could be used. As it is, we had to put up three state buildings in the vicinity of the Capitol and still don't have any room to put anything.

In the decades after Myers drew up his capitol plans for Colorado, the number of state institutions grew at a rate inconceivable to Gilded Age politicians and architects. Myers cannot be blamed for underestimating the unforeseen demands placed on his designs.[28]

Historians in the 1950s, a particularly difficult decade for the capitol structurally, expressed a kind of benign ambivalence toward the edifice. The Denver Posse of the Westerners, a group of amateur and professional historians, published two articles about the statehouse in their annual *Brand Book*, a collection of essays about western history. In the 1952 volume, Martin A. Wenger, the assistant Colorado state archivist, claimed that "one has some tendency to doubt the architect's judgment as he sips coffee in the gloomy basement lunch stand." Paul D. Harrison, writing during the gold rush centennial celebration in 1959, treated the capitol more kindly. He called it "perhaps the most significant public building in the Rocky Mountain West. Coloradoans hold it in high esteem not only on account of the important position it occupies in the state's history, but also because of the abundant natural, warm and simple charm that it possesses." Interpretations of the statehouse in the mid-twentieth century often took a "to each his own" approach.[29]

Two master's theses written about the capitol differ somewhat in their treatment of the building's design and the suitability of Myers's plans. The 1962 work of William R. Pyle contains an exceptional amount of factual information about the capitol and other state buildings, but he rarely looked at the deeper meaning of the structure. Still, Pyle did encourage his readers to think of the statehouse "as a monument and a shrine to Colorado's history, its people, and its natural resources, and not another mere office building." Clarice Eleanore Moffett similarly argued in her 1936 thesis that "Colorado's Capitol may not be the largest or the costliest or most ornamental in the country, but it is majestic, substantial and commodious." But these scholarly works often shied away from a great deal of interpretation or opinion, instead presenting a more factual account of the building.[30]

Not surprisingly, tour guide booklets have been kind to the capitol over the years. The reader often notices the relative ease with which these publications deliver their accolades in an almost natural, inevitable manner. The most comprehensive tourist book, Margaret Coel's *The Pride of Our People: The Colorado State Capitol*, expresses an appreciation for the use of classical architecture over more fanciful Victorian styles. Coel observed: "The Capitol they built is massive and dignified, yet graceful, its scale proportioned and humane. It connects us to our past, to what we have accomplished." Coel echoed this sentiment in a book coauthored with Gladys Doty and Karen Gilleland, *Under the Golden Dome: Colorado's State Capitol*, which described the building as a representation of permanence in a state that shortly before had consisted mostly of ramshackle mining towns. One of the first guidebooks, a state government directory printed in 1899 before construction concluded, considered the statehouse "a magnificent tribute to the liberality and progressiveness" of Coloradoans. The directory praised the building's similarities to the U.S. Capitol and its Corinthian design while declaring the dome's observation deck "a sight place that the visitor to Denver, and in fact the resident, should not neglect." A tour book published in 1939 reflected on the capitol with grand patriotism:

> In form, the Statehouse is an adaptation of the National Capitol which, in turn, was inspired by the architecture of ancient Rome. This monumental style was adopted by our Nation's builders as the one most consistent with the ideals of the young Republic. By the time Colorado was admitted to the Union, style and ideals were wellnigh inseparable. Colorado pioneers accepted without question the pillared tower and dome as traditional symbols of democratic power and dignity.

In the collective mind of the Centennial State, the capitol represented the rule of law and authority of the people enshrined in constitutional provisions.[31]

A recent interpretation of the Colorado statehouse came from Bill Handley, a volunteer at the capitol in the late 1990s. As an amateur architect who on several occasions portrayed Elijah Myers at Colorado Day celebrations, Handley proposed a theory about why the building feels so inviting. The porches and anterooms at the capitol's entrances provide a dark compression, released with the light-filled atriums and rotunda. Handley called the columns and arches "a forest effect," where a visitor can take refuge from the more open interior expanses. The complexity of the ornamentation balances the patterns of columns and materials, drawing the visitor farther into the building to see what lies around the next corner. As Handley commented, a visitor "knows there is a space beyond one's immediate view, but one must actually walk over there to see it." Handley believed Myers created "a building that is visually impressive, spatially rich, and instinctively satisfying." In this manner, Myers's design for the Colorado capitol leads visitors to search through the many recesses and expanses throughout the building. Mystery and uncertainty encourage exploration and ultimately provide a sense of discovery.[32]

Although some later critics lambasted Myers's design or the way in which the managers carried it out, contemporary audiences applauded the selection. Describing Colorado's statehouse plans in May 1886, *Harper's Weekly* paternalistically claimed that even though the state was "ridiculously rich and extremely young, Colorado was not led into wild architectural extravagances." Picking up on the ethnic and political sectionalism that often influenced life in Colorado, *Harper's* called the design "a compromise between the bonanza members of the north . . . and the southern members, whose income is largely derived from the 'bounty' paid on hawks' heads and wolves' scalps." The national newspaper credited state officials for their dedication to the use of Colorado materials and applauded the discovery of various stone resources statewide. In the meantime, the capitol board prepared to turn grandiose sketches into architectural reality. On January 2, 1886, Myers's firm submitted complete building specifications to the managers and confidently ensured them that the capitol would cost no more than the million-dollar legislative limit. Encapsulating his opinions on his winning design, Myers beamed: "The building, when completed, will be the finest in the State of Colorado, and one of the finest buildings in the country, of which every citizen of the State may be justly proud."[33]

The building designed by Elijah Myers and, over the next fifteen years, erected on the summit of Brown's Bluff must be understood through the lens of the late nineteenth century. The structure mimics the national Capitol, as do many statehouses of the period, all variations on a theme. In this sense, the Colorado State Capitol is not unique but instead is part of a trend intended to echo the sentiment of patriotism and the rule of law embodied in the federal edifice. It also transfers federal institutions to the state level, enshrining constitutional principles and supporting representative over executive authority. By touring other statehouses across the nation, the managers ensured that Colorado's structure would fit comfortably with those of its sister states, a symbolic method of establishing the Centennial State among the older members of the Union. The building's architectural competition might have unduly favored the most famous capitol architect of the day, but Coloradoans still won an impressive building, unparalleled in the region. Regardless of similarities to other capitols across the country or of criticism leveled against the structure in later years, the Colorado capitol represents all citizens of the state better than anything else does. Its design promised simplicity in function yet "dignity of appearance," fulfilling the needs of state government while providing an appropriate focus for the wealth, pride, and accomplishment of Colorado. All that remained was to build it.

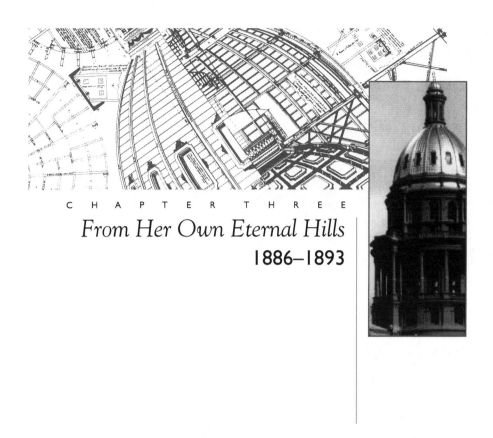

*From Her Own Eternal Hills*

1886–1893

F OR A QUARTER OF A CENTURY, the dream of a permanent home for
 Colorado's government had been just that, a dream. Records and furnishings traveled from town to town and building to building, giving
the impression of a transient state authority. But Coloradoans took steps
to settle their wandering government by establishing the capital at Denver in 1881 and creating the Board of Capitol Managers in 1883 to oversee statehouse construction. Three years later the managers possessed the
designs for the structure and the funds to build it, but the challenges
faced in the planning stages paled in comparison to countless difficulties
that hindered construction over the next fifteen years. The first period of
work, from 1886 to 1893, witnessed the completion of the building's exterior, boasting a facade of native stone "from her own eternal hills." The project
also served as a significant motivator for developing economies around the
state. Most important, as the walls and dome climbed from the dusty summit

of Brown's Bluff, the building's role as the representative symbol of Colorado took shape.

Several local and national economies prospered as a result of the capitol's construction during this period, yet the work also inspired troublesome contradictions. Although railroads shipped Colorado sandstone to the statehouse site as well as to lucrative markets in the Midwest and Great Plains states, Denverites opposed plans to lay tracks through their streets to facilitate construction. The Board of Capitol Managers promoted rural economies by using stone from isolated areas of the state but selected a Chicago firm for ironwork rather than utilize local industries. The project experienced the labor discontent sweeping across the nation in the late nineteenth century when quarrymen struck for better pay and shorter hours, slowing work in Denver. As the state's largest building project to date, the capitol work participated in many of the economic forces of the late nineteenth century. And even before stonecutters finished the exterior walls, the building started drawing Coloradoans to their common symbol, most notably during the 1890 cornerstone ceremony. From its earliest days, the statehouse served as a unifying agent for a western state that, like most others, needed some physical object to bring its disparate peoples and regions together. By 1893, with the superstructure complete and work set to begin on the interior, the populace could finally gaze upon the representation of its brief past, prosperous present, and hopeful future rising on the dusty ridge above Denver.

Initially, the capitol managers wanted one contractor to control all aspects of construction and help select materials for the structure. Five contractors submitted bids for the project on February 20, 1886, following the guidelines provided by architect Elijah Myers, although only one came in under the legislature's million-dollar limit. With little other choice the board picked thrifty William D. Richardson of Springfield, Illinois, and entrusted him with the task of erecting the statehouse. Richardson beat out a number of local bidders including Peter Gumry, who had directed construction of Denver's Arapahoe County Courthouse several years earlier and now worked for the managers as an architectural adviser. In March 1886 the managers gave Richardson his first assignment and asked him to investigate the possibility of using sandstone piers to support the building. The contractor studied four quarries in the state, one each in Fremont, Jefferson, Gunnison, and Las Animas counties. Unimpressed with those choices, Richardson looked north from Denver to new quarries nestled in the hogback of the Front Range.[1]

Massive cliffs of sandstone loomed over the valleys and plains below, tempting nearby settlers to take advantage of the substantial natural resource. Private citizens had hauled wagonloads of durable red and white sandstone to towns on the Cache la Poudre River throughout the 1870s and into the 1880s.

In 1882 William H.B. Stout organized two flagstone quarries in Spring Canyon, just behind the ridge to the west of Fort Collins, in the shadow of Horsetooth Mountain. Shortly thereafter, Stout sold his quarries to Henry C. Lett, superintendent of the stone division of the Union Pacific Railway Company. Within a year a subsidiary of the Union Pacific laid tracks through Bellvue up the valley to the Stout sandstone quarries. Superintendent Lett helped develop this industry into a powerful economic force, with contracts for paving stone coming in from cities like Denver, Omaha, Kansas City, and Topeka faster than quarrymen could ship it. The managers, along with Elijah Myers, Peter Gumry, and William Richardson, visited Stout on March 22, 1886, to determine the stone's suitability for the capitol subbasement supports. Impressed board member John Routt claimed "that a sufficient quantity of stone could be taken from the quarries to build a wall around the state as did the Chinese of old." A week later the managers and Richardson met in Denver and agreed to use the Stout stone, bringing a sense of pride and a lucrative contract to the sandstone industry above Fort Collins.[2]

In the early summer of 1886, laborers arrived in Denver and prepared for work on the statehouse. But before construction commenced, a personal conflict flared between Richardson and Myers, who had worked with each other before on several projects. Attempting to reduce the financial burden of building the capitol, Richardson suggested some changes to Myers's plans, such as omitting the elevators and three of the four entry porticoes. The contractor likely realized the difficulty of coming in under his low estimate for erecting the statehouse and started looking for ways to cut costs. Indignant at the challenge to his skill and ability, Myers vehemently opposed any alterations. He demanded that the managers appoint him supervising architect to ensure the complete execution of his design, and the board acquiesced. Worried about the developing feud between the architect and the contractor, the managers wanted a third man in charge to keep the peace. They appointed Peter Gumry superintendent to oversee all the work and to serve as an intermediary between Myers and Richardson. With three competent men heading the construction team, the managers felt confident as the project commenced.[3]

Shovels struck Brown's Bluff on July 6, 1886, almost ten years after statehood and just shy of thirty years after Denver's first log and sod cabins arose on the banks of Cherry Creek. Over the next two months crews excavated twenty feet into Brown's Bluff before reaching bedrock, eight feet deeper than originally expected. As September arrived, a crew of 250 worked at several ledges of sandstone at Arkins, part of the Stout quarry system on the ridge west of Buckhorn Creek. They extracted hundreds of slabs of the tan rock that would eventually support the upper floors of the capitol. Wagons carried the stone several miles to the Stout rail yard, and from there it was "shipped as fast as cars can be secured" down the line to Denver. By mid-spring 1887 laborers at the capitol site had finished work on the forty-two immense pillars, each six feet square. In the years that followed the Stout system flourished, providing paving and building stone to markets across the nation thanks to the Union Pacific's transportation facilities. The Spring Creek quarries and abandoned foundations of Stout's buildings rest at the bottom of Horsetooth Reservoir, although a sign on a Larimer County road marks the spot of the formerly booming area. The quarry at Arkins that provided the capitol's stone, however, still functions in the early twenty-first century, now managed by the Arkins Park Stone Corporation.[4]

All persons involved in the statehouse project expressed pleasure over the successful first year of labor as the summer of 1887 approached, but the amiable progress stumbled with the onset of the first major controversy regarding construction. Richardson petitioned the Denver City Council to allow the Union Pacific to build a line from its yards to the statehouse grounds, an act he claimed would save him $20,000 in transportation costs. Outraged local homeowners, who had built expensive mansions near the capitol site, worried that their property value would decrease by millions of dollars with a railroad line passing by their front doors. To ensure that their dusty streets did not become the next right-of-way for the Union Pacific, many residents gathered together to prevent the line from being built. These well-armed bands of vigilantes patrolled constantly to prevent crews from laying the track in the dead of night. Tense divisions emerged in the city between supporters of the capitol work and opponents of the railroad. Governor Benjamin H. Eaton pleaded with the enraged homeowners, telling them that a temporary rail line would expedite construction so the building would be finished sooner. Eventually, the Union Pacific decided against laying tracks to the capitol, and Richardson paid to haul stone and other material to the site by wagon.[5]

With the sandstone supports complete, Richardson checked with the managers and Myers about any final changes to the capitol before his crews set the foundation flooring in the late summer of 1887. Richardson selected a granite quarry named Brownville, high in the Rockies near Silver Plume, which had sent stone to Topeka for use in the Kansas State Capitol's exterior stairs. Owned by mining magnate and powerful state Republican politician William A. Hamill, Brownville sat near the Colorado Central Railroad, which presupposed the transportation difficulties faced by many other quarries. Several Colorado newspapers congratulated Richardson on his favorable employment policies, including the institution of an eight-hour day with ten-hour-day wages, which prevented quarry unions from protesting conditions at Brownville. Silver Plume's *Silver Standard* expected Richardson to employ thirty laborers at the quarry for at least three years and anticipated a boom in requests for the granite. The paper optimistically prophesized that most of the stone needed to build the capitol, not just the foundation, would eventually come from Brownville. Coloradoans, the *Silver Standard* believed, wanted "an edifice to be pointed to with pride, in preference to squandering a clean million and in return have a botch which would reflect discredit upon the state." Within a few weeks the Brownville operation started in earnest, with laborers dressing and shipping blocks of granite to Denver for installation in the capitol's foundation. Quarrymen and the local press predicted many years of productive work at the blossoming granite works, for as the *Silver Standard* casually remarked: "Prosperity Demands It."[6]

As the people of Silver Plume established a thriving new industry to bolster their substantial silver mining economy, in Denver William Richardson grew increasingly nervous. He realized that he had substantially misjudged the cost of erecting the capitol when a bill for over $45,000 arrived from the Brownville quarry. Richardson racked his brain to divine a solution and finally decided to shift the blame. Richardson accused Superintendent Gumry of approving the expensive Brownville granite instead of using rubble for foundation stone in the subbasement, as called for in Myers's plans. Gumry, who did not have the authorization to choose any construction materials, emphatically denied the charge, and Myers backed up the superintendent. Richardson demanded that the Board of Capitol Managers reimburse him for the expense, but the skeptical group sided with Gumry. In response, Richardson wrote a vitriolic letter to the managers accusing them of turning their backs on their contractor. He also blamed Myers for drawing plans that no one could possibly build for less than $1 million, likely a justifiable charge. Before returning home to Illinois to confer with his attorneys, Richardson fired all 200 laborers at the capitol site. On October 24, 1887, statehouse construction simply stopped.[7]

In the waning months of 1887 Richardson prepared to bring suit against the Board of Capitol Managers for over $72,000 to recoup his losses from Brownville, and the board consulted with Attorney General Alvin Marsh. The contractor promised that as soon as he received the money he would return to Denver and resume construction. Residents of Silver Plume expressed a great deal of worry about the matter as their quarry operations shuddered to a halt. The *Silver Standard* believed the managers would "keep on monkeying around until the state will fully decide not to have any Capitol Building." The board considered the situation disconcerting as well and worried about the future of the statehouse project. Taking a firm stance, the board demanded that Richardson appear before the managers on February 9, 1888, and explain himself. When Richardson failed to appear, the board declared his contract abandoned. To satisfy wage claims made by the workers Richardson had fired in 1887, the state legislature appropriated $5,000 several years later for a relief account, from which the board paid out until 1902. Richardson lost his lawsuit in the U.S. Circuit Court of Appeals in late 1888 and dejectedly boarded a train that took him home to Illinois.[8]

With the Richardson fiasco settled, the Board of Capitol Managers needed a new contractor to resume work at the capitol site. The managers placed advertisements in Denver newspapers and Chicago architectural journals in early March 1888 for a firm to complete the foundation of the statehouse. After carefully considering the proposals they received, the managers selected two young Denver businessmen for the task, William F. Geddes and David D. Seerie, on March 27. Unlike Richardson, however, Geddes and Seerie did not secure a contract to erect the entire statehouse. The managers decided to break up the capitol work among several firms instead of relying on one general contractor. This practice firmly entrenched the board's power over the statehouse project by ensuring that it made all major decisions concerning material and labor. This influence grew steadily over the next several decades and inadvertently transformed the board into one of the most influential agencies of state government.[9]

While the managers sorted out their new duties in the summer months of 1888, Geddes and Seerie waited patiently to hire laborers and resume work. The board allowed quarrymen at Brownville to ship enough stone to complete the foundation of the subbasement but refused to make a hasty decision on using that quarry further. Erecting the superstructure of the capitol, the next major task after finishing the foundation, required a decision regarding the kind of stone to use. Myers's plans called for white sandstone, smoothly cut for a dignified appearance. To that end, Superintendent Gumry and the state engineer, Edward Nettleton, had inspected a white sandstone deposit in Gunnison County in 1886. Months of negotiation followed, with Gunnison residents promised significant contracts for work at the statehouse on several occasions. But in the intervening two years the managers' tastes had changed, and many in Colorado recognized the porous white stone as an unwise choice, with the stacks belching coal smoke around Denver. The board decided instead "that for our chief building our best stone should be adopted," the strong and durable granite. The managers expressed concerns about using the Brownville quarry, which had unintentionally caused such chaos. They had received many other samples of granite over the years and knew of a number of Colorado sources of the durable stone.[10]

The board did not publicly declare its decision to use granite, and with good reason. Most estimates the managers received placed the likely cost of a sandstone statehouse at $388,456, whereas granite ran as high as $859,852.75.

But public pressure to resume work on the statehouse provided an excellent diversion for the managers. Silver Plume's *Silver Standard,* upset about the cessation of work at Brownville, had bemoaned the lack of progress in Denver: "At this rate the $1,000,000 structure will be multiplied three times and over before the walls rise to the second floor. At the next session of the legislature the outside counties will doubtless distinguish themselves by stirring into this mess with a sharp stick." The board allowed Geddes and Seerie to proceed with the foundation work and quietly gathered legislative support for increased funding to use granite instead of sandstone for the capitol's exterior. The efforts paid off, and in April 1889 Governor Job A. Cooper signed a bill authorizing more funding for the statehouse. To restore public faith in the project, shaken by the Richardson fracas, the legislature also reorganized the Board of Capitol Managers. Influential Republicans John Routt and Otto Mears secured two of the seats on the board, and Governor Cooper held the ex officio chairmanship. The managers reappointed Secretary Donald W. Campbell, who had served since the death of the first secretary, George Clark, in 1888. In August 1889, after less than a year as secretary, Campbell resigned, and the board selected Herman Lueders, an old friend of Mears's, to fill the position. The two men had worked together in 1873 on the Brunot Treaty, which constricted Ute lands in western Colorado, and afterward they escorted Chief Ouray and other Utes on a trip to Washington, D.C. For sixteen years after his 1889 appointment, Lueders provided essential leadership on the board and helped establish it as one of the most powerful agencies within Colorado government. The reorganized board also reflected a dominance of Republican membership that later led to numerous accusations of partisanship, favoritism, and corruption.[11]

After the legislature's modifications to the capitol project in 1889, the managers immediately took up the matter of granite for the statehouse. They published advertisements in Chaffee, Clear Creek, and Gunnison county newspapers requesting stone samples and instigated a frenzied competition among Colorado's quarries. Hoping to resurrect the local granite industry, Silver Plume's *Silver Standard* invited the managers to visit the Brownville quarry. Laborers there prepared the largest stone ever quarried in the state, weighing in at over thirty tons, to send to Denver as an example of what Silver Plume could offer. Meanwhile, in a dedicated effort to demonstrate his site's superiority, Frederick G. Zugelder cut a cubic foot of granite from his quarry southwest of Gunnison, strapped on his snowshoes, carried the granite out on his back, and brought it by rail to Denver for the board to inspect. Within weeks the managers received dozens of specimens, including some from Buena Vista, Monarch, Trinidad, and Platte Canyon, as well as those from Gunnison and Silver Plume.[12]

As the board debated among the granite submissions, heated arguments raged across the state. The *Gunnison Review-Press* commented on the cautiously optimistic spirit of the locals: "This is all Gunnison asks. The Gunnison granite combines strength and beauty unequalled by any other in competition." In the capital, Gunnison received support from the *Denver Republican*, which printed several editorials commenting on the superiority of the stone from Zugelder's quarry. That position drew fire from the *Silver Standard*, which accused the *Republican* of failing to understand the intricacies of determining granite quality. The *Silver Standard* grew more irate in late May 1889 when the *Republican* sent a reporter with the managers on a trip to visit several granite quarries, including Zugelder's and Brownville. Hopeful Gunnison citizens conducted a tour of the site six miles from town for the board. The managers also briefly visited a quarry north of Buena Vista and finally inspected the Brownville site before returning to Denver. By June they had concluded that either the Zugelder or the Brownville quarry would provide the stone for the statehouse.[13]

The managers employed scientific methods to help them decide between the Silver Plume and Gunnison granites. They sent samples from the two quarries to the U.S. Geologic Survey, and Chief Clerk James C. Pilling tested the stone. He called both samples "excellent building stones, but that from Sliver Plume is thought to be the better of the two." Lingering ill will from the Richardson fiasco soured the managers on the Brownville quarry, however. To absolve themselves of the burdensome decision, the managers signed a contract with Geddes and Seerie to build the superstructure and let their contractors select which stone they wanted to use. Since David Seerie had recently leased Zugelder's site and renamed it Aberdeen after the famous Scottish quarry, the contractors quickly made up their minds. William Geddes told the infuriated *Silver Standard* that "the stone can be got out of the Gunnison quarry with far less trouble" than was the case at Brownville—a blatant lie since the latter boasted a direct rail line, whereas Aberdeen sat six miles down a treacherous streambed from the nearest railroad. Aberdeen was a more attractive choice for Geddes and Seerie, since there they could operate on their terms without attempting to deal with a production system already in place. The *Silver Standard* suspected "a political scheme at work in the bush" but solaced its readers by touting the town's strong silver industry, an economic backup Gunnison lacked. The managers passed a resolution on June 26, 1889, stating "that the Zugelder quarry granite be, and is hereby selected as the granite to be used in the construction of the superstructure of the Colorado State Capitol Building." Two hundred miles southwest of Denver, Gunnison citizens let loose their jubilation. Perhaps the *Gunnison Review-Press* said it best: "We 'Got There!' General Rejoicing Among Our People— Hopeful Outlook for the Future. . . . The agony is over."[14]

While the board vacillated between Silver Plume and Gunnison granite for the capitol superstructure, yet another controversy erupted. To cover the added expense of changing the stone for the statehouse, the Seventh General Assembly had appropriated $2 million in early 1889 and pushed the completion date to January 1, 1893. Almost immediately, concerns arose among the managers over the increased capitol funds. As part of his contract, Myers received 2.5 percent of the final cost of the building as a salary. Some members of the legislature and the board thought Myers had purposely designed an overly complicated structure to get more money from the state. The assembly had granted the managers extensive powers to hire "an architect and a superintendent and all other employés," and with this legislative support the board took action. On June 1, 1889, the managers abruptly fired Myers, stating only that "in the opinion of this Board, the services of Mr. E. E. Myers, Architect, are no longer necessary, and he is hereby discharged." Superintendent Gumry found himself unexpectedly promoted to the post of supervising architect. The press went in search of answers as to why the board had treated the respected man so brusquely. When asked to comment by the *Denver Republican*, Otto Mears outlined the board's position:

> You see we don't need him. If he stays he gets the commission on the increased price of the building and that will make him a little fortune to which he has actually no right. The State has got his plans and they have paid for them. The law plainly says that we can dispense with his services whenever we desire. There is no use throwing money away, and so we have thought best to let him leave. . . . I have talked too much now. You don't get anything more out of me.[15]

The offended architect fired back at the managers, accusing them of reckless spending. Myers stated that he would challenge the decision and clearly expressed his frustration: "I have built more public buildings than any other man in the United States and at no time have I ever received such an indignity as was offered me to-day. . . . For a man of my age and experience this is a most unpleasant occurrence." Although Myers considered legal action against the board, the *Rocky Mountain News* called his threat "a big bluff" and blamed him solely for the problems with William Richardson. The *News* identified two possibilities, that "either Mr. Myers is incapable of estimating the cost of his own plans, and incompetent to supervise the erection of a building such as the state capitol is expected to be, or else he was in standing with Richardson and purposely deceived the board when he urged and advised the acceptance of [Richardson's] bid." Although Myers never sued the managers, he did not give up his position without a fight. He suggested changing the capitol designs to require less funding by adopting some of the options first offered by

Richardson in 1886. Myers did not, however, suggest a pay cut for himself. Several days after this proposal, Myers sent the board a haughty note: "Without any reflection upon the ability of Superintendent Gumry, who, without doubt, is as competent for the position as any man you could get . . . I feel frank to say, that the building cannot be constructed thoroughly satisfactorily, without me." The architect held out hope until 1896, when former governor Routt officially informed Myers that Colorado did not owe him anything.[16]

After the managers removed Myers from the Colorado project, the architect's career declined. Over the next decade his firm entered and lost a dozen competitions for county courthouses, and although Myers designed a winning plan for a territorial capitol in Utah, the Beehive State never executed the plans. Many sources also credit Myers for designing a parliament building for Brazil, which like the Utah attempt was never realized. Having reached the pinnacle of his career with the Texas capitol in the early 1880s, Myers and his firm were already well on the way to obscurity by the time Colorado sent him packing. Reflecting on the architect, Henry-Russell Hitchcock and William Seale remarked: "The Gilded Age in state capitols ended only when Myers left Denver, but in many respects its decline had begun long before. There would be no more palaces of his kind." In a less favorable opinion, Paul Goeldner described the reasons the architect perpetually encountered problems, most of which were self-inflicted:

> Myers so frequently insisted that his designs could be constructed within his estimates and the available appropriation, when they so rarely could, that he might well be accused of incompetence or dishonesty. Another possibility is that he so desperately wanted his designs to be built that he believed, and convinced others to believe, that his estimates were sound.

One of the most prominent architects of Gilded Age public buildings, Myers died in 1909, supposedly after losing one of many lawsuits instigated in his last years to reclaim lost wages and pride. Regardless of the architect's many failings, the Board of Capitol Managers' dismissive treatment of Elijah Myers remains a somewhat embarrassing event in the statehouse's history.[17]

With the controversy surrounding Myers concluded, the managers and contractors returned their attention to capitol construction. The Aberdeen site, tucked into a small valley in the sagebrush flats southwest of Gunnison, provided several problems that needed to be solved before work could resume in Denver. Getting the granite from the isolated quarry to the capitol site posed the first and most significant challenge. To aid in the transport of the stone and at the same time bolster its public image, the Denver and Rio Grande Railroad built a spur free of charge along South Beaver Creek from the main line to Aberdeen. In the meantime, Frederick Zugelder carted in supplies by

Massive cliff of granite at the Aberdeen quarry southwest of Gunnison, as it appeared in September 1998. Author's collection

wagon and hastily built several structures for the laborers, who worked to quarry as much granite as possible before winter's freezing temperatures descended on the site. The intensive work soon started with an influx of skilled men, including Swedes, Italians, and even Scots who had once toiled in the original Aberdeen quarry. When railroad employees had finished the spur, flatcars brought in steam boilers and derricks, many of which weighed five to ten tons. The first trainload of granite left Aberdeen for Denver on August 14, 1889. In the three years that the site produced capitol granite, the quarrymen produced an average of forty carloads a week. Once the blocks reached the statehouse site, an army of stonecutters from all over the country shaped the blocks for placement in the building. Myers's plans called for approximately 20,000 different sizes and shapes of granite pieces, which an overhead crane and mule team moved around the construction site. A crew of 250 laborers— including 160 stonecutters, 40 stone setters, and 50 bricklayers—worked steadily, and by November 1889 the exterior walls stood almost fifty feet high on the north side and just under thirty-five feet high on the south side.[18]

Other significant work took place in Denver while the men at Aberdeen hauled out the rock. In July 1889 local foundry owner W. J. Godfrey secured the contract for the decorative interior cast-iron pillars, which the Colorado Iron Company took up when Godfrey found the prospects too daunting for his business. Meanwhile, Lane Bridge and Iron Works of Chicago won the bid for the cast-iron floor support beams. Lane Bridge and Iron underbid local competition, and the board chose cost over state industry, dismissing the legislature's directive to use Colorado materials in the interest of saving money. Already a well-established commercial power, Chicago foundries and smelters used iron ore from the Upper Peninsula of Michigan and coal from southern Illinois to make cheaper cast iron for western markets, a process aided by Chicago's rail connections to the region.[19]

In the meantime, the quarrying at Aberdeen proceeded with alacrity. The *Gunnison Review-Press* described the charged atmosphere in September 1889. Three switches provided yard room for fifty cars, loaded by four steam derricks powered by two twelve-horsepower engines. The crew of fifty-five men earned wages ranging from $2.50 up to $8.00 per day, depending on the level of danger of their duties. Twelve blacksmiths worked at Aberdeen maintaining the many quarrying tools. The *Review-Press* described the "busy scene of activity," with laborers who "much resembled a swarm of bees flitting about here and there, each seeming to know just what is required of him." Granite production slowed in the winter of 1889 but proceeded at full speed once spring settled into the Gunnison country. In March 1890 a huge blast of dynamite separated enough stone from the rock face to keep crews busy splitting blocks into late May. Contractor David Seerie told the quarrymen of his recent visit to Aberdeen, Scotland. He proudly claimed Colorado's Aberdeen granite was "far superior; in color it is about the same, but . . . the Scotch granite has a great deal of iron whilst ours has none." The managers also visited the site, and they noted with satisfaction that the quarrying proceeded faster than the stone could be dressed and placed in Denver. Problems existed at the quarry even in the best of times, however. On May 19 a granite block slipped from a derrick and killed Frederick Anderson, a Swedish quarryman. The *Gunnison Review-Press* reported that "before the unfortunate man could escape his head was caught between the falling stone and one on the ground and his skull was crushed as if an egg shell. He was instantly killed." The accident reminded everyone of the dangerous nature of quarry work.[20]

The most immense stone ever quarried at Aberdeen, weighing in at twenty tons, became the center of attention on Independence Day 1890, when Coloradoans held their largest party to date. The *Rocky Mountain News* described the momentous day in Denver:

> Mr. Sol, in the joy of his heart, smiled one of his brightest smiles of bland encouragement over the brand new state to the north [Idaho], winked a wink of Democratic condolence to the discouraged territories on the south

[Arizona and New Mexico], cast a bowl of perspiration to the plains on the east, but let out and seemed to concentrate the whole vast radiance of his very hot beaming face on the cornerstone state of the great middle West— the state that was to lay the cornerstone of its own statehood on the national birthday in tons of mossy granite from her own eternal hills.

Trains pulled into Union Station that morning crowded with spectators from all over the state and region. The festivities started with a parade through Denver that stretched for several miles. A number of aging Colorado pioneers joined the procession, representing "sturdy oaks in the progress of our grand state," as well as dozens of fraternal and social organizations. Spectators clung to trees, fences, and telephone and electrical poles all along the route. An immense crowd gathered at the capitol site, the terminus of the parade. Estimates of 20,000 people counted only the fringe of the assembled, with the number pressed in close to the scaffolding for the ceremony on the northeast side of the building too great to count. The total number at the celebration possibly surpassed 60,000. Bunting, flowers, and evergreens covered the stage built around the statehouse's cornerstone, and an American flag draped the stone itself. After a Masonic choir with a thousand members—the largest such group ever assembled west of Chicago—sang "America," the official program began.[21]

Famed Coloradoan and former United States senator Horace Tabor conducted the ceremony dedicating the twenty-ton granite cornerstone. Those present on the stage included Board of Capitol Managers members Otto Mears, Charles J. Hughes Jr., and former governor John Routt, as well as judges James B. Belford and Wilbur F. Stone and Denver mayor Wolfe Londoner. The numerous pretty young girls gallantly given seats near the stage inspired more interest than the politicians, however. People climbed on top of the unfinished granite walls of the capitol and perched on the masonry shell of the rotunda and even on the roofs of the on-site stonecutters' sheds for the best views. After an invocation by the Masons and an optimistic speech by Tabor, the Colorado Grand Lodge conducted the ancient cornerstone ceremony, directed by the Most Worshipful Grand Master William Bridwell of Cañon City. The Masons set about sealing the stone, which enclosed a copper box containing all manner of 1890 Colorado memorabilia.* The News described the Masonic ceremony as the most impressive and beautiful imaginable.

Following the cornerstone rites Governor Cooper addressed the crowd, describing the construction progress and Denver's struggle for the capital designation. A speech by former governor Alva Adams followed Cooper's

*See Appendix A.

Thousands of Coloradoans, using umbrellas as shelter from the blazing sun, assembled to celebrate the cornerstone ceremony on July 4, 1890. The brick and stone shell of the rotunda rises in the distance behind derricks used to move granite blocks. Courtesy, Colorado Historical Society, F7490

somewhat uninspiring remarks. Stories of the adventurous and brave pioneers of Colorado filled Adams's chauvinistic speech. "Geographically," he declaimed, "Colorado is the most exalted state in the Union. Upon the apex of the continent our capitol becomes a lighthouse upon a great eminence, and from there it should radiate a never-fading glow of exalted principles, of high and patriotic examples." At the conclusion of the ceremony, in Lincoln Park just west of the capitol site revelers enjoyed the largest barbecue in Colorado history. They consumed 33,000 pounds of meat, 3,000 pounds of cheese, 15,000 pounds of bread, 10 barrels of pickles, and 500 gallons of lemonade. Officials hired over 200 waiters to facilitate the barbecue. Butchers slaughtered 350 sheep, 75 calves, and over 230 steers for the meal, enjoyed by about 40,000 Coloradoans. The *News* observed that the "loaves and fishes act would not have passed muster with that crowd." With a breathtaking barrage of fireworks launched from the upper ramparts of the capitol's shell that evening, the thrilling day came to a close.

Many capitols and other significant public buildings experienced similar cornerstone ceremonies. President George Washington set the precedent for such proceedings when he laid the cornerstone of the United States Capitol in his namesake city on September 18, 1793. As the former grand master of Virginia he conducted the Masonic ceremony, which followed a parade through the fledgling national capital and also included a celebratory barbecue on the building's grounds. Other states followed suit in later years. Michigan citizens laid the cornerstone of their statehouse in Lansing in October 1873. Like Colorado, they sealed a box of state memorabilia in the stone. The cornerstone of the Illinois State Capitol, laid in 1868, enclosed, among other things, some personal mementos of President Abraham Lincoln. In Cheyenne, Wyoming, on May 18, 1887, a massive public ceremony centered around the laying of the cornerstone made of Rawlins sandstone. Cornerstone ceremonies combined ancient tradition with popular enthusiasm and represented, in Colorado and elsewhere, the great popularity of fraternal organizations in late-nineteenth-century society.[22]

With the grand festivities of the cornerstone ceremony complete, the steady progress of quarrying granite and installing an inner iron skeleton resumed. But after four years of work, some Coloradoans expressed disappointment at the lethargic pace. The *Denver Republican* remarked: "For more than two years the people passing the capitol site have watched the slow rise of the stately pile that is to crown it and wondered at the tardiness of its erection." Several factors led to this impotence of construction. The managers spent a great deal of time considering designs for the four entry porticoes and Corinthian columns, and in September 1890 they viewed models for the west pediment, the dominant aspect of the building. Myers had supplied the board with guidelines for statuary to decorate the pediment in the late 1880s, calling for an ostentatious collection of virtuous individuals representing American settlement of Colorado, but the managers scaled back his proposal to correspond with their budget. The allegorical figures eventually selected represented a pioneer family and gold seekers struggling through the dangerous frontier to the welcoming lands of Colorado. Additionally, the board responded to repeated requests by Denver's city council to tidy the statehouse grounds, which were littered with construction sheds and a granite shaping facility. Superintendent Gumry's assistant, Robert C. Greiner, worked with Denver's most renowned landscape architect, Reinhard Schuetze, to draft a suitable plan for improving the site. However, Geddes and Seerie asked the board to wait until their crews finished the capitol's exterior before greening the grounds. The demands of construction meant that the managers considered no further beautification project for the next five years, to the dismay of Denverites.[23]

As the granite walls slowly but steadily rose from Brown's Bluff in early 1891, the managers prepared for another celebration at the capitol site. That spring president Benjamin Harrison toured much of the West by rail and stopped in Denver on May 12. Harrison spoke at the corner of Colfax Avenue and Broadway in the shadow of the rising statehouse to an estimated crowd of 25,000. Two large American flags fluttered over the proceedings from the cylindrical rotunda shell in the center of the granite hulk. Some of the same men prominent at the cornerstone ceremony the summer before joined Harrison at the podium, including Governor Routt and former governor Cooper and judges Wilbur Stone and James Belford. Postmaster General John Wanamaker spoke briefly on a topic of great significance to Colorado's economy—the free coinage of silver, which Harrison had ignored. The *Rocky Mountain News* acknowledged the delicacy of the subject: "Everybody thought the president would say something about free coinage. Mr. B. Harrison knows when to keep off the grass." The national debate over bimetallism, which allowed both gold and silver to back up the value of the dollar, attracted the attention of many in Colorado who recognized the disproportionate influence of silver in the state's economy. Although the mineral had revolutionized Colorado's industry in the 1870s and 1880s, it represented an overwhelming share of the regional economy, and any threat to federal silver purchase would result in catastrophe in the central Rockies. Harrison's reluctance to mention the controversial subject worried politicians, owners, and workers alike and cast a nervous pall over the throng assembled near the capitol site.[24]

Tensions other than those over silver also simmered in Colorado in the early 1890s. Labor unionism swept the nation as workers attempted to secure safer conditions and adequate pay in various industries. This dissatisfaction directly affected those working on the statehouse project. In 1877 a group of quarrymen had organized the National Union of Granite Cutters (NUGC) in Maine, and they set up a branch of the union in Denver in the late 1880s to serve the needs of laborers at the statehouse site. Members of the NUGC had struck at the Texas State Capitol several years earlier, and contractors in Austin had replaced the laborers with quarrymen imported from Aberdeen, Scotland. In April 1891 concerned workers at Colorado's Aberdeen established a branch of the Quarrymen's National Union (QNU), a specialized group chartered by the American Federation of Labor the year before. The goals of the union as expressed in the QNU's constitution echoed those of labor associations around the nation: "The maintenance of a fair rate of wages, the encouragement of good workmen, and to use every means which may tend to the elevation of quarrymen in the social scale of life." Suitably organized into effective bargaining units, the unions in Denver and Aberdeen hoped to improve the many hardships caused by their treacherous occupations.[25]

Members of the National Union of Granite Cutters gathered near their extensive stone-finishing facility at the capitol site in early 1892. The inset at upper left shows the exterior walls of the statehouse nearly complete. Courtesy, Colorado Historical Society, F3763

Shortly after setting up their branch of the QNU, Aberdeen's quarrymen resolved to strike on June 1, 1891, unless they received better wages and shorter hours for their often perilous work. The NUGC members in Denver announced that if Geddes and Seerie tried to replace the Aberdeen union men, they would refuse to shape the blocks or to travel to Gunnison to man the drills themselves. In exchange for their support, the NUGC encouraged the QNU members to end their blasphemous practice of working on Sundays. Aberdeen's union also received support from a QNU branch at Park Siding, a quarry along the South Platte River in Jefferson County, which sympathetically informed the quarrymen that "we are with you June 1st 91." Writing from the union's main office in New England, Secretary John J. Byron emphasized that all members of the organization stood in solidarity with their downtrodden brothers in Colorado. As the Board of Capitol Managers nervously awaited the outcome of this latest threat to the statehouse project, Geddes and Seerie meekly attempted to avert a strike.[26]

As May 1891 came to a close, Geddes and Seerie rejected repeated requests by the Aberdeen union members to discuss their differences. The contractors felt confident that the quarrymen would back down and did not want to appear weak by negotiating with laborers. Geddes and Seerie's recalcitrance forced the hand of the union men at Aberdeen, who concluded that they had no choice but to strike. On June 1, thirty members of Quarrymen's National Union Branch 46 walked off the job and returned to Gunnison. Some remained there to await the strike's outcome, and others boarded trains to seek quarry work elsewhere. The Park Siding branch struck in sympathy, but the owners of the Jefferson County quarry acquiesced quickly and the union's solidarity ended. Meanwhile, at Aberdeen quarry superintendent C. R. Hansard brought in replacement labor including "miners, ranchmen, cowboys, mule skinners, bullwhackers, and even hoboes" from all over Gunnison County to keep the work going. The Gunnison Tribune supported Geddes and Seerie and observed, "Work at the quarries was only suspended for two days and the strike will amount to nothing." Unconcerned by the NUGC members' threat to stop their work at the capitol site, the contractors expected to easily defeat the strike.[27]

A week after the Aberdeen union men abandoned their drills, the confident firm of Geddes and Seerie received a report from Superintendent Hansard concerning the replacement labor at the quarry. Instead of Aberdeen's usual weekly output of forty cars of granite, the hodgepodge of unskilled workers only managed to produce eight cars. The Board of Capitol Managers conferred with its contractors and emphatically encouraged them to settle the strike. When Alex MacDonald, president of Aberdeen's QNU Branch 46, received a message from Geddes and Seerie to commence negotiations, he immediately called a meeting in the waiting room of Gunnison's La Veta Hotel. Within hours representatives of the contractors and the QNU drew up the following agreement, much to the pleasure of the union men and the chagrin of Geddes and Seerie:

> We the Quarry-Mens Union do hereby agree to settle this strike and return to work on the following conditions. That 9 hrs. shall constitute a days work for every day in the week (sundays excepted) and that we receive therefore, the same pay that had been previously paid for 10 hrs. and that we further agree not to make any demands that will increase the cost of quarrying stone for the Capitol Building. In cases of emergency, where it shall be necessary to work overtime, members shall work for the same rate per hour as received per hr. by the day, and that we agree not to interfere with the Laborers and Engineers or other persons not members of our Union.

With the provisions accepted, William Geddes, David Seerie, President MacDonald, and Branch 46 secretary Peter Olsen signed the hastily scribbled document. The victorious laborers paraded through the streets of Gunnison in three wagons festooned with patriotic bunting before returning to work at Aberdeen.[28]

In the months after the end of the Aberdeen strike, the quarry's output resumed its previous average of forty carloads per week. But as laborers at the capitol site approached completion of the exterior walls, production at Aberdeen slowed correspondingly. In late 1891 and early 1892 Geddes and Seerie cut back the number of quarrymen so dramatically that QNU Branch 46 closed for lack of membership. The union members last met at Aberdeen on April 1, 1892, ending the branch's successful existence of less than a year. From April 7 to June 15 the quarry crew dropped to only four men including Frederick Zugelder, who had discovered and promoted the site in the 1880s. By the time granite extraction for the capitol concluded at Aberdeen in the summer of 1892, quarrymen had produced over 280,000 cubic feet of granite, weighing in at an estimated 30,000 tons. Former territorial secretary Frank Hall described the Board of Capitol Managers as "eminently well satisfied with the progress of the work, and with the integrity and skill of Messrs. Geddes & Seerie, two young men who have won a distinguished place in general esteem. That the building will when finished be a credit to them and to the State at large is a foregone conclusion." But without any other major contracts for the stone, the contractors abandoned the isolated quarry. The Denver and Rio Grande Railroad pulled up the tracks to Aberdeen in 1904, effectively cutting off the site from the rest of the world. Crews hauled out some stone by wagon in the early 1910s for the foundation of the Colorado State Museum, but no significant quarrying has taken place at Aberdeen since July 1912. It remains an obscure, tranquil, lovely site nestled in the South Beaver Creek Valley, surrounded by the granite debris of four years of frenzied labor.[29]

With the massive granite walls complete, many Colorado leaders believed the interior would require little additional time, and they pressured the managers to finish the statehouse. The building's first occupant, Superintendent Gumry, moved his office from a wooden shack on Colfax Avenue into temporary space on the first floor in October 1892. But a substantial amount of construction inside and out remained incomplete. Laborers assembled the massive slate roof, considered the largest in the world, over the granite superstructure and cast-iron skeleton before the winter of 1892–1893, and crews employed by Geddes and Seerie installed gutters and drains. The sheds formerly used by granite cutters at the site came down, with the planks laid on the expensive slate roof to protect it during construction of the most remarkable exterior feature—the dome. For three years the brick and stone rotunda

The finished exterior of the capitol from the north in the early 1890s, before the dome's first coat of gray paint. Compare the rapid expansion of Denver seen here with the photograph from 1882 on page 26. Courtesy, Colorado Historical Society, William Henry Jackson, CHSJ2616

shell towered more than 100 feet over the capitol site. The managers awarded the contract for erecting the dome above it, as well as contracts for the tin dome ceilings in the legislative chambers, to Chicago's Lane Bridge and Iron Works in late 1892. Within months the Chicago firm finished the intricate task of fabricating the cast-iron dome, completing the basic external appearance of the structure. Myers's plans called for an allegorical statue to surmount the dome, but growing legislative and executive pressure to finish the building forced the board to abandon the clay sculptures and sketches of attractive young women who wanted to serve as the statue's model. The managers recognized the need to put business before pleasure and returned their attention to the substantial amount of work remaining inside the statehouse.[30]

With the superstructure essentially complete, Colorado citizens looked with admiration upon the capitol built with material "from her own eternal hills." The building reflected a civil society transcending more than thirty years of nomadic authority. It represented an important boon to developing local economies in towns like Fort Collins, Silver Plume, and Gunnison. As evidenced by the magnificent cornerstone ceremony in 1890, the statehouse captured the attention of citizens from all over the state who had waited so long to see the symbol of their collective ability rise from the dust and tumbleweeds of Brown's Bluff. Yet excitement blended with several controversies in the first seven years of construction. State leaders battled with Denverites over potentially bothersome railroad access to the building site. A contractor unprepared for the substantial demands of the capitol project abandoned his responsibilities. The statehouse board fired the architect for legally sound but ethically questionable reasons. Quarrymen unhappy with their working conditions went on strike and succeeded in redressing their grievances. The first visit to the capitol site by an American president reflected many citizens' increasing fears concerning the state's lack of economic diversity. Coloradoans expressed satisfaction at the progress made to finally provide a home for their representative government but disapproved of the incremental rate of construction. By the end of the first seven years of labor, Coloradoans could finally behold the embodiment of their collective interests rising in Denver, but another eight years of both celebration and difficulties would pass before state officials and private contractors finished their capitol. The work at the statehouse could proceed with confidence as long as regional industries maintained their lucrative production rates. But all the challenges of the first seven years of construction provided only a sedate prologue for the obstacles ahead, when in 1893 national politicians knocked away the supports propping up Colorado's precarious economy.

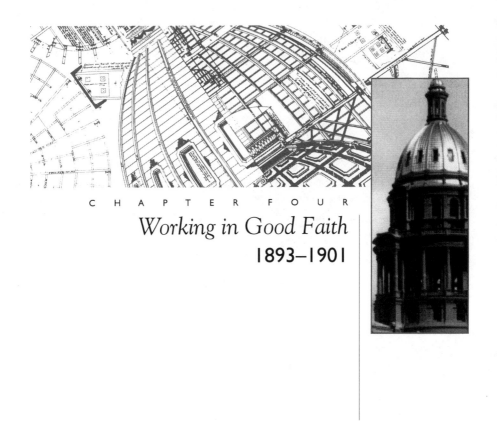

# Working in Good Faith
## 1893–1901

ISTORIANS OFTEN CONSIDER the last decade of the nineteenth century
a turning point for the western United States, and the same is true
for the Colorado State Capitol. In 1893, the year Frederick Jackson
Turner delivered his frontier thesis in Chicago, labor at the statehouse shifted
from the exterior to the interior, and new construction challenges developed. State leaders eagerly anticipated the day they could finally move into
their impressive headquarters and incessantly encouraged the Board of Capitol Managers to finish the structure. Numerous difficulties prolonged the
project, but the managers expressed their gratitude to contractors "working
in good faith" with the state. During the last eight years of construction on
the statehouse, however, scandals and lackadaisical progress consistently
endangered this camaraderie. All the while, the board's influence grew steadily
as the managers parceled out contracts individually and demanded oversight
on every aspect of the project. But the paramount obstacle to finishing the

statehouse developed after federal action devastated the state's silver industry and inspired a crippling economic collapse in Colorado in 1893. Although the final years of construction on the Colorado State Capitol ensured the completion of a dignified permanent center of government and a proper temple for the collective pride of the state, it came at a hefty financial and emotional price.

Coloradoans could look upon the statehouse in 1893, with its granite walls and cast-iron dome as a reflection of the state's general economic prosperity. Like several other regions in the state, the upper Clear Creek Valley, directly west of Denver and Golden, experienced exceptional wealth in the late nineteenth century from its substantial silver deposits. In early 1888 Silver Plume's *Silver Standard* prophetically editorialized the general feeling of many citizens:

> The State of Colorado is the producer of every imaginable article that is necessary to sustain the human body and soul; the population of the state is rapidly increasing every day, and millions of dollars are being annually extracted from the treasure vualts [sic] of the Rocky Mountains. The agricultural interests of the state are advancing year by year and manufacturing establishments are being erected in her central localities. Whatever may be done, it does not appear reasonable that any drawback to the industries of Colorado, can keep her from becoming the richest state in the Union within five years hence.

But at the end of those five years, instead of enjoying unparalleled prosperity, Colorado entered a period of economic catastrophe inconceivable when the *Silver Standard* optimistically gazed into the future. As the representative symbol of the state, the rising capitol suffered through the period alongside the citizenry.[1]

The Panic of 1893, part of a nationwide economic slump, hit Colorado perhaps harder than other states. Although the depression affected various parts of the country in different ways, in Colorado the vital silver industry suffered the greatest blow. President Grover Cleveland, anxious to stop a nationwide financial drain, called the U.S. Congress into session to repeal the Sherman Silver Purchase Act of 1890, dealing a terrific blow to the mineral that dictated the success or failure of many Colorado businesses. As the federal government abandoned silver in favor of gold to back up the nation's currency, mines in the Centennial State started to shut down. With the collapse of the state's most influential industry, other related enterprises had to close. Many banks, stores, and other establishments could no longer afford to remain open. Adding to the industrial woes, the state's agricultural community suffered several years of drought and harsh winters, resulting in tremendous devastation to livestock and crops. In this atmosphere of seemingly insurmountable difficulties, the Board of Capitol Managers pressed on with the expensive work of building a statehouse.

The sluggish pace of the first seven years of construction on the state capitol devolved into lethargy as the 1890s dragged on. The Panic of 1893 and the resulting depression, surprisingly, did not detrimentally affect the statehouse project, a remarkable exception to the rule in Colorado after the collapse of the silver industry. Completing the capitol, regardless of cost or time, filled a vacuum in the psyche of Centennial State citizens as they adopted an increased devotion to finish their symbol. Historians Carl Ubbelohde, Maxine Benson, and Duane A. Smith remarked that the Silver Panic forced Colorado to stabilize "the state's economy on a foundation other than a government-supported market for the product of its silver mines." The capitol project created jobs in rural economies in Gunnison and Pueblo counties, which provided jobs in the urban economy of Denver as raw materials arrived for installation on Brown's Bluff. Statehouse construction provided a symbolic contrast to contemporary challenges, an image of hope rising from the debris of industrial catastrophe. During the Civil War, President Abraham Lincoln had encouraged continued work on the U.S. Capitol as a representation of national determination. In much the same way, work on the Colorado State Capitol inspired citizens suffering through the worst economic conditions ever to hit the young state.[2]

With the essential exterior work and basic interior skeleton finished by 1893, the Board of Capitol Managers focused its attention on completing enough of the building to allow Colorado's government to finally occupy the structure. The first significant work on the interior resulted in a reevaluation of Elijah Myers's statehouse designs, which called for the use of polished hardwoods for floors and hallways to present the visitor with a rustic yet dignified western statehouse. But the danger of fire in a building filled with woodwork gnawed at politicians' minds. A disastrous blaze in 1863 had claimed much of Denver's fledgling business district and resulted in laws mandating the use of brick and other "fireproof" elements in city buildings. The devastating Great Chicago Fire of 1871 and blazes that destroyed statehouses in Minnesota and Texas in 1881 and in New Mexico in 1892 weighed heavily on the capitol managers' minds. Architectural thought of the period considered a structure fireproof if it was built primarily of materials that would not burn, such as stone. Few designers considered emergency exits an important part of a structure built of stone and often ignored the danger posed by flammable material within a building. Although these opinions would plague Colorado State Capitol caretakers a century later, they dominated contemporary construction methods. The legislature therefore considered the switch from hardwoods to marble an excellent step toward protecting the building and its inhabitants.

To allow for the time required to quarry and install stone, the legislature postponed the capitol's completion deadline to January 1, 1895. Most important, by choosing a resource found within Colorado, lawmakers responded to the Panic of 1893 by providing jobs for their constituents, since the state lacked adequate hardwoods to provide material for the interior. This alteration provided a popular response to the economic crisis in Colorado but also further complicated the statehouse project, with many resulting construction delays.[3]

Unlike the exterior stone debates in the 1880s over whether to use sandstone or granite, most Coloradoans recognized marble as the obvious choice for the interior of the capitol. In preparation for the new stone the managers divvied out a number of jobs. David Kelly's Denver Onyx and Marble Company won a contract for 140,000 square feet of reinforced concrete floors, over which marble could later be installed. A relatively new construction method in the 1890s, reinforced concrete offered a stronger and lighter method for erecting large buildings. The Denver Terra Cotta and Lumber Company manufactured bricks for the basic walls, which crews plastered over to divide the interior into office space. The managers allowed some decorative hardwoods in the building, awarding a contract of almost $50,000 for white oak from the Ozark Mountains for interior doors and window frames. The Denver Hardware Manufacturing Company fashioned distinctive doorknobs with the state seal and doorplates and hinges decorated with columbine patterns to further beautify the interior. Superintendent Peter Gumry directed several other tasks before marble installation commenced, including the construction of a tunnel under Fourteenth Avenue to a fuel-receiving vault from which coal could be brought directly to the boilers in the statehouse's subbasement. He also negotiated with Denver officials to connect the capitol to the city's sewer system. When the city neglected to respond in what Gumry considered a reasonable time, he linked the pipes himself, and the Denver Police arrested him for trespassing. The managers bailed Gumry out of jail and eventually paid the city over $1,600 to complete the connection and provide the statehouse with plumbing and sewage service.[4]

Shortly after the onset of depression in 1893, the managers opened contracts for marble flooring and wainscoting. On February 15, 1894, they granted the work to Denver Onyx and Marble. The managers hoped to have some parts of the building ready for occupation by the fall of 1894 and expected David Kelly's firm to finish the stone installation quickly. The board also responded to the concerns of some Coloradoans who questioned the extra expense of white marble in a period of economic difficulty. Reliable transportation made stone from Tennessee, Vermont, and even Carrara, Italy, cheaper than the remote Colorado marble, but state leaders kept the employment of their constituents foremost in mind. Governor Davis Waite, the board's chairman, remained dedicated to providing jobs for Coloradoans by using native materials as much as possible. On April 10, 1894, Waite issued a statement to the press saying "he had made up his mind not to consider any but Colorado marble, even if more had to be paid than for eastern material."[5]

High in the Rockies along Yule Creek, a tributary of the Crystal River, sat the white marble quarry Kelly intended to use for the capitol work. Prospectors searching for gold in the early 1870s stumbled upon the sizable quantity of stone, but little activity took place at the isolated site until 1884 when a small quarry opened. Even then the marble remained largely untouched, since no railroad or improved wagon road connected the site with the rest of the state. In 1894 the *Marble City Times* looked forward to using the capitol project as a source of employment and of advertising for the material: "Colorado people will have to pay for the capitol and it is no more than right that Colorado workmen should be benefited through its construction." As the Aberdeen quarry had promoted the Gunnison economy, boosters hoped providing marble for the capitol would do the same for the Crystal River Valley.[6]

While the Board of Capitol Managers drew up papers for white marble flooring, the members also contracted with Denver Onyx and Marble for the wainscot. The board members deliberated on the best stone to use for the decorative aspect of the interior, but as they had with their exterior stone contractors they left the final decision largely to Kelly's firm. After research into various sites around the state, Kelly leased a quarry of a striated red stone clinging to the cliffs amid the pine trees of the Wet Mountains above Beulah in Pueblo County. He suggested this stone, commonly known as Colorado rose onyx, to the managers as ideal for decorative use, and they agreed in April 1894. Quarrying the red stone proved exceptionally difficult at the small, remote site. Wedging techniques took the place of drills and dynamite, shaping the rose onyx by hand into manageable pieces. About a dozen men worked Kelly's rose onyx quarry for less than two dollars per ten-hour day. From the rugged site teamsters loaded the stone onto wagons for a two-day trip across the burnished plains to the Denver and Rio Grande Railroad at Pueblo. The board acquiesced on one stone and let Kelly's firm use a greenish-black serpentine quarried outside of Colorado for flooring trim along the walls.[7]

The most significant problem facing the work at both Marble and Beulah, and indeed a great deal of industry throughout the nineteenth-century American West, was transportation. Building a railroad to Beulah, a picturesque but isolated town, to move stone from the small quarry made little sense. Meanwhile, rumors of extending lines to Marble from Carbondale to the north or from Crested Butte to the south circulated for many years. John C. Osgood had established a rugged road along the Crystal River to his coal mines at Redstone in 1886. But sleds in the winter and wagons in the summer could

Laborers using mule teams to haul blocks of rose onyx from the quarry near Beulah to the railhead at Pueblo in the mid-1890s. Courtesy, Colorado State Capitol Tour Desk

only move small amounts of marble at a time along the treacherous route. For years newspapers wrote articles encouraging a railroad line to the marble quarries. The *Marble City Times* observed with exasperation in March 1894:

> The Denver papers state that D. J. Kelley [sic] is now opening the Beulah marble quarries and proposes to haul the stone by wagons a distance of 28 miles to the railroad. This shows what a man of energy can do. Why in thunder don't the quarry owners of this district follow this example and haul the stone to Carbondale? The distance is but a little longer. Once they commence to do this and prove up the marble thoroughly, a railroad would soon come to their assistance. This thing of talking marble for years and not attempt[ing] to place it upon the market is not of any material benefit to this section. We know we have the finest quality of marble here, therefore why not make an effort to introduce it? If it pays to haul marble by wagons a long distance in other sections why not here?[8]

The capitol board paid scant attention to the railroad controversies. Leaving such concerns to their contractor, the managers acquired furnishings and carpets for statehouse offices in the summer of 1894. Executive, legislative, and judicial authorities authorized funds for new desks, chairs, and other items, hoping to abandon the battered relics they had carted from town to town and building to building in the territory's and state's earliest days of government.

The Chicago firm A. H. Andrews and Company constructed gallery seats for the legislative chambers, and the Brunswick Balke Collender Company of Chicago fabricated desks for lawmakers and the presiding officers' rostrums, as well as benches for the supreme court and the court of appeals. Denver artist Manuel Hill decorated the tin legislative dome ceilings and the walls of the supreme court room with red, gold, and green Victorian stencil designs. Ensuring the capitol's position as the most modern structure in the state, the managers demanded electrical fixtures for the building. Several Denver firms, including the Hughes and Keith Plumbing and Chandelier Company, the Russell and Officer Electric Construction Company, and the Mountain Electric Company, won contracts to install fixtures throughout the capitol powered by both carbide gas and electricity. Hughes and Keith secured the most substantial contract, to construct the twin brass chandeliers in the legislative chambers and the chandelier in the supreme court room. The Crane Elevator Company of Chicago started work on the building's two hydraulic elevators in December 1894. Some offices received telephones, a technology less than two decades old. Although the adjutant general, state treasurer, secretary of state, and State Board of Land Commissioners, among other agencies, received telephones in the fall of 1894, the managers did not provide one for the governor's office for another year. To link state leaders with the rest of the world, the board ordered an Associated Press wire bulletin system. The capitol became a home to the latest and greatest technology at a suitable expense for the state's most prominent structure.[9]

Workers finished enough of the capitol's offices to allow some state leaders to move in by the fall of 1894. Executive staff, then meeting in quarters on the seventh floor of the Equitable Building in Denver, packed up and began what the *Rocky Mountain News* called their "Hegira" to the new statehouse. In late October 1894 the state auditor and state treasurer became the first political leaders to occupy the new building, in rooms with walls still tacky from fresh plaster. On November 12 Governor Waite and his staff joined the exodus to Brown's Bluff. A week later the supreme court convened in its second-floor courtroom. The *Rocky Mountain News* reported that the courtroom "is pronounced by persons who have traveled widely over the continent to be the most attractive in appearance of any court room in the United States, not excepting the room in which the supreme court at Washington holds its sessions." Employees of the court and the legislature moved 16,000 books and 15,000 pamphlets into the state and law libraries in the east wing of the second and third floors. These enormous rooms contained all of Colorado's official records as well as reports from the federal government and many other states. Librarians organized duplicates of their voluminous collections to send out across Colorado, encouraging literacy and education for all

citizens by promoting local libraries. The Board of Capitol Managers occupied the commodious space first used by Superintendent Gumry on the first
floor. In the meantime, decorative plaster and stucco work on walls and ceilings continued as the managers prepared the building for the first major test
of the new structure's abilities: the legislature's arrival for the Tenth General
Assembly.[10]

On January 2, 1895, the people's representatives came to the Colorado
State Capitol for the first time. After meeting in kitchens and pool halls, in
office buildings and Masonic lodge rooms, the legislature descended upon the
statehouse to take its rightful place on the second floor. Appropriately, the
first general assembly to meet in the capitol demonstrated changing political
thought within the state and the nation. The 1894 election had marked the
first in Colorado with universal suffrage. That November, voters elected three
women to positions in the House of Representatives, the first time women
had served in a state legislature in the nation's history. Additionally, the Tenth
General Assembly boasted the state's second African American legislator.
And in a twist of historical irony, the first legislature to meet in the capitol
also included James Brown, who had helped his father, Henry Brown, sue
Colorado in the 1880s to reclaim the donated statehouse property on Brown's
Bluff. The new home of state government received mixed reviews from legislators and the press. Editorials in the *Denver Times* praised the building, whereas
the *Rocky Mountain News* complained that the capitol's location, far from
downtown Denver, meant that fewer people would keep an eye on the assembly from the galleries. More optimistically, the Reverend Thomas A. Uzzell of
the People's Tabernacle gave a hopeful prayer to open the Senate and the
new capitol:

> We thank Thee for this magnificent building. We thank Thee that it has
> been honestly built, and that no charge of bribery has been made against
> the capitol managers. May this chamber never be disgraced by the scenes of
> lawlessness that have marred senate chambers elsewhere. Here in this
> solemn moment we dedicate to Thee and to useful legislation this beautiful
> chamber. May this be looked upon as the model session. May it redound to
> Thy glory and to the upbuilding of this state.

Coloradoans held great expectations for their legislators as well as for the
future uses of their new, still unfinished statehouse.[11]

Although the governmental role of the capitol remained the building's
preeminent purpose, citizens began considering it the city's best tourist destination as well, and rightfully so. Several basement rooms offered a bewildering
cornucopia of opportunities to learn about Colorado history, environment,
industry, and most any other aspect of the state at no charge to the visitor.

The largest and oldest of these agencies, the State Historical and Natural History Society, established in 1879, boasted extensive displays in the west wing. The collections included parts of the *Rocky Mountain News*'s press rescued after the 1864 Cherry Creek flood, machinery from the Clark, Gruber and Company mint, and dozens of oil portraits of the territory's and state's first settlers. In the late nineteenth century the exploration of prehistoric cliff dwellings in the southwestern corner of the state inspired a flurry of excitement for all Coloradoans, and the historical society put many artifacts from the Mesa Verde region on display in its polished oak and glass cabinets. Tourists gaped in amazement at the baskets, pottery, tools, and the shelves crammed full of skulls of the mysterious Anasazi people. Additionally, 500 stuffed birds perched near preserved bighorn sheep, bison, coyotes, bears, and many other animals, enticing over 120,000 people to visit the historical society in its first two years at the capitol. In nearby rooms, Civil War veteran Cecil A. Deane watched over the state's war relics, many of which he had donated in 1895. Captured Confederate cannons from the 1862 Battle of Glorieta Pass stood alongside Civil War banners and a silk flag made by pioneer women for Denver's 1860 Independence Day festivities. A state government directory published in 1899 praised the remarkable assemblage of "countless grim, savage missiles that man hurls in anger." The popularity of the war, historical, and natural history collections provided great satisfaction for the directors of those agencies and the capitol managers as well.[12]

But the statehouse's attractions did not end there. Colorado's extensive natural resources went on exhibit in the Bureau of Mines's and the State Horticultural Society's basement quarters as well. The latter offered a great deal of interest to agricultural enthusiasts; it included many samples of the state's trees, flowers, grain, and "fruits and vegetables fit for a king to eat, but none too good for good Americans." But when the flora attracted mice to the basement along with the tourists, the managers ordered the keepers of Colorado's horticultural collection to better isolate their samples. Down the hall, the mining collection boasted an immense color topographical map of the state created by Arthur Lakes of the Colorado School of Mines. Dozens of cabinets overflowed with stone and minerals including quartz, onyx, copper, silver, and gold. The capitol board donated many samples of granite, marble, and sandstone it had received over the years. Glittering, polished minerals and raw ore filled shelves in several large rooms and harkened back to the boom days of Colorado's mining industry before the economic collapse of 1893. That year the legislature had agreed to provide quarters in the capitol for the Grand Army of the Republic (GAR), a group of Union Civil War veterans that engaged in political and social activism in the late nineteenth and early twentieth centuries. The managers identified a room in the basement for the GAR

Rifles and artillery shells in the war relics collection in the capitol basement, with curator Cecil A. Deane at right. The Board of Capitol Managers fired him in 1902 for being "drunk too often" while on duty. Author's collection

to use for meetings but evicted the veterans in 1897 when their quarters became a haven for "card playing and carousel." To ensure the safety of visitors and politicians, the board hired a watchman to handle the building's security in 1895. The newly occupied capitol housed Colorado's government but also offered extensive displays of the state's history and natural resources, providing a source of pride for a society struggling to cope with economic failure.[13]

Even though the occupied statehouse helped boost the spirits of the many Coloradoans who visited Denver, certain elements of the capital city prevented it from attaining the respectability of established cities of the eastern states. Other Coloradoans recognized the need for improvements, such as this observation made by the *Gunnison Tribune* in April 1891: "Fourteen inches of snow fell in Denver Tuesday night and from ten inches to four feet of mud adorn the streets to the delight of pedestrians. Great city is the capital of Colorado. The city authorities are contemplating paving the streets in the next quarter of a century." Denverites needed to polish their image as well as their physical surroundings, and many considered the capitol the perfect place to start. Construction buildings, mud, and weeds surrounded the state's most prominent building instead of cultivated, dignified grounds. The managers had considered some improvements to Brown's Bluff in 1890 but postponed their decisions until exterior construction had concluded. Now with attention focused on the inner parts of the building, the managers agreed to transform the grounds into the proper setting for so remarkable a structure.[14]

After a spirited contest among local landscape architects, the managers awarded Reinhard Schuetze $150 for his simple yet stately design. An east-west axis from Broadway through the capitol to Grant Street dominated Schuetze's plan, with several curving walks on the capitol property. He incorporated a traffic and pedestrian circle around the building and a terraced west front down to Lincoln Street, which later served as a makeshift ski slope in winter months. American elms, lilac bushes, and evergreens dotted the perimeter of the grounds. Laborers toiled in the summer sun of 1895, and by the fall the Brown's Bluff site finally appeared like a proper setting for so impressive a structure. The movement at the turn of the twentieth century to recreate cities into grand metropolises with intricately designed parks began for Denver in the mind of a German immigrant who designed a dignified landscape around the people's democratic temple.[15]

The Board of Capitol Managers, still hard at work divvying up contracts to carry on the capitol project in 1895, proposed the first major change to the statehouse's interior that year. Unsatisfied with the cast-iron staircases in the north and south atriums then under construction, the managers decided on a more artful central ascent in the rotunda. To that end, they conferred with representatives of the Lane Bridge and Iron Works and instructed Superintendent Gumry to "commence tearing out and removing partitions, floors, portions of balcony, and change such wiring, gas and water piping and replace same as may be necessary." As the managers grew more experienced at their task, their architectural opinions solidified as well, encouraging them to make the most substantial alteration yet to Elijah Myers's designs. This change not only resulted in the demolition of work already under way, it also meant more construction delays for a project already nine years old. As they added to the building's timetable, the managers simultaneously expressed frustration with the Denver Onyx and Marble Company's slow pace. The board expressed general aggravation at the installation of white marble, which proceeded at an incremental rate. David Kelly brought a map of the Yule Creek area to a board meeting, blaming the delay on the poor wagon road from the quarries to the railroad at Carbondale. Unsatisfied, the managers asked Gumry to inspect the quarry himself. Before he could make the trip, however, events intervened that almost derailed the entire capitol project when Gumry and several other integral players in statehouse construction perished in the worst explosion and fire in Denver history.[16]

An incurable tinkerer and insomniac, Superintendent Gumry went to the basement boiler room of his hotel on Lawrence Street at around midnight on August 19, 1895, to check on the often intoxicated engineer, Elmer Loescher. Discovering the engineer's position abandoned, Gumry started fiddling with the boiler's controls. At 12:04 A.M. the boiler exploded, destroying the back half and center of the building, igniting a conflagration, and shattering windows for blocks around. Twenty-two people in the building died in the destructive fire, including Gumry, his assistant at the capitol, Robert Greiner, and Greiner's wife. One of the most famous Coloradoans of his day, General Charles Adams, a veteran of the Civil War and Indian treaties and friend of board members Otto Mears and Herman Lueders, also perished in the explosion. Lueders, who lived in the hotel, narrowly escaped with his life, as did representatives of the Denver Terra Cotta and Lumber Company and Chicago's Crane Elevator Company, who were staying at the Gumry Hotel while overseeing work at the statehouse. After Denver firefighters extinguished the blaze, they and city police spent several days recovering the survivors and the bodies of the deceased. When rescuers finally reached the flashpoint of the explosion, they came upon Peter Gumry's remains: "The body was in the most horrible condition of any of those that have yet been recognized. It was a mass of charred flesh and bones. The head resembled a heap of charcoal, but remained on the trunk as it was carried to the ambulance. The arms were taken out a piece at a time and placed beside the remains at the morgue." Denverites struggled to cope with the catastrophic events. They had known fires before, but never an explosive disaster like this. Capitol manager John Routt suggested that employees recently fired by Gumry blew up the hotel for revenge. Although no evidence surfaced to back up Routt's opinion, many Denverites shared his fears.[17]

The board members attended services and passed resolutions memorializing their lost colleagues, but they soon realized that serious problems demanded their immediate attention. After the debacle with William Richardson in the late 1880s, the board had decided against giving one individual or firm responsibility for the entire statehouse project. Instead, the managers contracted with many different companies for all manner of materials and tasks, creating a complex web of businesses and financial ledgers. Secretary Lueders knew more than anyone else about every aspect of the project, and if he had died in the hotel explosion the managers would have suffered incredibly to get the work moving again. Superintendent Gumry had served as the focus to organize physical labor at the capitol site and had also held the post of supervising architect since Elijah Myers's dismissal in 1889. The loss of Gumry and his assistant forced the managers to quickly find a dependable person to facilitate construction. They appointed James Murdoch as superintendent less than two weeks after the destruction of the Gumry Hotel. But even more than had been the case with Gumry, Superintendent Murdoch exercised only supervisory control, reflecting the managers' entrenched influence since Richardson and Myers left the capitol project. For his first major assignment, the board sent Murdoch to Marble in October 1895 to investigate the quarry. The progress of road construction from Carbondale and the purity of the Yule stone impressed the superintendent, who praised Denver Onyx and Marble "for the energetic manner in which they have proceeded with the work of getting access to these quarries." Murdoch reassured the managers that more capitol stone would soon arrive in Denver. Although the board remained somewhat skeptical, other details of construction relieved the immediate pressure on David Kelly's firm.[18]

The managers dealt with other matters in 1896. They chose Snead and Company Iron Works of Louisville, Kentucky, to manufacture brass railings for the atriums and rotunda, with spindles originally designed by Myers in the 1880s. Soon after, the board also approved a contract from L. Schriber and Sons Company of Cincinnati, Ohio, for oval brass railings that allowed for heat ventilation in the atriums. Not only did politicians and the managers want to provide jobs for Coloradoans through the statehouse project, they also wanted to create an opulent structure to embody the state's collective pride, reflecting the golden past in the shimmering railings even if that meant contracting with foreign firms. Representatives from the board also consulted with a respected local architect, Frank E. Edbrooke, on plans for the grand staircase and signed papers with M. J. Patterson of Milwaukee, Wisconsin, to construct the elaborate rotunda risers. Patterson also secured a contract to build stairs leading from the third floor to the observation decks in the dome. With the addition of an ornate railing around the interior of the observation deck platform, visitors ascended to the lofty heights and enjoyed the view of Denver and the Rockies as Myers had intended. Jerome C. Smiley offered this description of the panorama in 1901:

> The view from the Capitol dome embraces a domain larger than either of several eastern States. From the west where snow on the mountain summits is visible the whole year around, the eye may sweep away to the north over a fertile and beautiful agricultural region along the foothills; to the northeast where the South Platte winds its way, appearing like a ribbon of silver in its fringing of greenery; far to the east where the billowy plains roll to hazy distances until the sky bends down to meet them; to the south fifty miles away where the "divide" between the Platte and the Arkansas rivers stretches from the mountains far out on the plains, looking like one side of a flatly sloping roof. The city is spread out at the feet of the beholder who now appreciates its beauty, its extent, and the charm of its location as he never did, never could, before.

The vista observed from the capitol observation deck made the Colorado statehouse a unique and beloved public building.[19]

The managers enjoyed little spare time to appreciate the view from the dome. They ordered more changes to work previously finished, including raising the floors in the legislative chambers, which required stairs for higher lobbies at the back of the rooms. David Kelly suggested and the managers accepted that Italian marble be used for the new risers, since his firm could not provide Colorado stone in suitable sizes. In October 1896 the board sent Superintendent Murdoch to the marble quarries for the second time in as many years to investigate the lethargic pace of Kelly's Denver Onyx and Marble Company. Although a summer drought had slowed work along Yule Creek, Murdoch expected crews to extract enough stone to finish the statehouse floors by the onset of winter. But by the end of the year, when almost no marble had arrived in Denver, the managers called Kelly back and granted his firm an extension to finish the contract. On December 31 the managers issued an optimistic statement: "The Board knows from investigations that the contractor has encountered many obstacles, preventing it from executing the work with greater expedition, but is working in good faith with the State of Colorado." Denver Onyx and Marble tested that faith numerous times over the next few years, but the managers approved of the work finished thus far and felt comfortable in granting Kelly some leeway. Most significant, even in the face of mounting delays, the managers remained dedicated to supporting native industries and materials.[20]

The meeting of the Eleventh General Assembly in 1897 took place in a capitol-in-progress, just like the previous session had and, incidentally, one more to come. Among other business the legislature reorganized the Board of Capitol Managers, charging it with "supervising and directing the construction, completion, and furnishing" of the statehouse. The assembly gave the board a significant directive: "The care and control of the Capitol building and grounds shall be with the Board of Capitol Managers." Centralized jurisdiction meant the board controlled security, maintenance, and visitor services for the structure and eventually for the entire statehouse complex of buildings. The group remained a staunchly Republican body, which elicited little partisan concern at the time but would result in great tension within several years. Also, the legislature gave the managers the solitary authority to decide when their task was done and they should end their service, another provision that caused much conflict in the decades to come. The 1897 legislation also gave the managers statutory power even over elected officials in the capitol, which they exercised by parceling out office space according to their own opinions.[21]

The unease between the Board of Capitol Managers and the Denver Onyx and Marble Company grew increasingly hostile in the early fall of 1897. David

Kelly reported to the managers on the "slow progress" and "many difficulties" at both the Yule and Beulah quarries. He told them that his firm could not meet the completion deadline of December 31, 1897, weakening the "good faith" the managers had bestowed on his company. When the managers decided to replace temporary wooden stairs from the second floor to the third with permanent ones, they turned away from Denver Onyx and Marble in hopes of completing the minor job quickly. Denver Wire and Iron Works, a local company known for its ornamental metalwork, constructed the frame for the risers, and Frederick P. Bagley and Company of Chicago secured Italian stone wainscot and Vermont marble treads, much to Kelly's chagrin. The board's dedication to Colorado stone had resulted in excessive delays it had hoped to avoid by allowing Bagley's firm to use foreign material. Still, workers for Bagley took almost two years to install the stairways with stones that contrast dully with the brighter Colorado white marble and striated rose onyx in hallways nearby. But after eleven years of construction, the managers' patience grew thin as they focused on simply finishing the statehouse.[22]

Firmly in charge of the manmade symbol of the state, the board considered numerous proposals for capitol artwork in the late 1890s. In 1892 a group of Denver society ladies had gathered at the home of John and Eliza Routt to view a plaster model of a statue by University of Denver art professor Preston Powers. The representation portrayed an American Indian standing over a slain bison. The ladies' organization wanted the statue to decorate the capitol grounds and raised $10,000 from many supportive Denverites. Using the plaster model as a guide, foundries in Florence, Italy, cast the statue in bronze and returned it to the United States. Before it came to Colorado, the statue went on display for six months at the World's Columbian Exposition in Chicago in 1893. There it received its fitting moniker *The Closing Era*, acknowledging the end of the independent American Indian lifestyle. Presenting a historical paper at the exposition, Frederick Jackson Turner recognized "the closing of a great historic movement" with the end of the American frontier, and *The Closing Era*, sitting in an exhibition hall nearby, served as a bronze representation of this changing national existence.[23]

After the stop in Chicago in 1893 *The Closing Era* traveled to Denver, and the managers placed the statue in storage while they ordered improvements to the capitol grounds. When they accepted Schuetze's landscape plans in 1895, the managers did not discuss incorporating *The Closing Era* into the design. Finishing capitol construction took precedence over decoration for the grounds. The only change to the statehouse property they made after Schuetze's work had been completed, removing all the hitching posts in June 1897, reflected little more than a concern for public hygiene. Undaunted, the ladies' group pressured the managers that summer to install the artwork. The board announced that the first statuary on the statehouse property would be located at the west front of the building so *The Closing Era* could always see the end of the day with the sunset behind the mountains. Some pioneers in Denver, however, harbored ill feelings about American Indians from the 1860s conflicts. They considered such a prominent position unsuitable and lobbied against giving their old nemesis the prime location on the grounds. The managers bowed to pressure and ordered that *The Closing Era* be placed on the east, rear side of the building on a pedestal of Cotopaxi granite.[24]

Ironically, one of those early Colorado pioneers intricately involved with the 1860s conflict received a notable honor in the summer of 1897: he became the first person to lay in state. Territorial governor John Evans passed away on July 3, and three days later pallbearers carried his casket into the west wing and set it on a catafalque in the governor's reception room. Mourners passed by the coffin, dominated by an American flag–draped portrait of Evans, before interment at Riverside Cemetery. Installed a year after Evans's service, *The Closing Era* represented the transition from the dusty hill of Brown's Bluff to the meticulously preened capitol grounds, the end of the frontier existence for Colorado, and lingering ethnic hostilities from the earliest days of territorial settlement.[25]

Exercising one of their many statutory roles, the managers made several changes to the capitol staff in 1898. They had employed a night watchman since 1896, but increasing numbers of visitors demanded the creation of the first statehouse police force two years later, primarily "to stop fast bicycle riding around the building during evenings." Although bicycling emerged as one of the most popular fads of the late nineteenth century, the managers considered such behavior unseemly for the refined capitol grounds. Within a few years the board hired more watchmen and instructed them to "not remain together in any one place, engage in card playing, or . . . enter any office for the purpose of sleeping, but [to] be constantly on duty during their watch." The board's overconfidence grew in the late 1890s and resulted in the highhanded dismissal of Superintendent Murdoch in a fashion similar to the removal of Elijah Myers in 1889. But after struggling for three months to organize construction at the capitol the board acknowledged its error and hired Frank Edbrooke as architectural adviser and superintendent. Edbrooke had advised the managers on plans for the grand staircase several years earlier and ranked as Denver's preeminent architect of the period. He had designed the Brown Palace, Navarre, and Oxford hotels; the Tabor Grand Opera House; Central Presbyterian Church; the Masonic Building on Sixteenth Street; and many stately private homes, and he had submitted the second-place design for the capitol in 1886. Finally, the managers expanded the building's visitor services by hiring the first tour guide, Michael Wetzel, in September 1898.

*The Closing Era*, the first monument on the capitol grounds, placed on the east side in 1898 over the objections of pioneers who opposed recognizing American Indians at the statehouse. Courtesy, Charles T. Goodsell

Although the board occasionally believed the contractors might never finish the capitol, the managers proudly celebrated its essential role as Denver's most popular attraction.[26]

Shortly after hiring Superintendent Edbrooke, the managers asked him to investigate shocking reports about capitol construction printed in the *Denver Post* and the *Marble City Times*. The newspapers claimed David Kelly and Denver Onyx and Marble had been using foreign white marble, not Colorado stone, for the capitol. The board had allowed Kelly to use Italian marble for the stairs to the legislative chambers, but the newspapers' charges far exceeded that exception. A *Post* story entitled "Imported Marble for State Capitol?" released on August 27, 1898, read more like a pulp mystery than a news article. Crews reportedly unloaded railcars of marble from out-of-state quarries at Kelly's shops on Sundays with few witnesses at the site. The *Post* recorded accusations against company bondholder David H. Moffat, who stonecutters blamed for encouraging the firm's felonious behavior:

> This Dave Kelly who's got the contract has not only thrown out of work a lot of us here in Denver by bringing in stone already sawed and dressed, but

he has violated his contract by importing marble from points outside the state. . . . And it is Moffat's scheme to import the Vermont marble already worked, for it can be done in the East by Italians for little or nothing, and he can lay it down here ready for use, except a little dressing of the corners, about one-third cheaper than he can get the Colorado marble.

The subheadline for the *Post* article made the situation plain: "If Contractor Kelly Is Not Putting It in Contrary to Agreement, the Common Talk Among Stone Men Does Him an Injustice." Four days later the *Post* ran an editorial cartoon with a drawing of the capitol and the caption "How Will This Look? Colorado State Capitol Built Entirely of Colorado Material *Except the Marble*." The managers knew some stone in the building came from outside Colorado but were reeling over the possibility that Kelly had duped them into extending deadlines while he used foreign marble and charged Colorado taxpayers for more expensive native stone.[27]

Superintendent Edbrooke made a study of all the white marble in the capitol while Kelly emphatically denied the charges. Laborers kept working on the rose onyx wainscot, which all agreed came from Beulah, but Edbrooke ordered all marble installation halted. In November 1898 the superintendent reported variations in color and grain in marble tiling on the second and third floors and in the basement. The managers debated for several weeks and finally concluded that regardless of whether Kelly's firm used Colorado material, finishing the job took precedence. Residents in Marble fumed and accused the managers of injuring local workers and industries. The *Marble City Times* pointed to the root cause of the entire debacle—the fact that no railroad linked the quarry to the outside world, and the cost of shipping stone by wagon to Carbondale often proved overwhelming. In 1899 a legislative committee assembled to study the accusations but failed to resolve the situation in meetings that devolved into shouting contests between politicians and contractors. Adding to the tension, Kelly reported that his crew could not install full rose onyx wainscot in the basement without having quarrymen work in Beulah for at least the next decade. The firm placed rose onyx trim with white marble panels on the basement walls instead. The exasperated managers seethed at "the slow and unbusinessman-like manner in which the work is being done" and desired only to finish the building and end the chaos.[28]

A peculiar manifestation of the conflicts within the granite walls developed in early 1899, when a great explosion in the basement rattled the windows and nerves of all within the capitol. In the horticultural society's rooms, a valve left open over a weekend filled one of the fireproof vaults with gas. When an employee struck a match the next Monday morning, she ignited the fuel, which erupted in a tremendous blast. Windows shattered inside and out, and the building shook with such ferocity that some wondered if "anarchists had been at their deadly work." Governor Alva Adams, sitting one floor directly above the horticultural society, felt the substantial quake and rushed to the basement with his secretary. He and others stamped out the flames quickly spreading across the carpets. Describing the destruction, Governor Adams believed that "an explosion of the boiler could not have done more damage." Two horticultural society employees, including the unlucky instigator of the blast, suffered extensive injuries. Capitol engineers reminded staffers of the danger of entering vaults with lit matches and encouraged the managers to shut off the gas completely and only use electricity. The board, however, decided that as long as employees exercised caution, it should keep gas as an important fuel and refused to abandon this technology.[29]

When the legislature returned to the capitol in January 1899, the members encouraged the managers to clean up the mess in the basement as quickly as possible to prepare for a much-anticipated celebration at the statehouse. One of the most famous men in America, William Jennings Bryan, came to Denver on January 17 and addressed the legislature and hundreds of citizens in the House of Representatives chamber. The House's sergeants at arms joined forces with Denver police to limit the crowd, but nearly 2,000 people filled the chamber and gallery to overflowing. In his address Bryan called for free silver coinage, equal status with wealthier states, and the abolition of special interests in national politics. Men in the chamber cheered incessantly while women waved "a sudden snowstorm of white handkerchiefs." The raucous event marked the first time people gathered at the capitol to celebrate being not just Coloradoans but citizens of the West with common interests and concerns, with the statehouse serving as the appropriate setting for the popular rally.[30]

Other ceremonies in 1899 contrasted with the joyful reception Bryan received and traded solemn dignity for bombastic cheers. Two former chief executives passed away and received the honor of state memorial services that year. Job Cooper, the governor who had presided over the 1890 cornerstone ceremony, died in his home just across the street from the capitol, and his body lay in state in the governor's reception room on January 23. On December 4, territorial governor Samuel Elbert lay in state in the west wing corridor outside the governor's office. But a former U.S. senator, Colorado lieutenant governor, and at one time one of the wealthiest men in the state received the grandest tribute that year. Coloradoans honored Horace Tabor, whose fortunes had faded but whose fame remained high, with a state memorial service on April 13. Flowers filled the governor's reception room and surrounded the casket guarded by soldiers from nearby Fort Logan. As the nineteenth century drew to a close, the first generation of Coloradoans faded away, but not without a dignified farewell.[31]

The governor's reception room in the late 1890s, the site of several state memorial services. The room was converted into the governor's private office in the 1950s by renovations that obliterated or concealed much of its original style. Courtesy, Denver Public Library Western History Collection, Joseph Collier, C-51

Although a number of tasks inside the capitol still required completion, work in the rotunda demanded the most attention. After the General Assembly adjourned in 1899 the managers focused on finishing the grand staircase, a project under way for four years without much progress. M. J. Patterson of Milwaukee secured a new contract in July for the cast-iron frame and brass railings, and regarding the treads and wainscot the board once more heard aggravating excuses from Denver Onyx and Marble. David Kelly told the managers that he could not secure Yule marble blocks of appropriate size for the grand staircase. He suggested using either Tennessee or Italian marble, of which the board chose the latter. By November 1899 the board referred to the performance of Kelly's firm as "absolutely unsatisfactory," with only one worker in the capitol placing tiles and panels. Kelly informed the managers that he had sent his entire crew to Beulah to quarry all the rose onyx necessary to complete the statehouse, and he expected his laborers back in Denver soon. Governor Charles S. Thomas unhappily expected that the installation would "require several years, instead of having the work completed during his administration which was his desire." Denver Onyx and Marble made preparations for the final work on the grand staircase wainscot in January 1900. The extended construction time provided steady jobs in both rural and urban economies during a difficult period, but as the years passed politicians and citizens alike who wanted their statehouse finished grew increasingly frustrated with the seemingly endless project.[32]

To complete the rotunda the Board of Capitol Managers allowed itself the luxury of artistic debate. High in the dome, Elijah Myers had allotted space for sixteen round stained glass windows of Colorado scenery. Making another change to his proposals, the managers asked the curator of the State Historical Society, William C. Ferril, to come up with a list of deserving Colorado pioneers to have stained glass portraits in the dome. Ferril provided two lists with a total of 108 names. From those, the managers approved only 7 in a meeting on August 11, 1899. They chose 2 more the following November, finally selecting the remaining 7 names in July 1900.* Otto Mears accused some of his fellow managers of wanting "to put in this gallery the portrait of anybody who drove an ox across the plains in '59." Another obstacle the managers faced in choosing members for the Hall of Fame revolved around their reluctance to include women. As Colorado was the second state to grant universal suffrage, to many it seemed appropriate for women to have a place of honor in the capitol. The board received a petition from the Pioneer Ladies

---

*See Appendix B.

Aid Society recommending several women including Augusta Tabor and Eliza-beth Byers, wives of famous Colorado men and influential figures in their own right. As their last selection for the gallery, the managers begrudgingly approved philanthropist Frances Jacobs as representative of the state's pio-neer women, illustrating the board's gendered opinion. Meanwhile, the *Longmont Times* pointed out another divisive issue:

> The capitol board of managers are about to select subjects for portraits in the dome of the capitol building. Many living men and women have been suggested for places, but no one alive should be given a place. If the board desires to have some of the old pioneers, who are yet living, a few spaces could be left to be filled in years to come. There is no necessity, and it would not be just, to fill every niche at one time. The state capitol building was built as much for the future as the present. Let the board set the precedent that none but those who have closed an honorable career have a place in the gallery.

The managers disagreed with the *Times*'s policy, and of the 16 people chosen in 1899 and 1900 for the "Colorado Hall of Fame" windows, manufactured and installed by Denver's Copeland Glass Company, just over half were still alive.[33]

Once again, in 1899 a state celebration put out of mind for a little while the ongoing headaches of construction at the statehouse. When Colorado troops finally returned home from the Spanish-American War on September 14, the state held the largest celebration at the capitol since the cornerstone ceremony nine years earlier. Governor Thomas declared the day a state holi-day to welcome the fighting men home. Over 25,000 cheering citizens as-sembled on the west front to meet the soldiers returning from the Battle of Manila Bay in the Philippines, in which Colorado troops had particularly distinguished themselves. Coloradoans rallied around a towering flagpole placed on the capitol grounds a year earlier in honor of the troops fighting around the world, the first war memorial at the building. After a parade down Sixteenth Street, soldiers presented their regimental colors to Governor Tho-mas for display in the war relics collection. The Chaffee Light Artillery, the forerunner of the Colorado National Guard, fired an artillery salute using cannons that later found a permanent home on the statehouse grounds. In December a group of Coloradoans who fought in the Spanish-American War met in the statehouse basement to found the Army of the Philippines, an organization that several years later merged with similar groups into the Vet-erans of Foreign Wars. The capitol's role as a stage for the dramas of society coalesced through events like William Jennings Bryan's impassioned oration or the cheering of imperialist expansion at the end of the Spanish-American War. As the symbol of representative authority, the statehouse provided the

The grand staircase in the rotunda, the most substantial change to Elijah Myers's 1886 design, shortly after its completion at the end of the nineteenth century. Compare the original stencil designs on the first-floor walls with the murals on page 140. Courtesy, Denver Public Library Western History Collection, Louis Charles McClure, MCC-729

gathering point for Coloradoans to participate in a process that transformed them into a group conscious of their collective concerns and desires.[34]

The final year of the nineteenth century witnessed the gradual completion of all remaining construction at the Colorado State Capitol. Crews from

Denver Onyx and Marble installed the last stone slabs in the grand staircase, and Superintendent Edbrooke drew up plans for the brass balustrades of oak leaves and ivy, traditional symbols of strength. Laborers completed plaster and stucco work, including intricate ceiling decorations, throughout the building. Exhausted after fifteen years of chaos, despair, controversy, and excitement, the Board of Capitol Managers welcomed the closing of the century on December 31, 1900, with a great deal of satisfaction. When in January 1901 the legislature met for the fourth time in the statehouse, the members finally occupied a finished capitol for which so many people had struggled for so many years.[35]

The completion of the statehouse ended those long-active contracts for the interior stone quarries, but Marble and Beulah experienced different fates after providing stone for the capitol. The Yule marble developed into a major industry for northern Gunnison County for years afterward, even though much of the stone for the statehouse had been extracted by dynamite, which caused fracture problems in the quarry. When the Crystal River and San Juan Railroad finally arrived in November 1906, it made the marble affordable for many more projects. All across the state and nation, contractors used Yule marble for unknown numbers of structures. Hundreds of federal and state government buildings, memorials, private homes, and office structures incorporated the pure white stone. But a Vermont competitor bought and closed the Marble quarries in 1941, and they remained shut for almost half a century. The Yule site reopened in 1990 and daily produces remarkable building stone, making it the most successful of the quarries that provided capitol stone—ironic considering how much trouble it caused for the state in the late nineteenth century.[36]

By contrast, the difficulty of getting stone from the small Beulah quarry prevented its widespread use. Some local houses and the Pueblo County Courthouse incorporated pieces of rose onyx for interior decoration, but a lack of adequate transportation proved the site's downfall. David Kelly failed to recover his losses by turning the town into a resort community like General William Jackson Palmer had done with Colorado Springs. Many small pieces of stone remain at the isolated site above Beulah, but reopening the quarry would demand significant technological improvements. A wooden boom derrick still stands on the south lip of the quarry pit, but in the summer of 2001 vandals stole a large gear once used to lift the rose onyx boulders. Today the quarry serves as an unofficial Beulah park and a favorite site for hikers, nestled among the pine trees of the Wet Mountains.[37]

Herman Lueders, who served for sixteen tireless years as secretary of the Board of Capitol Managers, summarized the cost of the building in December 1900. Thus far the state had spent approximately $2.5 million to build the capitol, requiring both legislative appropriation and bonds, which the state paid back by 1904. The beautification of the grounds cost $60,000, and the board spent a little over $100,000 to furnish the building. Lueders calculated a total sum of $2,715,362.15 for constructing and furnishing the statehouse, with approximately an additional $200,000 spent in the six previous years for maintenance. Comparing these numbers with early-twenty-first century figures, the capitol's cost would easily surpass $60 million today.[38]

Opinions about the finished product varied greatly. The *Rocky Mountain News* referred to the capitol's interior as "the lining to the casket," a "bewildering maze of pillars, pilasters, and archways." Yet the *News* expressed admiration for the large atriums, which "shrink a man to pigmy size and compel him to regard his insignificance." Hidden alcoves, shimmering brass balustrades, and the sheer immensity of the capitol impressed any visitor who trod the marble floors. The statehouse received similar scrutiny from Beatrice Webb, an English socialist who toured the United States with her husband in the late 1890s. They wandered confusedly through the "pretentious" capitol as they sought out the executive suite. There the Webbs met the "uncultivated and muddle-headed" Governor Adams whose constantly ringing phone diverted his attention from his unimpressed guests. Adams managed to find time to conduct a tour of the statehouse for the Webbs, who expressed disappointment at the informal Colorado leaders they encountered. Beatrice described Secretary of State Charles Whipple as "an indifferent-looking clerk" but considered the supreme court justices "sensible sort[s] of persons." But like most chief executives, Adams could not neglect his office for long: "At this desk I am bound to listen to every man's complaint." The ostentation of the capitol, particularly in a period of economic difficulty for most Coloradoans, offended the English socialists and befuddled some locals who meandered uncertainly through the massive edifice.[39]

But these criticisms proved the exception rather than the rule to opinions about the completed capitol. The *Denver Times* considered the statehouse the preeminent national accomplishment of political architecture, "so suggestive of strength and endurance in its massive but perfectly harmonious proportions, with that beautiful impress of symmetry too often lacking in the great piles of stone, steel and mortar serving as seats of government in the commonwealths." The *Times* noted that the building's 12,000 bricks, if laid end to end, would reach from Denver to Topeka, Kansas. A train seventy-five miles long, from Denver to the foot of Pikes Peak, could hold the materials used in the capitol's construction, including over 280,000 cubic feet of granite and two acres of marble floor tiling. When running at peak efficiency, powering everything in the building at once, the boilers would require at least a ton of coal an hour. Rose onyx wainscot ran the equivalent of two miles, and estimates placed the weight of the building at approximately 300 million pounds. The *Times* also observed that the capitol stood exactly a mile above sea level, although not until a scientific measurement was conducted by students from the University of Denver in 1909 did the building's famous elevation receive proper recognition. Expressing the opinion of many Coloradoans, Jerome C. Smiley said this about the completed statehouse in 1901:

> Our Capitol with its great, lofty dome; massive walls, columns and portals, is an exceptionally handsome, dignified and well-proportioned edifice; few structures in this country are more pleasing in their aspects than it as it stands there on its commanding site in a splendid park that each passing year will make more beautiful. . . . Furthermore, it is an honestly built structure, the State having received full value for every dollar expended on it. . . . It would seem that a structure so stately, so dignified, so harmonious in all its lines and effects, should inspire higher, nobler and better things than some of the legislative performances that have been enacted within its walls.[40]

The state's preeminent building carried a hefty price tag, perhaps a bit extravagant to Coloradoans suffering in the wake of the Panic of 1893. Still, the project provided jobs in urban and rural economies and gave citizens something to raise their spirits and encourage state pride. The Board of Capitol Managers remained dedicated to using native stone regardless of cost or delay as a way to counteract the damage to Colorado industry. Yet the managers rarely acknowledged allowances made on other materials, such as brass and cast iron. The interior construction of the capitol served as a contrast between issues on which the managers would compromise and those on which they would not. At the same time, the board's influence increased dramatically as the nineteenth century drew to a close. By parceling out separate contracts for every detail of work and managing the maintenance and security of the building, the appointed managers often proved themselves more powerful even than elected officials.

For Coloradoans of the late nineteenth century, the statehouse project represented a source of continued employment and perseverance, with contractors and state officials "working in good faith," rather than a drawn-out, expensive debacle. As it had since the days of the 1890 cornerstone ceremony, the capitol served as the backdrop for significant events. In the late 1890s, however, activities at the statehouse adopted a broader context, reflecting both national and international interests. The capitol's role as a stage for the dramas of society as well as everyday political, social, and economic life crystallized as the building's construction concluded. The economic difficulties of the Silver Panic did not, could not, stop the state from pursuing its long-held dream. Through artwork as well as construction, the capitol also represented the end of the American frontier as traditionally identified by Frederick Jackson Turner and the beginning of a new regional identity in Colorado and the West. The building stood as a triumph of modern technology and common potential for many Coloradoans, responding to the perennial feeling of inferiority when they compared themselves to older parts of the Union. With their capitol finished, Coloradoans considered the frontier subdued and themselves able to stand as equals with their fellow Americans. After decades of waiting, wishing, and working, by the beginning of the twentieth century the people of the Centennial State could proudly gaze upon a permanent home for their representative government and a reflection of their collective abilities.

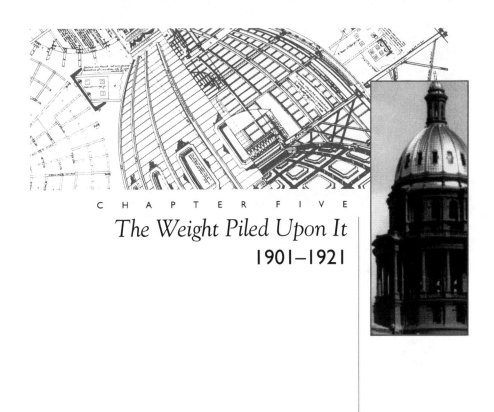

# The Weight Piled Upon It
## 1901–1921

T HE DAWNING OF THE TWENTIETH CENTURY HERALDED A NEW ERA for the Colorado State Capitol. After fifteen years of dust and noise, construction finally ended, and the statehouse settled into use as the seat of government. With the rapid expansion of state institutions in the Progressive Era to make a safer and more efficient society, the capitol experienced firsthand the evolution of a modern political community. The physical limitations of the building emerged as the dominant issue for caretakers in the early 1900s. At the same time, the place of the structure in the state's collective identity solidified. Instead of a newfangled attraction, the statehouse became part of Denver's accustomed landscape and a place for Coloradoans to gather to recognize their common interests. Celebrations and protests punctuated life at the building as citizens gradually came to accept and utilize the structure as their unifying symbol. Between increasing physical demands on the statehouse and the common acceptance of its purpose and symbolism, the capitol in the early decades of the twentieth century constantly felt "the weight piled upon it."

The most significant development at the completed statehouse in the first two decades of the twentieth century was its emergence as the accepted seat of authority in Colorado. The governor and supreme court worked in stately rooms equipped with modern technologies. Early every other year the legislature convened there and more often than not created new boards and commissions for which statehouse caretakers needed to find room. The Board of Capitol Managers entered the 1900s firmly in command of practically all aspects of the building. Republicans had dominated the board since its inception, but during this period its partisan nature instigated friction with many statehouse officials. The managers' participation in the building's partition among varying interests added to the hostility, but not until a major scandal broke did the managers' enemies possess the tools needed to reform the board. The first two decades at the finished building witnessed growing tension as new state agencies competed in bitter turf battles under the dome. The trend of expanding bureaucracy during the Progressive Era placed increasing demands on the capitol and its managing board and resulted in physical expansion into two new buildings near the statehouse. In the meantime, Denver city officials instituted massive construction projects that altered the physical appearance of the capitol's neighborhood, creating a parkland setting embodying a modern government and society. Although the period ended with the statehouse occupied by troops during World War I, the first two decades of the twentieth century represented the statehouse's best years. The parallel trends of the building's increasing symbolism and its growing physical pressures made the early twentieth century a time of both settling and tension in the capitol. Never since has it stood as strong or inspired more pride.

In the 1890s, groups of citizens calling themselves Populists organized around the country to respond to the needs of working-class and agrarian Americans. Colorado boasted a number of Populist successes. From electing a Populist governor, Davis Waite, to adopting women's suffrage, the state embraced the demands of the common man. Populism struggled to achieve nationwide success, however. In the early twentieth century a new movement called Progressivism, which included many disparate elements of society, adopted a number of Populism's social and economic causes. Aiming to make government more accountable and responsive to citizens' needs, Progressive-Era politicians in Colorado and elsewhere established many state boards to regulate all manner of industries and public needs. Instead of responding to pressing, basic concerns, as had the Populists, the Progressives enjoyed a relatively strong national economy that supported their efforts to ensure prosperity, health, and safety for all citizens. With national and local success the

Progressives created activist governments, providing a check on private enterprise in the interest of the collective society. Although the legacies of the silver collapse still affected Colorado's economy, the state experienced better times in the early twentieth century as a result of more diversified industry and agricultural production. As a result, the Progressive movement greatly impacted Colorado and by default the home of its representative authority, the capitol.

Even though construction was finished, state law made the capitol's caretakers responsible for the building's operations. One of the perennial, if mundane, concerns for the Board of Capitol Managers was purchasing coal for statehouse furnaces. Making the structure comfortable for state leaders, especially during the winter legislative sessions, ranked as a top priority. The managers spent much of their time in the early 1900s debating coal contracts, a shift in focus from construction issues of previous years. The board considered its choices carefully and only awarded the job to businesses it felt deserved the privilege of providing coal for the state capitol. The managers' cavalier nature, especially concerning the selection of coal suppliers, led to conflict between the board and members of the press, government, and ordinary citizens in the years to come. Yet the managers dealt impartially with personnel within the building. They promoted Patrick J. Boyle, who started as a floor tile installer with the Denver Onyx and Marble Company, to head janitor, a post he held until his death forty-three years later. The comfort of state politicians also demanded attention. On the second floor of the building several women sold cigars to legislators, and an African American man set up a shoeshine booth. Before their 1901 session some members of the General Assembly asked for a cafeteria in the building, considering the structure's distance from most Denver restaurants. The managers approved building a lunch counter in the north wing corridor of the basement, provided it did not sell alcohol. The counter closed after only a month, much to the dismay of the legislature, since it could not turn a profit by only serving politicians.[1]

An act of the Thirteenth General Assembly in 1901 unexpectedly instigated tension among the capitol managers, for the first time significantly threatening the body's collegiality. The Senate passed Concurrent Resolution 6 in March, providing for a stained glass portrait of Otto Mears in that chamber. The senators commended his "energy, zeal, and executive ability" during the capitol project, working to create "an enduring monument" for all Coloradoans. He had been recommended and rejected for a portrait in the dome's Hall of Fame, much to the dismay of many in southwestern Colorado, especially Mears himself. The task of ordering and installing the Senate's requested stained glass portrait fell to the capitol managers, and since Mears still served on the board, his peers expressed concern about what action they should take. The tension grew in November 1902 when Mears politely but firmly reminded his fellow managers that his window had not yet been made. Board member Joseph H. Thatcher argued that no person still alive should be honored with such a portrait, a claim he had made without success to oppose placing any living person's portrait in the Hall of Fame several years earlier. As a Democrat on the Republican-dominated board, Thatcher also politically opposed honoring Mears, one of the most prominent Republicans in the state. Temporarily subdued, Mears requested that the managers fulfill the Senate's resolution as soon as possible. This episode marked the beginning of private but intense infighting within one of the state's most powerful agencies, a signal of trouble ahead for the board.[2]

Other decorations proposed by the legislature resulted in discussions of a different nature for the board. In 1901 the General Assembly called for a fresh coat of gray paint for the dome and for a suitable covering to be placed on its outer surface. The assembly provided only minor appropriations, however, as many members felt unwilling to spend more money on the capitol, which had already taken fifteen years to complete. In the final years of the nineteenth century, as a temporary measure crews installed copper plates on the dome, which gave the building a shiny brown top. This solution failed to please citizens, who argued that copper mining had almost no history in the state, but the managers could not afford anything more suitable. Some people suggested a silver dome instead, a remarkably unpopular suggestion considering the collapse of the state's economy the previous decade—caused largely by Colorado's overdependence on silver mining. In response to the public pressure, the board recommended to the legislature a mineral with a much more popular image in the state's past—gold. The idea of a sparkling golden crown for the capitol struck a chord with many Coloradoans. Superintendent Frank Edbrooke reported that gold leaf, "although more expensive at first, is the only substance which will last for years, give a much better appearance, being more in harmony with the general color of the building, and lastly be a saving to the state." The managers received letters encouraging them to use gold for the dome, noting that Colorado had a history with the mineral that, perhaps aside from California, no other state could match. Many Coloradoans expressed increasing dissatisfaction with the copper dome as the plates oxidized and splotches of green appeared high above the capital city. Without funds, though, the managers could do little but sit back and watch the dome change colors.[3]

After tabling proposals for the building's pinnacle a decade earlier, the managers considered proposals for such work in the early 1900s. Elijah Myers had suggested an allegorical statue to top the structure in 1886, an element included in several of his designs, including Denver's Arapahoe County Court-house. But Superintendent Edbrooke suggested a large glass ball with lights instead, a popular new architectural feature he had viewed while visiting the Pan-American Exposition in Buffalo, New York, in 1901. It would cost less than a statue, be visible from as far away as Pikes Peak, and represent the power-ful contemporary faith in modern technology. As an added bonus, the *Den-ver Times* remarked that "by adopting this plan, the board would get out of a great deal of trouble which would surely come to it if it should attempt to place a figure on the dome and model it after any Colorado girl." Many people favored the glass ball over a statue, particularly since the arms of the statue on the courthouse had melted over the years as a result of several lightning strikes. But without suitable funds for any of the dome projects, the managers took no immediate action.[4]

The capitol, and its dome in particular, dominated the skyline of Denver and consequently the eyes and minds of all Coloradoans who passed through the Queen City of the Plains. Surpassing the Arapahoe County Courthouse as the tallest building in town, the statehouse towered over all prominent Denver structures. The dizzying height inspired artists, poets, tourists, and even lovers. On Christmas Day 1902 a watchman honored the signed order of Governor James B. Orman's secretary to let a couple ascend to the dome to get married, the first such ceremony in the building. The bride had her heart set on getting married before the state's most picturesque backdrop, and the guard commented that he had "heard of 'em getting married in a balloon and in lions' dens and things, but this certainly takes first prize." Edifices like the Brown Palace, Windsor, and Oxford hotels; Trinity Methodist and Central Presbyterian churches; Denver City Hall; the Mining Exchange; and the Eq-uitable Building stood proud in the city, but they all paled in comparison to the recently completed temple of republican government. The capitol's sym-bolism outranked all other structures in Denver and in the state as a place for both intimate and mass celebrations, a phenomenon that grew more power-ful as the twentieth century passed.[5]

Planning for the twentieth century's first large public ceremony at the capitol started with joy and ended in sorrow. President William McKinley, touring much of the country in the spring of 1901, planned a stop in Denver but canceled his visit when his wife fell ill and the entourage returned to Washington, D.C. Several months later the managers arranged for a different kind of ceremony in honor of President McKinley. In September 1901 capitol employees hung black bunting across the west front as part of nationwide mourning after McKinley's assassination in Buffalo, at the same exhibition Superintendent Edbrooke had recently visited. A memorial took place at the statehouse on September 19, part of simultaneous ceremonies at many public

The luxuriant new capitol offered a perfect stage for grand events, such as this ceremony for Denver banker and railroad executive David H. Moffat Jr. (*seated right*). In the governor's reception room in December 1904, his fellow citizens presented him with this silver cup, now owned by the Colorado Historical Society. Courtesy, Denver Public Library Western History Collection, Z-2883

places across the country. An estimated crowd of 40,000 sorrowful citizens assembled at the capitol for the solemn event. Black crepe on gray granite made the statehouse, the people's building, the perfect embodiment of Colorado's grief.[6]

Two years after the McKinley memorial the statehouse hosted more exuberant festivities. After the inauguration of Governor James H. Peabody in January 1903, thousands of Coloradoans brimming with spirit, both patriotic and fermented, packed the corridors for the building's first and only inaugural ball. Bunting and potted palms filled the atriums and hallways, and a fireworks spectacle on the west front thrilled the crowd. The *Rocky Mountain News* reported the attendance of over 25,000 "panting, jostling atoms of crushed humanity," which caused women to faint in the chaos while some escaped the throng by climbing out of windows. Several months later the state again welcomed the chance to host a chief executive at the capitol. President Theodore Roosevelt announced a trip to Colorado in the spring of

Forty thousand Coloradoans cheered President Theodore Roosevelt when he spoke at the capitol's west front on May 4, 1903. Courtesy, Colorado Historical Society, F31676

1903, and he agreed to speak at the statehouse. The managers instructed Superintendent Edbrooke to construct a wooden platform on the west steps from which Roosevelt could orate. When the president's entourage arrived on May 4, excitement filled the air. A parade escorted his automobile from Union Station to the capitol's east front, where many citizens gathered to catch a glimpse of the famous man. So many climbed on *The Closing Era* monument for a better view that the *Denver Post* remarked "it is a wonder it did not collapse under the weight piled upon it." After a stop in the executive office to chat with Governor Peabody, Roosevelt emerged at the west entrance to address a crowd of 40,000 Coloradoans. To allow the cheering throng to see him better, Roosevelt delivered the speech while standing on a chair. The nation's energetic chief executive, standing before Colorado's most significant collective accomplishment, combined to give the state a day to remember.[7]

After the bunting came down from the west front, the managers struggled with the many needs in the capitol, a task made difficult by the perennial lack of appropriations. The 1903 General Assembly encouraged the trend toward larger government by creating a number of new agencies, including the Labor Bureau, the State Traveling Library Association, and the Public Printing

Department. Pressure on capitol employees included increased demand for janitor service, furnishings, bathroom facilities, and the already overworked telephone system. But the ongoing issue of partisanship often distracted the managers from accomplishing their duties. The Republican-dominated board made a flagrant gesture against its opponents after the gubernatorial election in November 1904, which resulted in the most bizarre political event in Colorado history: the state had three governors in a twenty-four-hour period the following March. On March 17, 1905, during Governor Peabody's daylong second term, the managers met for little reason other than to show their preference for the Republican executive over his opponent, Democratic governor Alva Adams, ousted from office on March 16. Dominated by Otto Mears, an influential state Republican, the board rarely sided with Democrats even when the governor, as ex officio chairman, was a member of the latter party. With no time limits on their service, Republican appointees held their position for many years and often conducted their affairs to benefit fellow party members. Although this lopsided political representation had existed since the board's founding in 1883, it provided a source of increasing hostility in the early twentieth century. As Progressive-Era politicians crossed party lines to make government more efficient, controversial groups like the Board of Capitol Managers provided tempting targets for reform.[8]

A seemingly minor issue stoked the fires of partisan conflict and infighting among the managers in 1905. The board agreed to pay for a stained glass portrait of former U.S. senator Edward O. Wolcott in the Senate chamber, but when Denver's Copeland Glass Company presented another bill for a recently finished window of Otto Mears, some managers balked. Four years earlier the Senate had requested the window, resulting in tense arguments among Mears's colleagues. When the matter resurfaced in 1905, the managers almost came to fisticuffs over whether they should honor a person not only still living but also still serving on the statehouse board. Joseph Thatcher, a Democrat who opposed Mears's honor for both political and personal reasons, resigned from the board over the issue, ending much of the debate. Eventually, the managers grew tired of the bickering, and finally acquiescing to Mears's entreaties, they ordered his window installed later that year. But in response to their virulent debates, the managers never again honored someone, especially one of their own number, in like manner while he or she was alive. Over the next fifteen years workers hung three memorial windows in the capitol, all shortly after a noted citizen had passed away. Two other former members of the statehouse board and noted politicians joined the ranks in the years to come, Governor John Routt in 1909 and U.S. senator Charles J. Hughes Jr. in 1911. The third, also commissioned in 1911, honored Chief Justice Robert W. Steele and found a home above the bench in the supreme

The Senate chamber in the early twentieth century, with Otto Mears's stained glass portrait above the west gallery and the tin dome and skylight, which renovations sealed off in the 1950s. Courtesy, Denver Public Library Western History Collection, Joseph Collier, C-195

court's room on the second floor. Although their selection and installation inspired a great deal of heated debate, the cathedral-like artworks conveyed an interest in history and a passion for vibrant imagery in the cavernous chambers of the people's government to which later generations added in similar fashion.[9]

In the summer of 1905 the arrival in Denver of one of the nation's most patriotic organizations, the Grand Army of the Republic (GAR), inspired another artistic addition to the statehouse. Veterans attending the national encampment of the GAR reminisced among the statehouse's war relics and historical collections and gazed upon the flagpole honoring troops from the Spanish-American War on the west lawn. Yet the state boasted no memorial to soldiers from the Civil War. A territory during that conflict, Colorado played a regionally significant role, but its participation did not demand a large or expensive memorial such as those erected by eastern states. Pressured by the GAR, a Colorado Memorial Monument Board of Construction organized and suggested to the Board of Capitol Managers several possibilities for the plum exterior site at the statehouse—the west side facing the Rocky Mountains. Union veteran Irving W. Stanton of Pueblo conferred with Governor Jesse F. McDonald and other state officials, all of whom agreed that a humble yet dignified statue would best represent the state. In 1907 the managers contracted with the Seerie Brothers firm, an offshoot of Geddes and Seerie, which had quarried and assembled the capitol's exterior, for the Aberdeen granite pedestal. John D. Howland, a veteran of the First Colorado Volunteers and the Battle of Glorieta Pass, designed a statue of a dismounted cavalry soldier to cap the pedestal, which he finished in 1909. Before the last of the state's Civil War veterans had passed from the scene, the Centennial State recognized its role in the nation's greatest conflict. Those Colorado pioneers far preferred the Civil War monument on the capitol's west front to *The Closing Era*, even though the latter was a far more expressive memorial. Howland's statue, not unlike many others at county courthouses across the country, was attractive but much less compelling than *The Closing Era*. The placement of these two statues demonstrated the power of Colorado's earliest American settlers in capitol affairs, allowing ethnic intolerance to overpower historical and artistic symbolism.[10]

A change in the Board of Capitol Managers' office took statehouse caretakers by surprise in 1906. Herman Lueders, the secretary of the board since 1889, occupied the most influential position in one of the most powerful state agencies and more than any other individual deserved credit for the board's capability, success, and growing authority. Lueders suffered health problems in 1905 and took a leave of absence. Within a few months, though, his condition worsened, prompting Lueders's doctors to proclaim him "legally . . . of unsound mind" and to admit him to the state mental hospital in Pueblo. On February 7, 1906, the managers declared Lueders's office vacant and hired William K. Burschinell, a Civil War veteran and former sheriff of Arapahoe County, to fill the important post. The managers authored a lengthy resolution honoring Lueders, a man whom they saw as "efficient, honest, economical, and in every way commendable." In closing the tribute, which was much longer than such honors even for board members who died in office, they stated: "In the opinion of this Board he exhibited the best qualities of those who are called to public service, in devoting himself unselfishly to the discharge of important duties, with a desire solely to efficiently and honestly serve the State." For his unflagging efforts to facilitate the construction and occupation of the capitol, Lueders richly deserved the tribute from his colleagues and friends.[11]

Several other individuals with important connections to the statehouse received special honors in the early 1900s. First, after a distinguished career as a businessman in Denver, if a failure in the courtroom, Henry Brown passed away and received a state memorial service in the capitol. On March 11, 1906, 2,000 people filed past Brown's open casket in the governor's reception room, guarded by two capitol watchmen and surrounded by somber flags, streamers, and rosettes. From Governor McDonald to the Brown Palace Hotel's bellhops, many paid their respects to the man who donated the capitol site. A few years later James Brown, Henry's son, donated a large portrait of his father to the state to hang in perpetuity in the governor's private office in honor of Henry's statehouse property donation. Another memorial ceremony took place in August 1907, after the death of former governor and capitol manager John Routt. On August 15, pallbearers placed Routt's casket, attended by members of the Colorado National Guard, on a bier in the west wing corridor, draped with a flag and surrounded by palm leaves. After two hours of mourning, five former governors escorted Routt's casket from the building to a church service, and the capitol remained dark the rest of the day in honor of the deceased executive. The *Denver Post* called the capitol a "fitting setting for the obsequies," considering Routt's efforts as a capitol manager. The first generation of men and women involved with the statehouse gradually passed from the scene, and it remained for the next generation to maintain the building they left behind.[12]

This generational transformation of Colorado took many forms and included the landscape around the capitol in the first decade of the twentieth century. After years of conflict between the city and rural residents of Arapahoe County, Denver had achieved home rule as a city and county in 1904. Mayor Robert W. Speer promptly set out to remake Denver into a blend of civic pride and modern efficiency. He capitalized on the so-called City Beautiful movement then transforming urban areas across the nation, which called for grand public architecture and parklands that reflected the growth and purpose of government in the Progressive Era. In a period obsessed with remaking society in an enlightened manner, the physical appearance of civic institutions demanded close scrutiny. By altering Denver's urban landscape, Mayor Speer hoped to place the capital on par with the best cities in the United States and perhaps even in Europe. The capitol played an important role in this transformation. The west front of the statehouse, the primary facade of the capitol, looked out on grimy homes and the power plant for the Denver Tramway Company at the beginning of the twentieth century. At Speer's request, architect Frederick MacMonnies drew up plans in 1908 for a new civic center to replace the unattractive structures. He worked with a committee of twelve distinguished citizens, including businessman David H. Moffat and Reinhard Schuetze, the man who had designed the capitol grounds over a decade earlier. The group proposed a park extending west from the capitol to a new government building on Cherokee Street, which would consolidate all of the city and county's needs. Monuments and cultivated grounds in between would make Denver a world-class city, with the capitol dominating from its position atop Brown's Bluff. By 1912 Denver officials started purchasing and tearing down the structures west of the capitol to create a dignified landscape and center of political architecture for the city.[13]

Brooding from its perch above the city, the capitol's granite hulk dominated the skyline. Yet the building's most significant feature, the copper-covered dome, suffered repeated insults as a result of its splotchy green complexion. After years of discussion, in the years 1907–1909 the building's pinnacle finally received much-needed attention. Six years of proposals resulted in an appropriation for funds to gild the dome in 1907. Deposits of the mineral near Cripple Creek had reinvigorated the mining industry after the collapse of silver, and Colorado wanted to reflect that resurgent hope in its most important structure. Under the clear blue spring sky in 1908, two Denver men clung to the dizzying height and placed 200 ounces of Colorado gold, pounded into tissue-thin sheets, on the dome. At the same time, the board approved Superintendent Edbrooke's glass ball for the top of the building. Responding to criticism from some quarters about their decision, the managers remarked that "the thousands of visitors to Denver unanimously admire and commend this embellishment of a structure which is the pride of every loyal Coloradoan. The globe itself completes the symmetry of the Building and the illumination from the electric lamps is at once unique and a constant attraction at night." The capital city's dominant feature reflected the state's mining boom days of the nineteenth century and represented a beacon for citizens seeking the embodiment of their pride and aspirations.[14]

Visitors to the statehouse enjoyed the building's historical and cultural displays as well as its architecture and art. The crowded collections in the capitol basement demanded more than a passing glance. Well over a million and a half tourists had passed through the many rooms of historical and scientific curiosities since they opened in the 1890s. Visitors flocked to the Bureau of Mines' displays of gold and silver nuggets from all parts of the state, as well as building stones and rare pieces of strange minerals called uranium and vanadium from the Western Slope. Historical society curator William Ferril traveled the state collecting newspapers, books, and pamphlets for the archives and birds for the natural history displays. He also lectured to awestruck audiences of tourists and schoolchildren about many elements of Colorado's past. Even more excitement awaited in a rapidly expanding collection of the historical society:

> In another department of the basement is one of the most wonderful
> anthropological collections known to science. It contains a complete

assortment of all the utensils, wearing apparel, weapons, etc., pertaining to the Cliff Dwellers, who were among Colorado's earliest inhabitants. . . . The region in Montezuma [County] known as the Mesa Verde was their principal settlement. . . . In the collections of the State capitol are a number of mummies of these strange people. The mummies include both adults and children, and are remarkably well preserved, showing the hair and features, and, of course, the diminutive size, for they were a race of pygmies.

The *Post's* convoluted anthropology notwithstanding, displays in the capitol tantalized many people with artifacts from the state's first national park, Mesa Verde. Even more bizarre, in the subbasement rested an almost unknown attraction—the heads of Felipe and José Espinoza, notorious bandits from the San Luis Valley. Seeking a reward from territorial governor John Evans, scout Tom Tobin had killed and decapitated the two men in the 1860s. The heads arrived at the capitol in the 1890s with other gubernatorial paraphernalia and were placed in storage. The skulls remained in a box in the capitol's tunnels until sometime before the late 1930s, when crews cleaning out the subbasement incinerated them in the boiler furnaces, destroying forever the most grotesque artifacts ever to find a home in the statehouse.[15]

As the number of visitors to the capitol grew exponentially in the early twentieth century, the historical society and other agencies asked for more space to house their collections. Even though Elijah Myers had promised a statehouse capable of holding every conceivable element of state government, the evolutionary nature of civil authority placed increasing demands on the building's physical limitations. Progressive-Era politicians who considered an efficient government the best way to improve society only exacerbated the problem. After the Sixteenth General Assembly met in 1907, the managers needed twenty-two new offices to house a mighty list of agencies, including bureaus of Child and Animal Protection and Vital Statistics; commissions of Dairy, Insurance, Printing, Pure Food, and Water; inspectors of Building and Loan Associations and Oil; the public accountant; and the Colorado Prison Association. Two new Progressive agencies, the Civil Service Commission and the long-awaited Railroad Commission, promised to restore order to a chaotic system of government employees and corrupt officials often in the pocket of major railroad firms. The latter promised to end a great deal of bribery even in the legislative chambers, where railroad officials placed free passes on politicians' desks to secure votes for key issues. But for all the good these new agencies promised to do, they posed more problems for the statehouse caretakers. Since the managers could no longer comfortably house all state boards in the capitol, they recommended extending the east wing of the statehouse "as the only way out of the dilemma."[16]

Inspired by the thought of new construction, the managers set about laying the groundwork for legislative financial support. They asked Superintendent Edbrooke to create plans for an extension that would blend harmoniously with the existing structure and preferably use similar materials, especially Aberdeen granite. With hopes of revitalizing a local industry, Gunnison newspapers exaggerated reports that they needed few preparations to reopen the site. Since the entire east front could be disassembled and reassembled after installation of the new offices and floors, Edbrooke doubted the managers would need to ask for more than $300,000. Further encouraging the project, Republican governor Henry A. Buchtel supported the idea of extending the east wing. A change in political leadership in 1909, however, put all construction plans on hold. With Democrats in control of both the legislative purse strings and the executive office, the Republican-dominated managers failed to secure the needed appropriations. The new Democratic governor, John F. Shafroth, scrutinized the managers' actions more closely than Governor Buchtel had. Governor Shafroth, who supported Progressive reforms that forced the issue of statehouse office space, staunchly opposed an extension of the capitol. Nonetheless, he and the General Assembly began instituting government reforms that created many new agencies, making the problem worse. The new governor desired a larger and more proactive state authority but cared little about housing those boards and commissions.[17]

Only weeks after taking office, as Governor Shafroth received dozens of complaints from the heads of his cherished Progressive agencies, he realized he could no longer ignore the problem of space in the statehouse. Although he did not want to increase the authority of the powerful Board of Capitol Managers, which he and other reformers considered a dated and wasteful agency, the governor agreed to the plan to erect a new state building nearby to relieve the pressure in the capitol. Shafroth begrudgingly granted the managers the responsibility of putting up this new structure. Practically all state officials agreed that moving the historical and scientific displays out of the statehouse and using the basement for boards and commissions made the most sense. Historical society curators William Ferril and Jerome Smiley lobbied for the proposal, and the legislature agreed in early 1909. In May the managers purchased land on the southeast corner of Fourteenth Avenue and Sherman Street to provide the state's most popular tourist displays with a suitable new home. Superintendent Edbrooke and his draftsmen got to work immediately on the Colorado State Museum and presented final plans in October, when construction commenced on the state's second edifice on Brown's Bluff.[18]

As excavation for the state museum began south of the capitol, the managers prepared the statehouse for several notable visitors. A train bearing President William H. Taft arrived at Union Station on September 21, 1909, and paraded up Seventeenth Street to an excited throng of children on the state-house grounds. Once inside the capitol President Taft, Governor Shafroth, and U.S. senator Charles Hughes Jr. stood at the foot of the grand staircase and shook hands with a long line of citizens. Many who met him considered Taft's famous smile as bright as the new gold dome. A private reception in the governor's suite followed and included former governors Alva Adams, James Grant, and James Orman; the state supreme court justices; and former U.S. senator Henry M. Teller. A year later Colorado welcomed back to the capitol a popular figure, Taft's predecessor Theodore Roosevelt. On August 29, 1910, Roosevelt spoke to a joint session of the General Assembly in the House of Representatives chamber. A supporter of many Progressive reforms, he attacked politicians who reneged on campaign promises, as well as members of the press who wrote exaggerated stories to inflame public opinion. Legislators on the floor and spectators in the galleries enthusiastically cheered Roosevelt's remarks. From Taft's casual charm to Roosevelt's energetic oration, the capitol admirably fulfilled its role as the state's preeminent stage for political and social thought.[19]

Whereas the building's role as a backdrop for momentous events grew increasingly strong, opinion about the capitol managers steadily weakened. Many legislators wanted the board to declare its existence fulfilled and, most important, to free up its valuable office space on the first floor. But in the first decade of the twentieth century the managers exerted a great deal of influence over statehouse affairs. Through its power to grant or take away office space, the board often impacted the effectiveness of state officials—from the governor, legislature, and supreme court to the smallest commission—and its partisan nature only made things worse. In 1910 the board endured a number of attacks from political opponents. Democratic secretary of state James B. Pearce claimed that his office held statutory jurisdiction over the capitol and that the managers' tenure should end. Democratic attorney general John T. Barnett sided with his fellow partisan against the primarily Republican managers. Unexpectedly, Democratic state treasurer William J. Galligan broke party ranks and promised to honor the managers' vouchers as his office had in the past. The *Denver Republican*, politically supportive of the managers, pointed out that with the construction of the state museum under way, the managers could not realistically conclude their tenure. The *Denver Post* similarly considered the board's termination unlikely and recognized that the 1897 capitol managers' statute provided that only the board itself could "declare [that] it has finished the job and the time to retire has arrived." Regardless of opposition from elected officials, the board, having achieved significant influence over the entirety of state government, was not about to chop off its own head.[20]

In recognition of its unpopular position, the Board of Capitol Managers resolved that "the first and most economical thing to do is to complete the State Museum Building, and thus relieve the congested state of the Capitol." By alleviating the territorial battles under the gold dome, the managers hoped to diffuse some of the anger focused on them. The managers had become far more professional since the 1880s, but, as they had with the capitol project, they parceled out museum jobs individually instead of trusting a single contractor and relied on Superintendent Edbrooke's expertise to guide construction. The board awarded numerous contracts in 1911 and 1912 for the state museum, including ones for brick, concrete, and iron work. Seerie Brothers won a contract for $25,000 to construct the museum's foundation of Aberdeen granite, specially quarried from the now closed site, to blend with the statehouse to the north. Underneath the museum Edbrooke designed a new heating plant to replace the capitol's aging boilers. He also recommending discontinuing the use of carbide gas for light, a decision made easier after an explosion in 1912 that shattered a pillar in the statehouse. For the museum's superstructure, the Colorado Yule Marble Company erected Edbrooke's neoclassical design with stone from the same quarries used for much of the capitol flooring. The building included military and mineral exhibit rooms in the basement and on the first floor, a memorial hall at the main entrance on Fourteenth Street, exhibit and lecture rooms on the second and third floors, and an art gallery and a library. Edbrooke's final major commission capped an exemplary career as Denver's best architect of the era. After six years of steady work the Colorado State Museum opened to the public on September 2, 1915, a spacious home to honor the state's past.[21]

As the state museum rose, contemporary events overshadowed the ongoing problem of office space at the capitol. Coal miners in southern Colorado went on strike in September 1913 for better wages, safer working conditions, and other traditional labor concerns. The aggrieved members of the United Mine Workers union lived in tent colonies near the mines while firms like the Colorado Fuel and Iron Company struggled to find replacement employees. As the strike dragged on, the federal government appointed a committee of five U.S. congressmen from various states to come to Colorado and investigate the situation. They assembled in the Senate chamber in February 1914 and heard testimony from representatives of labor unions and the mining and steel industry for several days. When Deputy State Labor Commissioner Edwin V. Brake accused industrial leaders in Huerfano and Las Animas counties of bribing authorities, intimidating miners, and preventing the exercise of justice, supporters of the coal companies jeered from the galleries. Union representatives claimed the state militia, sent to the strike zone by Governor Elias M. Ammons to keep the peace, only increased tension between the parties.

After several days the committee adjourned to Trinidad, where the members visited with miners and industrialists, and then returned to Washington, D.C., to discuss their findings. But instead of the pressure having been alleviated, the situation in southern Colorado worsened with each passing day. Events reached a deadly climax at Ludlow on April 20 when militiamen attempted to remove the strikers from the tent colonies. A gun battle ensued that killed people on both sides and started a fire in the laborers' camp. By day's end over a dozen women and children had died from burns or asphyxiation. The violence of what became known as the Ludlow Massacre shocked many in the state and around the country.[22]

As the representative symbol of all Coloradoans, the capitol served as the focus for public reaction to Ludlow. On April 23, 1914, the Woman's Peace Association met in the House of Representatives chamber and approved several resolutions to present to Governor Ammons, including the removal of the militia from the strike zone, state seizure of the mines, and an appeal to President Woodrow Wilson for federal intervention. Public anger erupted two days later when, as the *Denver Post* reported, "500 Women Storm Capitol, Corner Squirming Governor, and Demand Strike War End." Women and children clogged the hallways, atriums, and rotunda while a delegation appealed for Ammons's presence in the House chamber. Under armed escort he made his way to the second floor and promised action to the assembled throng. Unconvinced, many women camped in the governor's office until he dispatched a telegram to President Wilson asking for help. The *Post* commended the effort, noting a new kind of political participation for women that proved "they can demand, instead of politely resolving and requesting." The next day 5,000 union members marched on the capitol and denounced Ammons as a traitor to his fellow Coloradoans. The crowd stood in the pouring rain while they listened to eighty-year-old socialist activist Mother Jones encourage the impeachment of the man she called "this governor thing of yours." A week after the Ludlow deaths a group of women trapped Ammons in his office and demanded that he make a stronger plea to Wilson for federal relief. Humiliated at his inability to avoid the women's dictates, the governor acquiesced and soldiers arrived at the mines three days later. Events as shocking as the violence at Ludlow inspired the most virulent and effective protests the capitol would witness for decades.[23]

By December 1914, representatives from labor and management had settled the violent coal strike. Coloradoans desperately wanted to put the whole affair behind them. But that month the *Denver Post* exposed a scandal with statewide ramifications, and the controversial Board of Capitol Managers stood at the center of it all. Under what the *Post* called a "gentleman's agreement," the Leyden Coal Company had served the statehouse's fuel needs

BY NEWSBOYS,
ON TRAINS.
★ THE BEST NEWSPAPER IN THE U. S. A. ★
16 PAGE
3D EDITI
DENVER, COLO., WEDNESDAY, DECEMBER 23, 1914.
WE PROMISE TO GET BUSY, FINISH OUR WORK AND GO HOME AND PUT IN OUR CROPS — THE LEGISLATURE
RESIGNATION OF THE BOARD OF CAPITOL MANAGERS
WE PROMISE TO DO OUR BEST TO PUT PEOPLE ON OUR VACANT LANDS! SIGNED State Land Board.
WE PLEDGE OURSELVES TO GIVE COLORADO AN HONEST, CLEAN AND EFFICIENT ADMINISTRATION. SIGNED STATE OFFICERS ELECT.
We heartily agree to have mutual Good fellowship and Peace for 1915!! Signed Labor Capital
SOME CHRISTMAS PRESENTS MISS COLORADO WOULD APPRECIATE!

Front-page editorial cartoon in the *Denver Post*, December 23, 1914, encouraging many government reforms, including the Board of Capitol Managers' resignation, to brighten the holiday season for Coloradoans. Author's collection

since 1906, suspiciously the same year William Burschinell took over as secretary of the board, although the *Post* found no direct evidence to accuse him of wrongdoing. Contrary to statutory guidelines the board had not sought competitive bids, and during the coal strike it had bought fuel under an expired contract to avoid public negotiations. The board's partisan enemies finally possessed the ammunition with which to launch a full assault. But several weeks before the scandal came to light, voters had reacted against Governor Ammons's handling of the coal strike by returning the Republicans to power with a legislative majority and placing George A. Carlson in the governor's office, thus giving the managers a temporary reprieve. Two years later, though, the coal controversy proved too powerful for the board to survive unscathed when Democrats reclaimed the governor's office and both houses of legislature. In 1917 the Democrat-controlled Twenty-first General Assembly limited the managers' influence to caretaker status and introduced term limits of eight years for the members of the board. They also lost their large office on the first floor and moved to a small corner of the basement once occupied by the statehouse carpenter. Although they remained in existence for nineteen more years, the managers lost most of the influence they had accumulated over four decades. State officials finally brought to heel a recalcitrant, partisan agency.[24]

Even after the coal scandal the managers still coordinated important events in the building, including the most somber honors the state could bestow. In the 1910s they arranged for numerous memorial services, including one for perhaps the most famous man in the world. Colonel William F. "Buffalo Bill" Cody passed away at his sister's house in Denver in early 1917. On January 14 pallbearers placed his casket, draped with an American flag, at the foot of the grand staircase, surrounded by floral arrangements sent from all over the world. During a three-hour period, 18,000 people passed by the master showman, and guards turned away another 12,000 at the end of the day. Many dignitaries came to view Cody's remains. Former governor Jesse McDonald, current governor Julius C. Gunter, members of the state supreme court, Mayor Speer, Wyoming governor Frank Houx, Nebraska lieutenant governor Edgar Howard, and the mayors of Cody, Wyoming, and North Platte, Nebraska, joined the somber ranks. As perhaps the most famous individual to ever lay in state in the capitol, Cody's service and subsequent burial on Lookout Mountain west of Denver incorporated pomp and commemoration well worthy of the master showman.[25]

Perhaps the most solemn duty of the capitol, state memorial services occurred with notable regularity in the first decades of the twentieth century. Politicians and businessmen who brought Colorado from territorial status to statehood and shared in the boom of the 1880s and the bust of the 1890s deserved special recognition for their role in the state's history. In 1911 three such men received the honor of a memorial service in the capitol. U.S. senator Charles Hughes Jr., a former member of the Board of Capitol Managers, died in office and lay in state at the foot of the grand staircase on January 13. On March 23 state officials paid honor to banker and railroad entrepreneur

Dignitaries and mourners in the rotunda around the coffin of Colonel William F. "Buffalo Bill" Cody, laying in state on January 14, 1917. Courtesy, Colorado Historical Society, F303

David H. Moffat with a memorial service witnessed by 10,000 mourners. The casket of former governor James Grant also rested in the rotunda, on November 4. On February 25, 1914, former U.S. senator Henry Teller received a memorial service, as did former governor James Peabody on November 25, 1917. No more dignified tribute to the most famous individuals of Colorado existed than to lay in state in the people's building.[26]

William Cody's memorial service in the rotunda foreshadowed the entry of the United States into the most destructive war yet known to civilization. World War I had dragged on with ghastly carnage around the world since 1914. Hoping the U.S. entrance would bring the conflict to a speedy conclusion, Coloradoans determined to make a significant contribution to the war effort. To that end, state leaders created a number of new agencies that impacted the capitol in various ways. Governor Gunter established a defense council to ensure the state's preparedness, and the Board of Capitol Managers expanded statehouse switchboards to handle telephones for War Department offices in the building. The board purchased lots north of the capitol on Sherman Street and Colfax Avenue, and the rapidly expanding Adjutant General's Department took over a former home on the northeast corner of the intersection. Officials from several federal agencies, including the United

States Army, moved in with the adjutant general while the managers found room for state preparedness councils, the provost marshal, and the United States Fuel Administration, among other groups. Recognizing ongoing concerns about space in the building, the board also asked the legislature to review options for postwar office needs. But for the moment turf battles in the capitol quieted as state officials acquiesced to the demands of a society at war.[27]

The capitol experienced the changes of wartime in other ways as well. Executive officials ordered the dome closed in December 1917 as a wartime precaution, and it did not reopen for visitors until 1920. Many groups used rooms in the statehouse for patriotic meetings, at times as frequent as ten per week. The most significant such gathering, the Colorado War Conference, took place in early May 1918. For two days interested citizens listened as speakers including Governor Gunter, opportunity school founder Emily Griffith, and Colorado Agricultural College president Charles A. Lory discussed ways to help the war effort. Eager audiences filled the legislative chambers and committee rooms to consider topics such as food conservation, women in industry, military science, and the evils of "pan-Germany." As the state's most important building, the capitol filled an appropriate local role in the promotion of victory and eventual peace.[28]

With the armistice in November 1918, Coloradoans celebrated the end of World War I along with the rest of the world. No amount of flag waving or fireworks, however, could top a visit from the victorious chief executive, Woodrow Wilson. On a cross-country trip promoting the League of Nations, the president's proposal for an international body to resolve differences peacefully, Wilson came to Colorado on September 25, 1919. Before he addressed a large crowd at the Denver Auditorium, Wilson's entourage drove to the capitol so the president could greet 30,000 schoolchildren assembled there. Wilson stood and addressed the crowd: "I cannot pass by my fellow citizens and young fellow citizens without telling those within the sound of my voice how glad an old schoolmaster is to be welcomed to Denver." After shaking hands with some of the thousands gathered on the grounds, Wilson rode off with his wife and Governor Oliver H. Shoup to his speaking engagement. After an address later that day in Pueblo, Wilson collapsed from exhaustion, and his train quickly returned to Washington, D.C., where he suffered a massive stroke a week later. On that sunny day in September 1919, the capitol provided a stage for one of the last public appearances of the man who tried to make the world safe for democracy.[29]

Even as the nation considered joining a new world order, old problems remained unresolved at the statehouse. Debates over the physical space needed by government resumed after the end of World War I. The capitol's new superintendent, James Merrick, hired in 1917, continually bemoaned the number of offices crammed into the capitol. Many state leaders agreed that the demands placed on the statehouse during the war required a physical expansion of state government. In 1919 the General Assembly appropriated funds for the State Office Building, a "c"-shaped structure designed by Denver architect William N. Bowman, on the northeast corner of Colfax Avenue and Sherman Street. At the request of Governor Shoup, Colorado manufacturers provided as many of the building's elements as possible, although some ornamental stone originated in Tennessee, Vermont, and Italy. In an effort to aid Colorado's war heroes newly returned from the fields of France, Shoup and the legislature asked that veterans be considered first for work on the State Office Building. In the meantime, Superintendent Merrick conceived of a new addition to the labyrinthine subbasement—an 800-foot-long tunnel from the state museum to the new office structure, crossing the capitol under the east steps, to provide heat and electricity to all three buildings. On June 5, 1920, almost thirty Masonic lodges laid the cornerstone of the State Office Building, and only a year later crews finished the structure after a little more than two years of construction, freeing up fifteen legislative committee rooms in the statehouse. State leaders considered the office space problem solved for at least a few years.[30]

As the capitol complex grew, Denver resumed work on the parkland west of the statehouse. Mayor Speer brought landscape architect Edward H. Bennett from Chicago to revitalize the civic center project, and by the end of the 1910s the park setting in front of the capitol included frontier statuary and Greek colonnades. Banker John H. Voorhies donated over $100,000 for a memorial and fountain on the north side of the park. In the Greek amphitheatre to the south, Allen T. True painted murals in honor of former attorney general Charles Toll. Plans languished for a new central administrative building for Denver, the need for which grew after both the city hall and county courthouse had been declared fire dangers in 1915. But by the time the 1920s dawned in Denver, the setting near the state capitol had been transformed from isolated prairie to ramshackle homes to a dignified focus for city, county, and state architecture. As Speer had envisioned, the dream of building a "Paris on the Platte" was well on its way to reality.[31]

In the years shortly after World War I, these grand expressions of public authority experienced threats unlike any seen before. Anarchists had long worried those charged with public safety, and after the overthrow of the Russian government by socialists in 1917, many Americans expressed fears about similar uprisings in the United States, a phenomenon known as the Red Scare. As the capitol was the most visible symbol of state authority, caretakers grew increasingly concerned about the building's security. In response to unfounded rumors of anarchism, Governor Shoup ordered fifteen members of the Colorado National Guard to patrol the statehouse corridors and grounds in November 1919. State leaders' fears turned the capitol into an armed camp. The group that caused by far the most anxiety in the American West was the "one big union" of laborers, the Industrial Workers of the World (IWW). Organized in 1905 to encourage energetic collective action, the IWW used revolutionary rhetoric to promote socialist reforms. The union's disapproval of national participation in World War I resulted in public opposition and government attacks. By 1917 the IWW's influence had waned precipitously, but its constituents still used the union's radical image to spread chaos. Fueling the fires of paranoia in Colorado, members plastered stickers that read "Join the IWW. We Don't Want Any Scabs" on doors and walls in the capitol on New Year's Eve 1919. Superintendent Merrick considered the vandalism a practical joke, but Governor Shoup and the Board of Capitol Managers failed to find anything amusing about the prank. For a while, fears lingered in everyone's minds, but by the end of 1920 the situation at the capitol had calmed, and the guardsmen departed from the building.[32]

When President Warren Harding took office in 1921 he promised a "return to normalcy," back to the peaceful days before the United States entered World War I. In much the same way, after Colorado National Guard troops left the capitol, the building returned to normal use. For much of the twenty years after construction concluded in 1901, statehouse caretakers performed the double task of encouraging the structure's place as a unifying symbol and establishing it as a working office building. Yet state leaders encountered difficulties in accomplishing both goals. The Progressive Era, with its exponential growth of commissions and civil servants, made a substantial impact on the capitol and its environs. Although Elijah Myers had designed the capitol to hold every office imaginable for a state government, by 1921 the structure could no longer comfortably house the growing bureaucracy. To combat vitriolic competition for space in the statehouse, the government physically grew with the Colorado State Museum and the State Office Building. Additionally, Denver officials created a parkland setting for civic authority, with the statehouse dominating and coexisting with city government. The building honored the first generation of Coloradoans through memorial services, the penultimate tribute from a grateful state. Whereas the capitol provided a forum for artistic and patriotic expressions, best witnessed by the addition of stained glass windows and the Civil War memorial, it also served as a setting for controversy. The coal strike of 1913–1914 resulted in federal hearings and massive public demonstrations that effectively shaped state policy. Also, after the 1914 coal scandal the Board of Capitol Managers' partisan opponents finally succeeded in restricting the board's influence. Never since has an agency enjoyed as much power over state government or the capitol. The perilous days of World War I brought increased demands on the building and threats as well, with troops patrolling the grounds, turning the statehouse into a granite fortress and contradicting all concepts of an accessible government.

As Colorado entered the 1920s the completed statehouse had crowned Brown's Bluff for two decades, flanked to the north and south by granite and marble representations of the growing needs of early-twentieth-century society. No longer controlled by the tight fist of a domineering agency, the Colorado State Capitol weathered controversies and welcomed celebrations to successfully reflect its dual role as the embodiment of the state's collective identity and the home to its representative government. Never since has the statehouse functioned so well under "the weight piled upon it."

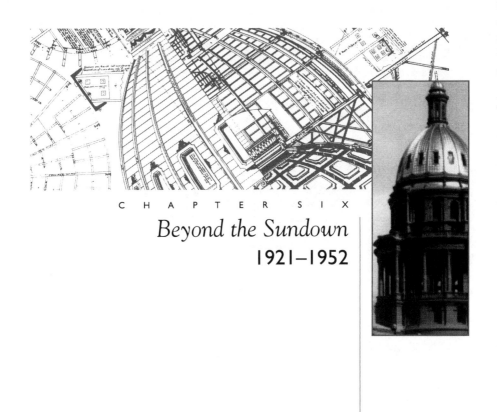

*Beyond the Sundown*
1921–1952

A S THE TWENTIETH CENTURY PROGRESSED, the capitol settled comfortably
into a position of steady use and an accepted part of the state's
manmade landscape. Two decades after completion, it still housed
most agencies of Colorado authority, even taking the state museum and office
building into account. The statehouse represented the wealth of Colorado's
greatest boom period and harkened back to the best in the state's past. It
stood no longer as a novelty but instead as a necessary and important part of
Colorado life. With the biennial legislative meetings and ongoing work of
the executive and judicial branches, the capitol aged gracefully as the midpoint of the twentieth century approached. Carrying a bright destiny from
the first decades of occupation, the capitol experienced a kind of sunset as the
first generation of Colorado political leaders and statehouse employees departed
from the scene. "Beyond the sundown is Tomorrow's Wisdom," the state's
poet laureate philosophized in 1938, expressing the hope that the challenges

of today would be translated into success tomorrow. From 1921 to 1952 the building's story revolved around the constancy of events, the regular cycle of legislatures and executives, with occasional changes to the structure and its environs. Although occasional problems for the statehouse and the people in it demanded attention, the capitol's dominant position in the state's collective heart and mind remained constant.

Between 1921 and 1952, events at the capitol reflected an evolving society to a greater extent than before. During the building's construction the statehouse had emerged as a driving force in state economics and society, leading the way for new ideas and technologies. But as the twentieth century passed the nature of the capitol's existence changed to a more detached role of echoing events taking place within and without its walls, serving as a benign stage for playing out the dramas of Colorado life. Looming over Denver's completed Civic Center, the capitol was the dominant structure of Colorado's Forum, coexisting with the public structures around it. The edifice experienced firsthand the Ku Klux Klan craze during the 1920s and suffered neglect during the economic collapse of the 1930s. The statehouse expressed growing federal power, both in Colorado and in the nation generally, by housing a number of New Deal agencies. As the most significant building in the state, the capitol's symbolic role increased during World War II as it provided a focus for patriotic unity, an image carefully cultivated by statehouse caretakers. As the first half of the twentieth century came to a close, the state expressed hope for the future through a new gold dome and provided visitors with an unprecedented guide service. In this period the statehouse no longer inspired change through its novelty but was instead carried along on the tides of history, like the citizens it represented. The uniform nature of everyday life in the capitol over these three decades meant it could reflect Colorado's changing society in a neutral, representative way, befitting its purpose as the home of the people's government.

With three buildings in the capitol complex, Colorado officials managed to get through the 1920s with fewer space problems than before. After a period of intense expansion in the Progressive Era, the third full decade of the twentieth century seemed relatively calm. Although the Progressive ideal of reshaping society through efficient government waned after the shock of the Great War, the legislature continued to create new bodies in the 1920s, but with less zeal. The decade also witnessed an ongoing trend from earlier in the century as the capitol hosted several more state memorial services. John Shafroth, former governor and U.S. senator, lay in state in the rotunda with a military guard on February 22, 1922. Less than a year later U.S. senator Samuel D. Nicholson died in office, and family members returned his body to Colorado for a state ceremony on January 30, 1923. Former governor George

Carlson also received the honor of laying in state on December 7, 1926. With fewer iconic pioneers to honor, state memorial services took place with much less frequency, but they still served as the most powerful tribute Coloradoans could bestow upon their fallen leaders and fellow citizens.[1]

The tradition of using the capitol as a rallying point to welcome distinguished guests also remained strong in the 1920s. Queen Marie of Romania visited Denver in November 1926 and during her trip reviewed a group of 15,000 youths from the quasi-military organization the Olinger Highlanders who marched past her in formation on the west lawn. The next summer, after his historic flight across the Atlantic Ocean, Charles A. Lindbergh came to Colorado and paraded through the streets of Denver and around the capitol circle as thousands of citizens cheered and waved flags. Whether in solemn dignity or enthusiastic abandon, Coloradoans came to their capitol in the 1920s to participate in the momentous events of society.[2]

With only a fraction of the influence it had enjoyed a decade earlier, the Board of Capitol Managers grew increasingly inconsequential in the 1920s. As a result of significant reform by the legislature in 1917, the board changed at a greater rate than ever before. Members who could recall the vibrant, exciting, domineering days of the early twentieth century gradually retired. The last member of the board's old order, Otto Mears, finally resigned in 1920, ending an unmatched record of thirty-one years of service for the managers. In 1922 the board's secretary, William Burschinell, vacated his post after a sixteen-year tenure marred by the 1914 coal scandal. To replace him the managers hired their first female secretary, Margaret McDermott. Newer board members limited their efforts to managing employees and decorating the statehouse. To the Senate's four stained glass windows they added portraits of David Moffat and Samuel Nicholson, yet they also harkened back to the dedication to use state industries by awarding the contract for the intricate work to Denver's McMurtry Manufacturing Company instead of the Tiffany Company of New York City. The board also approved plaques for the building's exterior honoring President Abraham Lincoln's "Gettysburg Address," General John A. Logan's Memorial Day order, and educator and soldier General Irving Hale. To make the building's most prominent feature more dramatic at night, they instructed crews to replace the thousands of small white lights that outlined beams on the dome with floodlights to illuminate the top of the building. Pleased with the public reception to this new spectacle, the managers reported "much favorable comment not only by our Colorado residents, but by many of the Eastern and Western visitors to our State" regarding the dome's radiance. But another light in the Colorado night sky, visible to the west from the statehouse observation decks, warned of a much more frightening development in the 1920s.[3]

Governor Clarence J. Morley in his business office in the mid-1920s, which three decades later the executive branch converted into the governor's reception room. Courtesy, Denver Public Library Western History Department, Harry M. Rhoads, Rh-238

Weekly cross burnings on Lookout Mountain, on Denver land used by permission of Mayor Benjamin F. Stapleton, cast shadows of hatred and violence across the capital city in the 1920s. Capitalizing on the fears of many ethnic and religious groups in the years after the Great War, the Ku Klux Klan increased in both membership and influence across the state. By the middle of the decade Colorado voters allowed these ideological flames to flicker in the halls of the capitol. In the 1924 election, with candidates primarily running on the Republican ticket, the Klan seized control of the state House of Representatives, as well as many Denver city and county positions, and elected Clarence J. Morley as a puppet governor of Colorado. For the next two years the Klan's state leader, Grand Dragon John G. Locke, kept Governor Morley on a tight leash. Messengers traveled constantly between the statehouse and Locke's offices on Glenarm Place. "Every man under the capitol dome is a klansman," Morley proudly proclaimed. Following Locke's orders, the governor fired an African American messenger who had worked for several chief executives. From their desks in the legislative chambers, many Democrats and moderate Republicans exchanged nervous glances across the aisle as they feared for the state's political and social institutions. In the meantime, the capitol found itself besmirched by the tinge of state-sponsored racism and religious hostility.[4]

Tension between and within the branches of government brought the sinister ideology of the Klan into the marble hallways of the capitol. Threatening newspapers published by the Klan found their way onto some legislators' desks. In private meetings Governor Morley promised to veto any bill authored or supported by the Klan's opponents. Morley and his associates attempted to make practically every employee of state government subject to gubernatorial approval. Morley and the House of Representatives targeted, among other agencies, the Civil Service Commission, the State Industrial Commission, the Board of Corrections, and the State Tax Commission. Yet some members of Colorado's government refused to grant the Klan its desired power. Led by Senator William H. Adams, a Democrat from the San Luis Valley, several Republicans joined their Democrat colleagues and created a legislative roadblock during the Twenty-fifth General Assembly, which met in the spring of 1925. The state Senate routinely blocked officeholders and judges appointed by Morley. Even former opponents joined forces to thwart the Klan, particularly when Democrats rejected the governor's proposal to eliminate the Board of Capitol Managers in 1925. Perhaps the only potential benefit for the statehouse of Morley's two-year administration was an attempt to decrease the size of state government by abolishing superfluous agencies, including the dated Board of Horseshoe Examiners. After Grand Dragon Locke resigned his position, the Klan's influence in Colorado dwindled, and Morley lost his bid for a second term in 1926 to Senator Adams. As the decade ended the Klan fizzled into insignificance in Colorado, restoring the image of a temperate authority at work in the capitol.[5]

When the 1920s came to a close, Coloradoans looked back on a difficult decade with little hope of better times in sight. Two years under Governor Morley and Klan domination had left little long-term impact but remained an unpleasant experience for those who worked in the capitol complex. Added to this, mining and agriculture progressed at a sluggish pace at best. Dry summers and winters resulted in poor harvests, and the population of many rural counties stagnated as failing farms reverted to impoverished tenancy. Mining had never fully recovered following the silver collapse of 1893 and the coal strikes during the 1910s. The stock market plunge in 1929 brought the United States fully into the Great Depression, but for years Colorado had mired in an economic slump that the larger crisis could only exacerbate. Pledging a massive

Helping to promote the fuel efficiency of Harley-Davidson motorcycles, Governor William H. "Billy" Adams, the younger brother of former governor Alva Adams, posed on a bike with friends at the capitol's west entrance in the late 1920s. Courtesy, Denver Public Library Western History Collection, Harry M. Rhoads, Rh-88

effort to combat the nation's difficulties, Franklin Roosevelt won the presidency in 1932 and pushed through Congress a series of programs collectively called the New Deal, aimed at getting Americans back to work through government agencies. In the 1930s Coloradoans joined the ranks of the Federal Emergency Relief Administration (later replaced by the Works Progress Administration), the Soil Conservation Service, the Public Works Administration, and the Civilian Conservation Corps, among many other programs. Through these efforts citizens revived agricultural production, improved public lands, built and decorated government buildings, and created displays for the Colorado State Museum. The mining industry experienced mild growth when the federal government increased the fixed price of gold and started purchasing silver again in the early 1930s. Some state politicians, however, compared President Roosevelt's employment programs to socialism. Unlike the 1890s, when state leaders responded to dire economic conditions by us-

ing the capitol construction to fuel rural and urban industries, Colorado politicians in the 1930s stubbornly refused to aid their constituents by encouraging employment programs.[6]

State leaders' limited response to the Great Depression often followed
the Progressive-Era model of creating agencies to encourage economic development. Unfortunately the state's halfhearted efforts often proved ineffec-
tual. In the meantime, the Board of Capitol Managers desperately searched
to find space in the complex for a rapidly expanding government. Several
New Deal agencies received space in the capitol and the museum, forcing
other employees to struggle for adequate space. The managers shifted groups
like the Oil Inspector, the State Labor Commission, the Automobile Driver's
License Department, and the Colorado National Guard around the statehouse. The State Hail Insurance Department, State Veterinarian, State Meat
and Slaughterhouse Inspector, and other agencies moved to the State Office
Building. Superintendent James Merrick lobbied for a new office structure
near the statehouse, inspiring the *Denver Post* to look back fondly on the days
"when government in Colorado was a simpler if not more effective machine."
Writing in the 1920s, Harlean James identified the problem of many contemporary capitols: "The monumental domed structure may always appeal to the
people as a fitting expression of their State governments, but it seems clear
that the expanding business of the important corporations of the States demands more space and housing than can profitably be accommodated in a
single classical building."[7]

The growing tension in the statehouse stood in marked contrast to the
excitement in Denver as the Civic Center, Mayor Robert Speer's grand vision of a modern government campus, added the crown jewel among its buildings. With the completion of the City and County Building in 1932, Denver
offices were consolidated in a new structure across a manicured parkland from
the capitol. The crumbling city hall on Larimer Street and the dilapidated
courthouse at Court Place and Sixteenth Street had been replaced by a shimmering, immense structure that cost almost $4.65 million to build. Later schol-
ars contrasted the two structures in opposing ways. Don and Carolyn Etter
claimed the City and County Building completed Reinhard Schuetze's landscape design stretching west from the capitol. The curved front of the city
structure embraced the axis across the park, providing the visitor with a sense
of totality. Henry-Russell Hitchcock and William Seale argued differently.
They claimed "the rising Renaissance façade of the new City and County
Building glared scornfully at the Myers Capitol with its gold-leafed dome, a
relic of the rambunctious boom days that Denver liked to forget." With the
completion of the imposing new edifice, officials decided to remove the old
public buildings from downtown Denver. After it had stood proudly as the

tallest structure in the city until the capitol's erection, crews tore down the old Arapahoe County Courthouse in 1933. The first of two Denver buildings designed by Elijah Myers, the sandstone courthouse had fallen into disrepair, and its demolition served as a public works project for Denver, putting unemployed men to work in an effort to combat the effects of the Great Depression. Over the next several months the aged structure disappeared from the city's horizon, making the statehouse the only edifice designed by Myers left in Colorado.[8]

The year 1933 marked the end of another legacy in Colorado, closing the book on one of the most controversial elements of state authority. After fifty years of directing construction, maintenance, and utilization of the statehouse and surrounding buildings, the Board of Capitol Managers finally faded into history. President Roosevelt's New Deal programs provided a philosophical model for reform in individual states as well. The arrival of Edwin C. Johnson in the governor's office in 1933 resulted in sweeping alterations to Colorado government. A five-member executive council consolidated the leadership of almost four dozen agencies and encouraged the review of many practices within state authority. After the coal scandals of 1914, the managers had transformed from one of the most influential, domineering, effective, contentious, and partisan elements of state government to a simple caretaker agency. By 1933 enough politicians agreed that the board's time to retire had finally come. James Merrick became superintendent of public buildings, answering directly to the governor with instructions to "exercise all the rights and powers and perform the duties vested and imposed by law in and upon the Board of Capitol Managers." Secretary McDermott stayed on for twelve years as an assistant to Merrick. With the stroke of a pen on an enormous bill entitled "Administrative Code," Governor Johnson quietly finished off the board. The remaining managers, none of whom had served during the board's heyday in the early twentieth century, held their last meeting on June 21, 1933, with no fanfare, ending fifty years, three months, and twenty-six days of service to the state.[9]

The biennial legislature of 1933–1934, derisively nicknamed the "Twiddling Twenty-ninth," proved incapable of responding to the Great Depression. Governor Johnson, a Democrat who unlike many of his fellow partisans accepted President Roosevelt's programs "only kicking and screaming," nonetheless expressed concern when the federal government announced that Colorado would not receive further aid unless the state contributed to the coffers. The General Assembly failed to respond to the threat, forcing Johnson to call two special sessions of the legislature in 1933 at which state leaders bitterly hammered out an agreement for limited taxes to help fund federal projects in Colorado. Many citizens complained about the halting efforts of

Construction in the House of Representatives chamber in the 1930s, before acoustic tiles covered the stencil designs on the walls and ceiling. Author's collection

state authority. Some members of the press took advantage of the public hostility to produce sensational and highly exaggerated stories intended to inflame state and national audiences. Frank Clay Cross wrote an article in *The Nation* in February 1934 that falsely reported a march on the statehouse by unemployed persons who took over the legislative chambers and convened "the first Communist meeting to be held under the dome of any Capitol in the United States." Reacting to this claim, Senate chaplain Edgar M. Wahlberg retorted that "there was no revolution in Colorado," a position supported by the event's mysterious absence from any reputable news source of the period. In the depths of the Great Depression many citizens gathered at the statehouse to petition officials, making their arguments in a respectable fashion as befitted the dignified but influential symbolism of their capitol. As Governor Johnson told one such crowd, "It is your building as well as mine." Even in the midst of great social and economic turmoil, while agitating for reform citizens behaved in a considerate manner that emphasized the capitol's egalitarian atmosphere.[10]

Although the managers had passed from the scene, the problems they had battled lingered for Superintendent Merrick, now in sole command of the building's condition. In his 1934 biennial report Merrick commented that postponing necessary work in the capitol could result in higher costs and physical danger in the future. The federal government offered what help it could, including assigning members of the Civil Works Administration to clean and polish the gold dome that year. But legislators refused to fund what they considered nonessential statehouse repairs in the midst of the Great Depression. Although the General Assembly opposed appropriations to fix minor problems in the building, the House of Representatives spent money to improve its chamber in the 1930s. Members of the House added a public address system to improve audibility in the cavernous room, among several other projects intended to increase legislators' comfort during their biennial sessions. The legislature also approved funds to replace the aging elevators with safer automatic lifts and to install eight brass elevator doors richly decorated with images of western history, such as railroad engines, cogwheels, and mining and agricultural tools. The executive branch expressed more concern for the capitol's condition. In the darkest days of the economic crisis Governor Johnson proposed a solution that would combat the dwindling maintenance funds. Through an executive order he required all state agencies that collected fees, from the Game and Fish Department to the Board of Barber Examiners to the Boxing Commission, to pay rent for their office space. Johnson threatened the affected departments with eviction if they did not contribute to the state's meager coffers. Even with added funds from the fees, though, Merrick consistently requested more money for increasingly extensive repairs needed for the aging building.[11]

Even in times of difficulty, the capitol experienced some exciting moments when people gathered at their building in celebration. One of the most enthusiastic events took place in October 1936, when President Roosevelt traveled to Colorado while campaigning for reelection. Statehouse caretakers eagerly welcomed the opportunity to host another chief executive. Superintendent Merrick and his crew built a large platform in front of the Civil War monument from which the president could address citizens of the Centennial State. When Roosevelt's motorcade approached the capitol, national guard units fired a twenty-one-gun salute from Brown's Bluff, and a band from the University of Colorado played "Happy Days Are Here Again." Governor Johnson, a longtime political opponent of the president's, begrudgingly joined Roosevelt for the ceremonies, along with Secretary of Agriculture Henry A. Wallace and Denver mayor Ben Stapleton. More than 50,000 spectators witnessed Roosevelt's speech, which focused on important Colorado issues such as livestock, water conservation, sugar beets, and a revival of the mining industry. Behind the president stood the capitol, a flag hanging from every window, providing a dignified backdrop for yet another national executive.[12]

Only weeks after his visit to the capitol, President Roosevelt handily won a second term in 1936 while Colorado voters sent Governor Johnson to the United States Senate. Succeeding him was Teller Ammons (son of former governor Elias Ammons), a Democrat who clashed openly with his immediate predecessor. This conflict resulted in one of the most infamous events in the capitol's history, when deceitful activities rocked the corridors of state authority. In December 1936 political opponents of Governor-elect Ammons enlisted the help of Governor Johnson's secretary to install hidden microphones in air ducts of the executive office so they could listen in on Ammons's conversations. A maze of wires snaked through the building to a telephone in the third-floor press room, set up by a *Denver Post* reporter, that connected to a nearby apartment belonging to a private investigator. During the day a secretary would transcribe every word transmitted through the remarkably clear connection, and at night recording devices preserved discussions in the executive suite. In early March 1937 members of Ammons's staff accidentally discovered the microphones and secretly carried out an investigation into their origin. On March 19 the *Rocky Mountain News* broke the story with a banner front-page headline "Statehouse Spy Plot Bared." Ammons treated the scandal in a casual manner, remarking, "Nothing has been said in this office which cannot bear full publicity." Even so, the governor asked Attorney General Byron G. Rogers to conduct an inquiry. Worried that the new administration might blame him for the affair, Senator Johnson sent word from Washington, D.C., that even though he and Ammons often disagreed, the former governor had no knowledge of the plot to monitor his successor's actions. In the meantime, Coloradoans waited anxiously for Attorney General Rogers to uncover the persons responsible for this shocking act.[13]

Within weeks state authorities identified Denver lawyer Erl H. Ellis as the instigator of the eavesdropping plot. Ellis remarked that as a concerned citizen he wanted to monitor state government's honesty, and he considered the microphones perfectly ethical. The state supreme court disagreed and disbarred Ellis. Dissatisfied with the state's conclusions, in June the Denver district attorney's office called a grand jury to investigate the matter thoroughly. The jury studied evidence and heard testimony from Governor Ammons, his staff, Ellis, and others during the summer of 1937 and gradually adopted some of Ellis's concerns about state affairs. The *Rocky Mountain News* commented that "the jury was exploring the widespread ramifications of the politico-business alliance at the Statehouse, the lobbying activities of many persons during the late [legislative] session, and particularly those affecting liquor and public utility legislation and the administration of state civil service."

At the end of August the grand jury indicted nine individuals—including three state representatives and a state senator—on charges of bribery, perjury, and eavesdropping. The jury surprised many Coloradoans by encouraging law enforcement to investigate Governor Ammons and his associates, as it had found sufficient evidence to suspect corruption at the state's highest levels. The *Denver Post*, eager to justify the actions of its reporter who had helped the capitol plotters, claimed on August 29 that "the special grand jury found SOME 'fire' under the 'smoke' from the statehouse microphone scandal. . . . Somebody else may go hunting again with microphones in another effort to expose the political corruption which so many people strongly suspect does exist." But little evidence surfaced to accuse Ammons of any wrongdoing. He only served one term, and the suspicion surrounding his administration, never fully proved or disproved, clouds his legacy. In the meantime, the capitol returned to an atmosphere of trust after the most controversial scandal in its history.[14]

Although the investigations into Governor Ammons's administration failed to turn up any incriminating evidence, many people in the state remained convinced of corruption at the highest levels. Angry at what they considered reckless spending and a lack of accountability, several groups of Coloradoans marched on the statehouse in late 1937. First, a group of realtors from the Denver area gathered at the capitol on December 12. Reacting to a proposal to erect yet another structure to house the burgeoning state government, they demanded that legislators abolish some agencies if current buildings could not hold them all. Three days later Denver businessmen came to the people's building to protest spending policies and the growing state bureaucracy. The unimpressed state treasurer, Homer Bedford, exclaimed, "If the state capitol were to close tomorrow, and with it all functions of the state government, it would only slightly relieve their tax burden." The protestors' demands clearly fell on deaf ears. In the depths of the Great Depression three years earlier, citizens had marched to the statehouse to demand more government aid, and now others used the same means to ask the state to cut back. But Colorado officials expressed little interest in constricting the plethora of state agencies. Instead they looked once again for an architectural solution to the perennial problem of space in the statehouse complex.[15]

The rapid expansion of state authority during the New Deal Era, as in the Progressive period before it, swamped the abilities of capitol caretakers. Something had to be done or, more to the point, had to be built. After initial reluctance to the New Deal, Colorado leaders decided to use some federal programs to the state's advantage. In the mid-1930s Governor Johnson had suggested a site southwest of the capitol for a structure modeled after the State Office Building, with agencies paying rent to use the new edifice to defray construction costs. Attorney General Rogers negotiated purchase of the land, and Superintendent Merrick suggested a new heating plant to replace the twenty-year-old boilers under the museum. Merrick submitted a request for $600,000 to the Public Works Administration, which federal officials quickly granted. Construction on the office building, named the State Capitol Annex, and heating plant, both designed by Denver architect Gordon White, began in the waning days of 1937. The F. J. Kirchof Construction Company of Denver won the contract to erect the structures, with Minnesota granite bases and Colorado Yule marble for the exterior walls. The high price of marble and of quarrying and shipping the stone meant the state could have found cheaper material elsewhere. But like the capitol project in the 1890s, the annex job employed distressed citizens in a rural economy. After three years of construction, the annex and heating plant stood as the last two major buildings constructed with Yule marble for much of the twentieth century, after a competitor's buyout closed the quarry in 1941. Historian William R. Pyle claimed the new structures represented "two important buildings at bargain rates" as a result of federal assistance. They stand as streamlined contrasts to the classically inspired capitol, Colorado State Museum, and State Office Building, although all five buildings coexist peacefully as a record of changing architectural tastes in the state.[16]

As the annex and heating plant rose to the south of the capitol, artists worked inside the statehouse to replace passé stencil designs in the rotunda. Allen True—who had created artwork for the Civic Center colonnades; the Brown Palace Hotel; the state capitols in Cheyenne, Wyoming, and Jefferson City, Missouri; and Denver's City and County Building—suggested eight murals portraying the significance of water in Colorado history. The Boettcher Foundation, a philanthropic agency established in 1937 and funded by Charles Boettcher's sugar beet money, paid for the project. Over the next year and a half True illustrated a historical poem written by Thomas Hornsby Ferril chronicling the story of water in the West. Decades earlier the poet had spent many happy hours in the capitol with his father, William Ferril, a former curator of the historical society. In the summer of 1940 crews hung True's canvas murals with Ferril's poem depicting the chronology of life in the arid region. Superintendent James Merrick noted the immediate popularity of the new artwork in his 1940 biennial report. Later in the twentieth century former state legislator John C. Buechner referred to Ferril's poem as "a force for education within the Capitol" and claimed that visitors reading the stanzas developed a clearer understanding of landscape and of Colorado's history. Their prominent location in the rotunda indicates the importance placed on water in Colorado from the earliest inhabitants to the present day. The installation of the murals ended the 1930s at the capitol on a positive note. Transcending

Three of the eight murals portraying the importance of water in the history of Colorado, hung in the rotunda in 1940. Author's collection

the difficulties of the moment, hope for the future resonated in Ferril's final stanza:

> Beyond the sundown is Tomorrow's Wisdom
> today is going to be long long ago.[17]

A year after the water murals arrived at the capitol, the dawning of the day at several faraway American military installations was reflected in a similar image—the unmistakable red sun emblazoned on Japanese aircraft. A surprise attack on U.S. forces in Pearl Harbor, Hawaii, captured the attention of the entire country, and once again the nation entered into a global conflict. World War II profoundly impacted the state. Historians Carl Ubbelohde, Maxine Benson, and Duane A. Smith described the period: "No other single event in the state's history and no other national crisis—not the Civil War, not World War I, not the Great Depression—transformed Colorado to the extent that World War II did." Construction around Denver added facilities like the Rocky Mountain Arsenal and the Denver Federal Center, large installations for war production. The conflict greatly affected the capitol, as had the previous world war. In 1941 Superintendent Merrick became the head of the newly created Division of Public Buildings, and he shifted state and federal agencies around the limited space in the capitol complex. But as the federal government began building its own structures around Denver to house employees for the war effort, they gradually depended less on state officials for space. Instead, as the unifying symbol of Coloradoans and the home of their civil authority, the capitol experienced World War II's impact through the pervasive influence of social programs and patriotic propaganda.[18]

Protecting Colorado's dominant building became the top priority of statehouse caretakers. Superintendent Merrick recommended establishing the State Capitol Buildings Civil Defense Unit, with air raid wardens in each office and plans for fire suppression and first aid training in case of attack. Merrick drew up intricate procedures for watchmen to black out the capitol during an air raid. Although the odds that Nazi Germans, Italian fascists, or Japanese soldiers would march on Brown's Bluff remained relatively low, Denver worried about attacks as much as any other large population center. Merrick also found many ways to encourage capitol employees to contribute to the war effort. He allowed the Denver Salvage Committee to take old machinery and storage shelving from the subbasement to melt down to fabricate airplanes, tanks, and other equipment. Agencies in the statehouse complex donated typewriters to federal boards around Denver for writing war-related correspondence and documents. Governor John C. Vivian even requested that department heads use the postal service for official communications, instead of the telephone or telegraph, after the federal government asked states to keep long-distance lines free for official war messages crossing the country. More than physical space, World War II demanded temporary inconveniences for Coloradoans working in the capitol in the long-term interests of victory.[19]

The most significant wartime development at the statehouse involved raising money for the war. Departments competed for donations in good-natured contests, and governors Ralph C. Carr and John Vivian encouraged the friendly rivalries. Campaigns to sell federal war bonds dominated social programs at the capitol. Superintendent Merrick installed a large billboard on the west lawn advertising the bonds and made space in the statehouse for the Colorado War Bond Committee, patriotic employees working diligently to raise money for soldiers fighting thousands of miles away. The committee published newsletters and posted them in the capitol encouraging state employees to donate, many with slogans intended to inspire aid for the war: "Defense Bonds Buy Japanese Bondage," "Dollars for Mac Throw Japs on Their Back," "Buy a Bond for Across the Pond," "Bullets and Powder Make Japanese Chowder." Whether going to or coming from work, at home, or in their offices in the capitol complex, state employees constantly encountered requests to help their nation's soldiers.[20]

The increased activity in the capitol complex once again stretched the five state buildings to their limits and put new demands on state employees. In 1943, to consolidate the papers and books in the statehouse and surrounding buildings, the legislature created the Colorado State Archives. Unnecessary papers, after the approval of the attorney general and state archivist, could be destroyed, whereas those of value to Colorado filled boxes and files around the complex. The legislature directed archives staff to put as many records as possible on microfilm, which State Archivist Herbert O. Brayer claimed would free 98 percent of the storage space previously needed. Although they often identified records of value to the state, perhaps the archives staff's most immediately significant task was to set aside those suitable for reuse. In their first two years the archives staff provided over fifty tons of wastepaper—well over 12 million documents—to a federal recycling program. At the same time, a significant number of state employees left the capitol complex to serve in the military. Janitors, watchmen, and elevator pilots departed to join the struggle in Europe and the Pacific and left Superintendent Merrick scrambling to operate the capitol. Although Merrick protested the impact on his tight budget, Governor Vivian ordered the superintendent to increase wages for the positions to hire quality temporary employees. Once the war concluded, however, the state welcomed any former members of the capitol staff with honorable discharge papers back to their jobs, replacing the stopgap staff at the higher pay rate. The statehouse did not suffer a repeat of the indignity of military occupation like the one that followed World War I, but the century's second great conflict nevertheless impacted numerous aspects of life at the capitol in the 1940s.[21]

With the war successfully concluded the capitol returned to a condition of calm, steady use that had characterized the early twentieth century for the building. But moments of celebration occasionally punctuated the regularity of government affairs. One of the most energetic came in the fall of 1948 when President Harry Truman addressed 25,000 Coloradoans from the west lawn of the statehouse. Traveling on a nationwide reelection campaign, the president and his family arrived at Union Station on September 20. They paraded through the city while thousands of citizens lined the streets as they had for several other chief executives. Before speaking to the large crowd in Civic Center, President Truman addressed the Inter-American Conference on Conservation of Renewable Natural Resources meeting in the House of Representatives chamber. A predominantly Spanish-speaking group of scientists from all over the Western Hemisphere, the conference attendees filled the chamber with the cry "Viva Truman!" In his speech on the west front, the president described himself as a "modern Paul Revere," warning Coloradoans against his political opponents' principles and encouraging them to vote Democrat in the 1948 election. Many citizens eagerly heard the address and delivered Colorado's electoral votes to the incumbent chief executive that November. The plainspoken man from Missouri brought to the capitol an electric style of speaking not seen since William Jennings Bryan's voice reverberated through the House chamber decades earlier.[22]

Gradually, as the twentieth century passed the ceremonial nature of the statehouse had become less significant, as the building primarily served the business of government while infrequently providing a stage for public events. The capitol rarely hosted the most somber of these events, the state memorial service, after the 1920s. But in 1950 the capitol once again performed its most solemn duty in honor of a fallen leader. The race for Colorado's chief executive that year pitted two powerful rivals, Republican former governor Ralph Carr and Democratic governor Walter W. Johnson, against each other. Carr unexpectedly passed away in late September 1950, and Governor Johnson set aside political differences to pay tribute to a fellow Coloradoan. On September 26 Carr's casket rested on a bier at the foot of the grand staircase, flanked by honor guards from the Colorado Highway Patrol. Johnson's magnanimity failed to win him votes, however, and he lost the governor's race in 1950 to Carr's last-minute replacement on the Republican ticket, Gunnison cattle rancher Dan Thornton. Carr's memorial service, a rare example of the state's highest tribute during the period, reminded citizens of the symbolic and historic nature of their capitol.[23]

High above the solemn scene of a memorial service, the capitol's dome had not fared well over the years. Holes in the gold showed the copper plates underneath and caused one Denver newspaper in the early 1940s to describe the dome as "moth-eaten." The difficult economic period of the Great Depression and the wartime needs of society during World War II, however, forced the state's attention away from such a superficial task as regilding the dome. By the late 1940s, though, with the state's economy growing, several Coloradoans took up the issue of sprucing up the crown of the state's most important symbol. Idaho Springs mayor LeRoy Giles and state senator J. Price Briscoe suggested a campaign to collect donated gold from Colorado mines. Many citizens saw the dilapidated dome as an unpleasant reminder of the difficult times just past and wanted to create a reflection of prosperity and hope for the future with a restored statehouse dome. When the legislature refused to appropriate funds for the work, Superintendent Merrick and Governor Johnson raised $19,000 from the public to pay Robert Muessel to gild the dome in the late summer of 1950 with the gold collected by Giles and Briscoe. On October 11, 1950, after the Colorado School of Mines band had played and the Colorado National Guard had fired a salute, state officials spoke at the dome's rededication ceremony. Governor Johnson harkened back to the days of hearty Colorado pioneers, and Senator Briscoe reminded the assembled citizens: "It's your dome, it's your gold—may it shine there a long, long time." Perhaps *Denver Post* reporter Bert Hanna, another vocal supporter of the regilding project, best summed up the capitol's importance: "You look at this fine old building and you think of all the tremendous work and pride that went into it. It is the heart of Colorado."[24]

Even with a brilliant new gold dome, the capitol and its surrounding buildings paled in the eyes of cramped civil servants. Only a decade after completion of the State Capitol Annex, officials considered erecting yet another addition to the capitol complex. In the postwar era the Colorado State Museum and State Office Building made room for patriotic groups like the American Legion and the Veterans of Foreign Wars in space once used by New Deal agencies. In the capitol, of the three dozen committee rooms originally envisioned by Elijah Myers, only four remained vacant for legislative debate. Superintendent Merrick suggested a postwar study to determine the future needs of a government forever outgrowing its physical limits, a proposal similar to one made by the Board of Capitol Managers after World War I. Governor Johnson suggested building four new structures at once, since state rent on Denver-area office buildings was approaching $200,000 a year. Merrick suggested a five-story edifice on the capitol's east lawn, where *The Closing Era* monument sits, but legislators quickly rejected that suggestion. For the time being, politicians and civil servants coped with increasingly meager accommodations in the five buildings of the statehouse complex.[25]

The dawning of the 1950s started the capitol in a new direction. Ever since the final days of the Board of Capitol Managers, the statehouse had muddled along without amenities for tourists and schoolchildren. Watchmen and a dome attendant answered questions, but visitors wandered around the corridors and galleries without real direction. Lieutenant Governor Homer L. Pearson bemoaned the situation while recalling his youth: "I remember as a child I visited the State Capitol with my Sunday School class. At that time a guide showed us through the building and told us all about the colorful history of the state. I thought it was swell." One proposal recommended hiring American Indians in full regalia to lead tourists through the marble hallways. But in 1951 a man decked out in cowboy boots and a crisp Stetson arrived at the capitol and resolved the issue. Governor Dan Thornton entered office as the second half of the twentieth century began. He recognized the statehouse as the perfect place to implement his program of promoting Colorado tourism. Thornton called for several college-age girls dressed in western attire to lead tourists around the building. In June guides Catherine J. Rankin and Rachel D. Root became the first statehouse employees in decades directed solely to serve visitors' needs. Thornton helped improve the capitol's image

Governor Dan Thornton with capitol tour guides at the Civil War monument in the summer of 1951. Courtesy, Colorado Historical Society

through visitor services that, combined with the sparkling new dome, conveyed a pleasant scene to every awestruck individual who walked through the bronze doors.[26]

The United States in 1952 represented a society of contrasts. The contented peace of the "baby boom" and the growth of the suburbs coexisted with ongoing war in Korea and simmering tensions with the Soviet Union. The Colorado State Capitol also represented a great contrast. Colorado's dignified symbol of civil authority still dominated the capital city, but the fears of the Cold War era cast a shadow over the edifice. Colorado officials authorized nuclear attack drills using the subbasement tunnels as bomb shelters. The capitol's deteriorating structural condition coexisted with these international concerns. With a shiny gold dome for the first time in years and information presented to visitors by attractive coeds, many citizens did not recognize the dangers of their aging statehouse. Superficial repairs over the years had temporarily addressed problems, but lingering under the surface, serious structural dangers awaited discovery. Still, the capitol had survived many challenges in the three previous decades. Physical pressures of a steadily expanding government, political tension between racist doctrinaires and level-headed statesmen, espionage to uncover political corruption, and public service during wartime made the statehouse a stage for great events of local and national importance. The capitol entered the second half of the twentieth century with hope that the building's next generation would care for it as well as the previous ones had.

The glistening dome represented for Coloradoans a triumph over recent difficult decades and the promise of a golden future. In a prosperous era, with its role as the representative symbol of the people stronger than ever, the statehouse could anticipate aging in a comfortable, dignified manner. But even though no one yet knew it, the building had reached its zenith and would henceforth decline both physically and symbolically. For the capitol in the years to come, grand hopes manifested themselves into neglect, abuse, disintegration, and despair. "Beyond the sundown" dawned a dark, cold day.

CHAPTER SEVEN

# Vandalism in the Name of Progress
## 1952–1990

A S THE SECOND HALF OF THE TWENTIETH CENTURY BEGAN, many
Coloradoans considered the future of their state capitol to be as bright
as the new gold dome. The building had stood proud and strong on
Brown's Bluff for over fifty years, and few people worried about the robust
granite hulk dominating Denver's skyline. But in the span of four decades the
statehouse's deteriorating physical condition grew more acute as "vandalism
in the name of progress" constantly threatened the structure. Overuse and at
times outright abuse by politicians and citizens alike made the period from
1952 to 1990 exceptionally dangerous for the capitol, an era when structural
threats went unanswered and the building's historical integrity was nearly
destroyed time and again. In essence, the statehouse aged in the three decades before the twentieth century's midpoint and became old in the four
decades that followed. The capitol's role as a stage for expressing the interests
of various Coloradoans remained strong in this period as citizens gathered to

147

agitate for social, economic, and political reform and altered some aspects of the building to reflect the state's diverse cultural heritage. But such activism focused on the needs of the moment while ignoring the capitol's equally significant symbolic position as the legacy of past generations and the hope for future ones. As Coloradoans struggled to understand the ties that bound them together, they ironically neglected the most important representation of their collective identity.

The years 1952 to 1990 marked a steady deterioration of the statehouse's physical and symbolic condition, with only occasional efforts to combat the building's decay and a focus instead on modernization of the structure. As this period started the capitol experienced several grave threats to its historical integrity as state officials considered plans to destroy part or all of the statehouse. By the 1960s the shocking proposals of the previous decade had resulted in a greater desire to protect the capitol by transforming it and the complex of neighboring state buildings into a home of modern government. Such plans revealed an attempt to extend the Progressive principles that created the Civic Center by rebuilding much of the area into a campus of efficient authority, but high costs prevented any serious action. At the same time, social activism during the 1960s centered around the statehouse. Hispanics, African Americans, and college students rallied on the grounds to lobby for political reform locally and to debate national policies, often focusing on the war in Vietnam. Whereas other parts of the complex received much-needed improvements in the 1970s and 1980s, many state officials opposed the inconvenience work on the capitol would create. By 1990 the statehouse stood as outwardly enduring as ever, but serious problems within the structure, exacerbated by both apathy and ignorance over the previous four decades, demanded attention.

Two events within a week of each other in March 1952 foreshadowed the difficult years ahead for the capitol. First, on March 11 an inmate recently paroled from a state correctional facility threatened Governor Dan Thornton on the west steps as he left his office for the day. Waving a broken wine bottle in front of the governor, the man ran off when Thornton's bodyguard rushed to the scene. Although politicians had seen many such displays of bravado before, Colorado governors had never encountered such brazen threats on the grounds of the people's building. But several days later the fugitive's actions paled in comparison with the building's first and, to date, only suicide, perhaps the most infamous event in the capitol's history. On March 18 Benton F. Marshall, a steamfitter from Missouri, paced in the third-floor rotunda as he gazed up to the inner dome and down to the grand staircase. Ignoring shouts from state employees he climbed over the rail, fifty feet above the first floor, shouted "I'm going to commit suicide," and jumped. He landed on the grand staircase, cracking the first step off the first floor, which made a horrendous noise that brought people rushing from all over the capitol. Paramedics whisked Marshall to Denver General Hospital where he died of severe internal injuries two hours after his plunge. The *Rocky Mountain News* published grisly front-page photographs of the incident but failed to uncover the precise reason for Marshall's suicide, which remains a mystery to this day. In response to the stunning event, Superintendent James Merrick directed all building employees to watch out for others who might try to hurt themselves in a similar manner, added regular guard patrols in the rotunda's upper levels, and installed gates that could be closed to prevent access to the room. The capitol naturally drew people who wanted to make a dramatic statement, but it had never before been witness to so violent an act.[1]

After the events of March 1952 life in the capitol calmed somewhat, although the building experienced steadily increasing use as the General Assembly began meeting every year and gubernatorial terms changed from two to four years. With politicians inhabiting the statehouse more consistently, many thought of ways to improve their quarters. Unfortunately, most ideas lacked respect for the building's historical integrity. Several committee rooms became permanent offices for legislative leadership, indicating the growing authority of the General Assembly and contradicting the ideals of late-nineteenth-century Coloradoans who had intended for the body to remain a limited, amateur group that would not remain in session too long. Within the legislative chambers some members considered removing the twin chandeliers, described as "more impressive than functional," after they terrified legislators by creaking and swaying during a minor earthquake. Public outcry combined with pressure from capitol newsmen convinced the legislators to retain the fixtures, but they sacrificed the stenciled ceilings and walls in exchange for beige acoustic tiles to create better audibility in the chambers, giving the cavernous rooms a far more sterile appearance. Legislators also removed from their chambers distinctive furnishings present since the General Assembly first met in the building, the spittoons. Two floors below, the condition of the capitol's basement cafeteria created hostility among employees in the building. For several years inspectors and customers had bemoaned the lack of appropriate space to accommodate the amount of business the lunch counter did. Superintendent Merrick worried about sanitation in the restaurant, which some state employees nicknamed the "roachateria." In 1955 the legislature passed a resolution complaining about what it considered a filthy, expensive lunch counter. One representative called the cafeteria "a stink hole and an eyesore," and Senator Neal Bishop pointed to "the grime of the ages" surrounding the entire works. Accordingly, health officials closed the cafeteria in May 1955, and shortly afterward the Colorado Industries for the Blind opened a more efficient and tidy facility in the basement.[2]

The restaurant debacle and acoustic tile installation illustrated the declining concern for the capitol's historical integrity in the 1950s, with alterations that often dismissed out of hand the building's structural legacy. But work on the first floor demonstrated even more harshly the inconsiderate architectural changes forced upon the statehouse in that decade. Reflecting the growing strength of the chief executive, in 1957 Governor Steve McNichols approved a sweeping project that swapped his private office for the reception room, giving the governor much more personal space. After an expenditure of almost a quarter of a million dollars, the executive suite discarded Elijah Myers's Corinthian decor in favor of a sleeker look. African wood paneling covered the original pilasters, and the office shone in many colors: gold flecks in the acoustic ceiling tiles, gold and persimmon drapes, turquoise carpet, a burnt orange leather couch, and beige and blue tiles in the new private bathroom. Reflecting the capitol's position at the forefront of technological innovation in Colorado, the new executive suite provided many modern conveniences. Governor McNichols's office boasted redesigned chandeliers, a movie screen, and the first color television in the state. At the same time some state employees suggested dividing the supreme court chamber into two floors or moving the judicial branch into its own building nearby. All these changes in the statehouse reflected a spirit in Colorado in the 1950s that buried the old and celebrated the new. With the state's population skyrocketing and its economy booming, many Coloradoans celebrated the remaking of the capitol instead of preserving their symbol of collective identity.[3]

This phenomenon of modernization impacted the statehouse as the lack of space for a growing state government—a perennial problem throughout the twentieth century—demanded attention in the 1950s. Denver architect Jared Morse responded to the situation with a proposal so radical that it shocked Colorado officials who had previously been eager to remake the statehouse into a hallmark of contemporary comfort. Morse suggested tearing down the capitol and replacing it with a plaza of immense, unadorned, stolid buildings on the three blocks of statehouse grounds. When some citizens protested the idea of the capitol's destruction, Morse suggested that some materials from the structure could be used to build a miniature replica statehouse as a tourist display. What his plan lacked in historical appreciation it more than made up for in architectural novelty. Still, the desire to create an "atomic age" statehouse reflective of modernity and progress tempted officials more interested in the future than in the past. Shying away from Morse's scheme, state leaders returned to the idea of building a new structure in the capitol complex to alleviate pressure on state agencies. Architects G. Meredith

The capitol complex (*lower right*) and the rapidly expanding city of Denver, in architectural transition as skyscrapers rose to the northwest of the statehouse, as viewed in 1960. Courtesy, Denver Public Library Western History Department, Otto Roach, X-29145

Musick and T. H. Buell and Company of Denver drew up plans for the State Services Building to rise on land northwest of the capitol, reflecting the sleek lines of the State Capitol Annex just as the State Office Building's design echoed the classical lines of the Colorado State Museum and the capitol. After two years of work, construction on the $4 million structure of Vermont marble was finished in the summer of 1960. Governor McNichols dedicated the State Services Building to Superintendent Merrick, who retired in 1959 after more than forty years in the capitol complex, and to former state controller James A. Noonan, a civil servant for half a century. But the edifice still failed to meet the needs of the state, as historian William Pyle commented: "Colorado's new, beautiful, 180,000 square foot office building was too small on opening day."[4]

The mid-century physical alterations to the capitol that endangered and at times eliminated historic interiors coincided with an architectural development in many national and world cities. Ever since the gold rush days,

Denver had sprawled over the prairie with little sense of organized development, but this tendency started to change in the 1930s. Older structures had been torn down since the Great Depression, and owners subdivided large homes near the statehouse into apartment buildings. An improved economy in the 1950s resulted in a great deal of development in Denver, and new buildings stretched toward the sky as well as to the horizon. Banks and insurance firms, stores, and offices of every kind invested in towering new skyscrapers. As the city rose above it, the predominance of the capitol waned in the collective mind of Coloradoans. The Tours Hotel battle served as a clear example of this change. The Security Life and Accident Company purchased the hotel, on Colfax Avenue between Lincoln Street and Broadway, intending to replace it with a thirty-one-story skyscraper. This development would have blocked the capitol's view down Sixteenth Street and detracted from its looming presence over the Civic Center. When Governor McNichols protested, the insurance firm replied in a flowery manner: "The beauty of the shimmering gold of the aspen in the fall is not marred by the snowcapped peaks above, but is enhanced thereby. . . . The matter of aesthetic value is an individual one. We cannot imagine how any modern building could detract from our beautiful Capitol." The state eventually succeeded in securing the Tours Hotel property and preserving the view, but the battle represented a general lack of concern for historical landscapes and structures in Denver. William Pyle suggested in 1962 that a height restriction be imposed for edifices near the capitol. "The dignity of the Capitol and the State would suffer," he remarked, "if large, tall buildings were allowed to dwarf and crowd-in the venerable structure." But events in the 1950s proved time and again that many Coloradoans preferred modernization to preservation of their representative symbol and its neighborhood.[5]

The turbulent era did not pass without celebration at the statehouse, however. In 1959 Coloradoans commemorated the "Rush to the Rockies" centennial, marking 100 years since the lure of gold brought settlers by the thousands to the banks of Colorado's streams and rivers. As the people's building, regardless of its physical condition, the capitol stood as a gold-domed monument to the legacy of those argonauts. On the grounds to the west of the statehouse, laborers assembled structures from across the state to create a "Pioneer Village." The most exciting was an old wooden cabin from Colorado City proudly proclaiming "Old Capitol Building" on the front. The Broadmoor Hotel donated the structure, which it had bought and preserved in 1927, and Governor McNichols happily accepted the cabin. Soon after its donation, however, Colorado historians began debating the authenticity of the building's claim to fame. Many primary accounts refuted the idea that the cabin ever served as a territorial capitol. For weeks, newspapers carried evidence regarding the authenticity of the "capitol" moniker. Most scholars concluded that the cabin had not been a territorial capitol, but historical accuracy failed to impress state officials. The fake statehouse arrived in Denver in December 1958, and the governor presided over dedication ceremonies for the building jointly with his brother, Denver mayor Bill McNichols. Governor McNichols even addressed a special session of the Forty-second General Assembly in front of the old "capitol" in Lincoln Park with the statehouse towering behind. As a *Denver Post* headline noted two years later as the weathered structure still sagged in front of the statehouse: "First Capitol or Not, Old Log Cabin Sits It Out." Crews finally returned the fake capitol to Colorado City in April 1961.[6]

Mixing the old with the new, technology played a significant role in the "Rush to the Rockies" centennial at the capitol, perpetuating the trend to honor innovation in the people's building. Crews erected temporary counters in the first floor's north wing to hold an International Business Machine (IBM) computer that served as a popular tourist attraction during the celebration. Employees of the Department of Revenue punched answers to 1,500 questions about Colorado history onto computer cards. Visitors to the statehouse submitted queries to the computer's operator, who entered them into the machine. The computer, named RAMAC (Random Access Method of Accounting Control), printed out the answer on "Rush to the Rockies" letterhead bearing the computer-generated signature of Governor McNichols. The month-long display proved popular with visitors and demonstrated once again the essential role of technology in the capitol. Unlike other changes to the building in the 1950s, though, the IBM computer moved on to other festivals while the capitol languished under inconsiderate structural changes made throughout the decade.[7]

After the abuse the statehouse endured during much of the 1950s, the early 1960s seemed fairly peaceful. Life in the capitol plodded on as citizens and politicians carried out the day-to-day business of government. Still, as the symbol of representative authority and the home of collective pride, events both pleasant and distressing around the state and the nation found expression within the building's marble halls. One November day in 1963, students and administrators from Colorado State University gathered at a Joint Budget Committee hearing to fight for their share of the taxpayers' money. During the meeting an aide announced to the chair that President John F. Kennedy had been assassinated. Silence fell over the room as the university's president, William E. Morgan, and State Board of Agriculture Secretary Charles Terrell dashed to Governor John A. Love's office. The governor remained at his desk with communications links to state and federal defense agencies while other employees clustered around a radio in the basement cafeteria for updates. A silent witness to the unfolding of history, the capitol provided a comforting and secure refuge in times of crisis.[8]

Over the decades since the capitol's completion, many state officials had considered proposals regarding the future of the structure and its surrounding complex. Unsympathetic alterations in the 1950s forced many to reconsider the statehouse's long-term needs. Indicative of the pressing nature of the situation, legislators had started discussing flooring over the capitol's atriums in the north and south wings to create more office space, but they could not solve the logistical and financial problems of such a project. During the mid-1960s Colorado officials undertook the first serious studies of the capitol's fate. In July 1965 an article in the *Rocky Mountain News* publicized the building's deteriorating condition. Charles Roos titled his article "Statehouse Showing Signs of Wear," one of the first overt calls to arms about the capitol. He decried the state of visitors' services, acknowledging the utility of tours but noting that if a tourist did not find the guide, he or she could wander amid pillars for hours. Bemoaning the "Stone Age rest rooms" and lack of public parking, Roos pointed out that the legislature and the governor had renovated their portions of the structure while doing little for the public areas. He issued a challenge to his fellow Coloradoans: "It is not too much to ask of us, in the interest of the future, to preserve what we inherited in this most important of state landmarks and to leave it a little better than we found it." A year later *News* writer Robert L. Chase took issue with the notion of a perpetually growing government and pleaded for an intelligent study of the state's future needs. Hoping to limit officials to the physical space they occupied, Chase warned that "if the expansion doesn't stop somewhere we'll one day have more citizens on public payrolls than we have paying the taxes to support them." The debate over the building's physical strength and a perennially expanding bureaucracy had finally entered the public arena.[9]

With the statehouse problems now common knowledge, Colorado leaders took an aggressive stance on finding a solution. In 1967 the Division of Public Works hired S.U.A. Inc. of Beverly Hills, California, to create a master plan for the future needs of Colorado's government, citizens, and capitol. Several months later the architects presented their conclusions to state leaders and the public. Like other suggestions made over the years, S.U.A. Inc. harkened back to the Progressive Era, suggesting an immense campus of buildings. Proposals included tearing down apartments and churches and extending the capitol grounds east to Pearl Street, as well as erecting a large supreme court building in the middle of Pennsylvania Street. To fulfill office needs the state would build four large structures on Thirteenth Avenue, and a twin of the State Services Building would replace the State Office Building north of the capitol. The new campus would provide 1.3 million square feet of office space to meet the needs of an expanding government. The ambitious plan would cost $60 million to complete and received reluctant support from Governor Love and the legislators. But many officials considered S.U.A. Inc.'s proposal a modern, exciting, historic solution to an ongoing problem.[10]

Myriad activities filled the capitol with life as state leaders pored over plans for the complex's future. The basement cafeteria closed temporarily in 1968, not in connection with health violations but because of the building's entry into filmmaking. Actor Van Johnson, filming a movie called *The Protectors*, graced the statehouse for several scenes of a feature made for television. In later years, scenes of several television shows were also shot in the capitol, including *Diagnosis: Murder* and *Perry Mason*, the latter of which featured Raymond Burr's title character arguing cases in the supreme court room. Changing tastes in personal grooming also demanded attention at the statehouse. In the 1950s new clothing styles had attracted the curmudgeonly disapproval of Governor Edwin Johnson, back in the chief executive's office after his service in the U.S. Senate. He opposed Governor Thornton's choice of apparel for the statehouse guides and sent several notes to Superintendent Merrick complaining about the situation. For example, Governor Johnson remarked: "Can you have the Capitol Guide dress as [a] Young Lady should dress? Please do something about getting her back in skirts." A decade later women's clothing choices still perturbed the old-fashioned men in state government. In 1969 the House of Representatives passed the first capitol dress code, forbidding the scandalously short miniskirts worn by its numerous women employees. Governor Love sarcastically sidestepped the issue: "I think it would be a very serious violation of the separate powers if I were to comment in any way." Contemporary social change outside the capitol, however, proved far more inflammatory than the thighs of legislative interns.[11]

The late 1960s, one of the greatest periods of social tumult in American history, transformed the statehouse neighborhood. The population of the Denver metropolitan area grew at a remarkable rate, and the region developed all the problems of congestion, pollution, and ethnic tension seen in other urban areas. Stretching east from the Civic Center, Colfax Avenue evolved from a popular shopping district into a street filled with prostitutes, pornography outlets, and transients that "demoralized" the region. The era also brought to the capitol a more colorful collection of protestors than ever before. As the natural gathering spot for people with axes to grind, the statehouse served as a backdrop for many cultural and ethnic demonstrations. No venue better suited the needs of idealistic, hopeful citizens than the people's building. Many groups took advantage of the capitol's automatic visibility to convey their desires, often ones of racial or ethnic struggle cloaked in opposition to the Vietnam War. In late 1968 members of the Black Panthers, supporting the rights of African Americans, gathered many "hippie-type teen-agers" on the west front to protest the behavior of Denver law enforcement. At times they also sat in the Senate gallery, quietly watching the proceedings below as nervous legislators looked over their shoulders. But in Colorado black activism remained comparatively limited when contrasted with other major cities.[12]

The most active minority group in the state, Chicanos, borrowed from African American efforts elsewhere to rail against Anglo dominance in Colorado politics and economics. Decades of discrimination in Colorado resulted in a great deal of seething anger, harkening back to the sectionalism of territorial days between the Anglo northern counties and Hispanic southern ones. Chicanos found a leader in Rodolfo Gonzales, who founded the Crusade for Justice to promote their interests in the state. A frequent visitor to the capitol, Gonzales lived only a few blocks away so he could keep in close connection with the state's most powerful political backdrop. Although the Crusade for Justice often sponsored peaceful demonstrations, including appearing in the House of Representatives gallery to support farm labor legislation, the group also conducted powerful protests outside. The Mexican Independence Day in September provided an annual opportunity to assemble at the capitol and agitate for reform. In 1969 almost 4,000 Chicanos gathered on the west front. Several climbed onto the Civil War monument and attached a Mexican flag to the cavalryman's rifle. They protested low minority performance in public education, and the crowd sang in Spanish and chanted slogans such as "Chicano power!" and "Viva la Raza!" Gonzales proudly admired the assembled throng and remarked, "I think this is the greatest thing that ever happened to Denver. . . . We didn't come to tear anything down. We came to build a new Chicano movement." His comments failed to impress worried capitol caretakers who, fearing damage to the structure, refused to let the marchers inside. A similar rally brought 2,000 Chicanos to the capitol grounds three years later. The state's two ethnic leaders, Gonzales for the Chicanos and Lauren Watson of the Black Panthers, joined forces with their friends in higher education in April 1969 for a large show of solidarity on the capitol grounds. One of the most radical youths of the period, Tom Hayden of Columbia University's Students for a Democratic Society, spoke at the rally, encouraging the struggle against war and oppression. The capitol provided the perfect stage for thousands to express their desire for a more equal and peaceful society.[13]

Governor Love, the chief executive with an ironic name who watched often rabid protests outside his office window, once ducked a brick thrown through that window by a particularly distressed activist. As a result, the Colorado State Patrol ordered that the governor's windows be immediately replaced with bulletproof glass. But Love often expressed gratitude and pride

Chicanos perched on the Civil War monument during the massive Mexican Independence Day rally on September 16, 1969. Courtesy, Denver Public Library Western History Department, John Gordon, X-21609

toward the many citizens who came to the capitol and argued for reform in a dignified and orderly fashion. Indeed, most statehouse protests of the period remained relatively peaceful. One notable exception marred the capitol's dignity in 1969, the year of the greatest social tension in the corridors of state power. Unsatisfied with more traditional protests, fourteen Colorado Communist Party members hijacked the Senate on May 7. Breaking in on an executive session through a side door, they ignored Lieutenant Governor Mark Hogan's requests to leave and denounced the body as "illegitimate." Most senators scurried out of the chamber, although one Republican and five Democratic members stayed to listen. Senator Frank Gill, determined to preserve the integrity of his position and the chamber, remained out of duty, not out of sympathy: "I was elected to sit in this chair, and I plan to sit here, regardless of who comes along and tells me not to." After almost an hour Denver police stormed the chamber and arrested the protestors, carrying out all but one as the Communist Party members sang "We Shall Overcome."[14]

Protests in Colorado and across the nation died down after President Richard Nixon altered the Selective Service Act in 1969, drafting eighteen-year-olds before older men, which meant senior college students were less affected. Although their opposition to the Vietnam War remained strong, fewer college students appeared in mass gatherings. But in May 1970, events in Ohio fanned the flames once more. During a protest at Kent State University, four students were shot and killed by members of the national guard, enraging youths across the country. Students at several Colorado colleges and universities went on strike to protest the deaths in Ohio, and at Colorado State University, Old Main burned down in a suspicious fire coinciding with the nationwide unrest. On May 7 more than 500 students gathered at the capitol and lowered the state and national flags to half-staff in honor of their fallen colleagues. Their actions had not been approved by state officials, but Lieutenant Governor Hogan quickly issued an order approving the flag lowering in an effort to prevent any conflict between the students and statehouse employees. Two days later a "peaceful protest" of 12,000 students was held on the capitol's west front, although some more radical groups attempted to change the tenor of the gathering. A member of one such faction affixed a red flag to the rifle on the Civil War monument and began shouting "Maoist rhetoric" to the assembled throng. Regardless, the massive group remained calm but dedicated to its principles as attendees listened to speakers while sitting on the lawn and perching in the trees on the grounds. Although many groups used the statehouse as a stage for demonstrations, by the end of 1970 the building had seen some of its most zealous gatherings ever.[15]

The protests and activism of the late 1960s and early 1970 could not detract from the ongoing demands of business in and around the capitol. Once again the state responded to the growing pressures of government by adding a building to the complex. Officials purchased a structure built in 1952 by the Farmer's Union Insurance Company north of the State Services Building on Sherman Street. The new addition complemented the complex well and received a new moniker, the State Social Services Building. Additionally, the legislature encouraged more long-range planning but shied away from the immense, costly plans drawn up by S.U.A. Inc. in 1967. As the 1970s began, the General Assembly called for an expanded complex with new quarters for the supreme court, which would provide the added benefit of space in the capitol for private offices for all legislators. Some proposed changes stayed on the drawing board, however, reflecting the last vestiges of the principle of an impermanent legislature. For example, conflict between the executive and legislative branches ended discussions of central air conditioning in the capitol. Governor John D. Vanderhoof argued that such technology drained state resources, a significant concern during the energy crisis in the early 1970s that substantially increased the price of utilities across the nation. The governor pointed out even more importantly that without air conditioning the General Assembly would leave the capitol and not remain to enact legislation throughout the hot summer months, a concept in harmony with those of Colorado's founders.

The ongoing debate over modernization contrasted with the traditional roles of the building, including another state memorial service, a much less frequent ceremony as the century passed. The body of Edwin Johnson, the only man to serve Colorado for three terms both as governor and U.S. senator, lay in state at the foot of the grand staircase on June 1, 1970, as hundreds of Coloradoans paid their final respects to "Big Ed." Several years later the Senate honored him with a stained glass window above the third-floor gallery. Occasionally, the capitol's historical nature reasserted itself within the ongoing dangers of modernization.[16]

New personalities dominated life at the statehouse as the 1970s progressed. Phyllis Woodard joined the staff as a tour guide in 1971 and directed the program for the next seventeen years. The building became a classroom unto itself under the care of Woodard, who professionalized visitor services during her tenure. Control over the capitol shifted in 1975 from the Division of Public Works, formerly Superintendent Merrick's Division of Public Buildings, to the executive branch's Office of State Planning and Budgeting. This change further distanced statehouse management from a group dedicated to the complex to an assemblage of political appointees with many tasks that left little time for the capitol's needs. The most influential individual in the capitol in the 1970s was state senator Hugh Fowler of Littleton, first elected in 1968. Always conscious of the statehouse's position as the people's building,

Senator Fowler regularly encouraged his fellow politicians to undertake improvements to the structure. Although his suggestions did not always reflect historical integrity, Fowler offered the strongest voice in decades fighting for the capitol's protection. Without his efforts the building likely could have seen another decade as physically damaging as the 1950s. Even so, a significant amount of structural change took place within the granite walls during the 1970s. Preservationists hollered when crews broke several precious rose onyx slabs in the lieutenant governor's office as they replaced the Corinthian decor with modern paneling. *Denver Post* columnist Joanne Ditmer referred to the project as "neither restoration [n]or refurbishing, but Modernization with a capital M." She made her argument plain:

> It is a terrible precedent to have it so easy to demolish the original character of this unique building, our State Capitol, by individuals who may well be "here today, gone tomorrow." Yet their vandalism-in-the-name-of-progress remains long after they are forgotten. We would never build a structure such as this today, but since it is our legacy, we shouldn't treat it so shoddily as to try to make a nondescript copy of a modern building. It ends up with the merits of neither.

Although many people championed the building as a center of technology and modern convenience in the state, the loss of historical integrity worried many others.[17]

In response to the social movements of the previous decade, the 1970s witnessed a great deal of legislative recognition of revisionist Colorado history. After the Senate resolved in 1974 to honor former governor Love with a stained glass portrait, some politicians noticed a trend of male-dominated tributes in the capitol. Indeed, the window of Frances Jacobs in the dome's Hall of Fame, installed at the turn of the twentieth century, remained the only memorial to a woman in the building seventy years later, and the legislature determined to more appropriately honor the role of Colorado women in the capitol. A group of female politicians selected two pioneering ladies in the state's history, opportunity school founder Emily Griffith and former state treasurer Virginia Neal Blue, to honor with stained glass portraits. The Elysian Stained Glass Company of Englewood crafted the Love, Griffith, and Blue windows and installed them before the dedication ceremony in 1976. Additionally, an intricate tribute to women took shape during the year, directed by Eva Mackintosh and Geraldine Merrill. They oversaw work on a tapestry named "Women's Gold" that honored nineteen Colorado women. Inscribed with the slogan "Their Heritage Gives Colorado Women Faith in the Future," the tapestry found a permanent home on the capitol's first floor in 1977. With two stained glass portraits and the immense tapestry, the statehouse's new artwork reflected increasing social awareness in the state.[18]

The celebrations marking Colorado's statehood centennial seemed sub-dued when contrasted with the bombastic celebrations of the nation's bicen-tennial in 1976. Coloradoans cheered their notable anniversary, but most local events paled in comparison to the national commemoration. Unlike the excitement that surrounded the "Rush to the Rockies" events in 1959, the capitol marked 100 years of statehood in an artistic manner in 1976. For example, the House of Representatives added its first stained glass portrait, of African American territorial businessman and political activist Barney Ford. Another recognition of the state's centennial involved erecting a new office building just south of the heating plant on Sherman Street to help relieve pressure on executive offices, the twentieth century's most familiar variation on a theme. The legislature named this new structure the State Centennial Building, and Governor Richard D. Lamm dedicated the functional but drab edifice in a ceremony on October 25, 1976. Unfortunately, the state's newest creation reflected a downward spiral in design for structures within the com-plex. The capitol still towered supreme, flanked by the attractive Colorado State Museum and State Office Building. Although modernistic, the State Capitol Annex and heating plant, State Services Building, and State Social Services Building augment the complex well. In contrast, the State Centen-nial Building stands as perhaps the homeliest structure ever erected near the statehouse. The commemoration of Colorado's 100th anniversary of state-hood offered only a few reasons to celebrate at the capitol.[19]

Colorado leaders provided other architectural responses to the perennial problem of housing state authority in the 1970s. In 1973 the legislature had recommended moving the judicial branch out of the statehouse. Long con-sidered the element of government most expendable in terms of office space, many states and even the federal government had moved their high courts from capitols to suit the needs of the rest of civil authority. Colorado's Gen-eral Assembly encouraged construction of a new museum building and wanted to relocate the high court and historical society somewhere within the capi-tol neighborhood. To satisfy the legislature's increasing sense of permanence, the justices found themselves served with an eviction notice: they were to move out as soon as the General Assembly could pay for the erection of a new building. On land just south of Lincoln Park two new structures arose, includ-ing a low, sloping, brown brick building for the historical society, leaving the museum south of the capitol temporarily vacant. Although the unconven-tional design of the "Heritage Center" generated some controversy, most people leveled their criticism at the supreme court's new building. This "box on stilts," with a breezeway underneath and a skylight for the basement law library, marked a shocking architectural departure from anything built near the capi-tol. It joined the modern design of the new Denver Art Museum, built in

Supreme court law library in the east wing of the second floor in the mid-1970s, shortly before the high court moved out of the capitol. Courtesy, Martha Campbell

1971 south of the Civic Center, as trendy structures that often clashed with the classical lines of nearby government buildings and monuments.[20]

Although the justices seemed happy with their spacious new quarters, they could not abandon their former home altogether. Before they left, some on the high court asked to take something with them—the capitol courtroom's immense two-ton chandelier. Their request started an argument between two branches of state government. Senator Fowler, concerned about the courtroom's future as a hearing room for the legislature, bemoaned the thought of losing the chandelier. Senator Harold McCormick of Cañon City agreed, claiming the "historical integrity of the building is involved," but other legislators expressed doubts that the fixture deserved the fracas. After months of posturing and heated debate, Senator Fowler negotiated a compromise with the high court. The chandelier stayed, preserving to a great extent the character of the room, but the court secured the stained glass window of Chief Justice Robert Steele for its new quarters. The justices also took a bust by Preston Powers—who had designed *The Closing Era* monument—of the state's first chief justice, Henry C. Thatcher, which rested on a pedestal behind the court's bench in the capitol. By 1977 the justices had settled into their new structure southwest of the capitol, and librarians finished shuttling hundreds

Old supreme court room as it looked in 2003, with the one-ton chandelier and Heritage Windows above the benches now used for public hearings. Author's collection

of volumes from the law library on the second floor to the research room in the basement of the new building. Over the next several years crews transformed the courtroom into a public hearing room complete with a new red decor one former court employee described as "pure whorehouse." But the battle over the chandelier represented a victory for historic preservation in the capitol even as modernization continued in other parts of the edifice.[21]

Shortly after the Supreme Court left the statehouse, a group of Coloradoans decided to add five ethnic windows to the building's collection of stained glass images. The "Heritage Windows" provided a vibrant addition to the political and social portraits in the capitol. In late January 1977 laborers unveiled the first two windows that honored Chicanos and African Americans, one a gloriously colored portrait of mapmaker Don Miera y Pacheco and the Dominguez-Escalante Expedition of 1776 and the other an abstract window honoring Clara Brown, a territorial businesswoman in Colorado. Portraits of Ute chiefs Jack House and Buckskin Charlie and Asian Americans represented by Chinese businessman Chin Lin Sou and Japanese entrepreneur Naoichi Hokazono arrived several weeks later. A final window honoring territorial governor Alexander Hunt and Ute chief Ouray replaced Chief Justice Steele's portrait. In the meantime, the General Assembly remodeled the second and third floors of the statehouse, securing for the first time office space for all legislators in the capitol. Responding to public opposition, members denied that their offices represented a step toward a full-time legislature, which Colorado's founders had feared and many citizens had opposed over the course of the twentieth century. The legislature also transformed the east wing's law library into office space and divided basement rooms with walls and drop ceilings, obscuring or destroying the original oak and marble. The renovation was finished in 1979 and provided offices and committee rooms at the expense of many historical elements of the building in favor of modern comforts for lawmakers.[22]

The capitol grounds languished in the late 1970s as the building's interior underwent superficial work. As the neighborhood around the statehouse and along Colfax Avenue deteriorated into one of violence and tawdry sex, the building suffered from the social decay. When night fell over the granite hulk on Brown's Bluff, young male prostitutes worked the streets in its shadow and often used the statehouse park to conduct their affairs. Several hundred young men solicited around the capitol, giving the building's surrounding driveway the nickname "Sodomy Circle." Additionally, reports of rapes, bomb threats, purse snatchings, and assaults in the area increased steadily over the years. Fear and anger simmered throughout the marble corridors of the capitol. The situation worsened on January 4, 1979, when an assailant stabbed Legislative Council Director Lyle C. Kyle with a knife in the capitol's basement restroom. Although Kyle recovered, the incident demanded a review of the building's security. The General Assembly gave Denver police liberal reign around the complex to help protect the building and grounds, whereas the Colorado State Patrol retained control over executive security. Within several years the state discontinued the capitol watchmen, a historic but increasingly ineffective group that had protected the statehouse since the 1890s. But state leaders failed to agree on a proposal for a more organized and capable security staff in the 1980s as partisan politics often interfered with safeguarding the people's building.[23]

Public concerns about the capitol's structural stability received increasing attention as Colorado leaders scrutinized the building's security. A 1978 article in the *Rocky Mountain News* pointed to a general apathy about the statehouse, for "much like the view of the Rockies or the turning of the Aspen—the State Capitol building is taken for granted by most everyone in Colorado except thousands of school children while they tour it as a part of their schoolwork." But in the 1970s the demolition of historic structures in the capital city became commonplace as the Denver Urban Renewal Authority attempted to rid the city of blight by tearing down old structures throughout the city. The threat to many historic buildings in Denver, such as the destruction of David Moffat's mansion and the near loss of the Daniels and Fisher clock tower, encouraged many citizens to rally against the destructive nature of urban renewal. After the federal government approved the National Historic Preservation Act of 1966, interest in protecting old structures and landscapes grew around the country. In Colorado members of the press often supported the effort to restore instead of demolish the architectural legacy of the past. A series of preservation articles in the *Denver Post* in 1979 included one calling to save the statehouse not only from violence and prostitution but also from the wear and tear of the ages:

> For 85 years the State Capitol has been the august symbol of the Colorado government. Visitors and school children by the thousands tour its stately halls. Legislators gather annually to determine the direction of the state. There are demonstrations against, and celebrations for, various ideals. The Capitol has seen the good times and the bad, and always it is there as evidence of continuity and strength, whatever the situation, mood or economy.

To save the statehouse for future generations, the building's physical condition demanded some measure of preservation. Although support for such work received only slight attention from Colorado officials, some media outlets maintained a steady interest in the capitol's situation.[24]

State leaders approved repairs to the building's most visible expression of historic pride in 1980. After thirty years the gold dome had once again chipped and tarnished to the point of embarrassment for many Coloradoans. Jay Otto and John Radford, who had regilded the Wyoming State Capitol's dome several years earlier, spent several weeks that fall dangling from boatswain's chairs, ropes, and ladders to replace Colorado's gold dome. The two men endured ferocious winds and a hair-raising lightning strike that forced Otto to "hang on and take the shock." By November they had finished the $595,997 job of covering the 7,200-square-foot dome with forty-two ounces of gold. At the same time, capitol caretakers repaired the building's roof, which leaked so badly that some senators had started bringing umbrellas into their chambers to ward off drips from the ceiling. Meanwhile a much more significant problem, the archaic electrical wiring, demanded the largest amount of construction work in the building since its completion eight decades earlier. Fans ran continually in the subbasement to keep the nineteenth-century wires cool during the summer months when window-mounted air conditioning units added to the strain on the building's electrical system. Senator Hugh Fowler had first pointed out this potentially catastrophic fire danger in 1976, but not until 1982 did crews begin replacing the statehouse's frayed, melted, brittle, sparking wires. The work took six months and required the use of 1890s plaster and paint techniques to blend with the rest of the structure, giving the building a historic, brilliant shine with safe new wiring and freshly refinished walls. When faced with immediate danger, the statehouse finally received much-needed attention.[25]

The deteriorating condition of the entire capitol complex made front-page headlines in 1983 when Governor Richard Lamm ordered the State Office Building closed as a fire hazard and asked for $4.5 million to bring it up to code. The Democratic chief executive warned that he would have the building torn down if the Republican majority in the General Assembly could not find the funds to repair it. Instead of a total renovation, the legislature appropriated money for "life safety" repairs, and within two years work was finished that retained the State Office Building's outer shell and boasted a rebuilt interior that preserved much of the edifice's historic architecture. After the office building's initial closing, concerned state leaders organized a committee to study the entire capitol complex. As E. Robert Turner, director of the Department of Administration, commented: "There's a major problem in every building."

In late 1983 the Capitol Complex Commission met to investigate the deterioration of all the state buildings on Brown's Bluff and within several months submitted a $33 million proposal to fix the complex. The commission suggested renovations of the State Services, State Social Services, and State Centennial buildings. The members successfully lobbied to turn the former state museum into the Legislative Services Building, which reopened

Civic Center from the observation deck, with the Colorado Veterans Monument in the foreground and the view west toward the Rocky Mountains, as it looked in 1998. Author's collection

in 1986 and boasted new quarters for the legislature's Joint Budget Committee and various agencies of the General Assembly. A year later crews finished a renovation project on the State Social Services Building. A third of the commission's recommended funds would go to the Department of Revenue for a new building near the crumbling State Capitol Annex, an idea vehemently opposed by the Joint Budget Committee. Senator Cliff Dodge of Denver, the committee's chair, responded tersely: "We're not going to build them an empire. We're not building Taj Mahals any more." Colorado officials no longer possessed the inclination or the ability to erect structures like those built by previous generations. But the Capitol Complex Committee made no recommendations to preserve the aging capitol, which was in the worst condition of any building in the complex after nine decades of use and abuse.[26]

As some state buildings received much-needed physical attention in the 1980s, capitol caretakers attempted to restore the statehouse's position in the eyes of many Coloradoans after years of neglect. Citizens worked with the state to erect several monuments on the statehouse grounds to commemorate Coloradoans' service during times of conflict beyond the Civil War statue and the Spanish-American War flagpole. After a number of delays in the late 1980s, construction was finished on an obelisk of red sandstone from Lyons in Lincoln Park west of the capitol. The Colorado Veterans Monument stood in contrast to the gray columns of the Civic Center but provided a backdrop for yearly ceremonies honoring the service of all Colorado troops. Memorials installed on the east side of the statehouse honored the Pearl Harbor Survivors Association, the USS *Colorado*, the World War II–era Japanese American internment camp Amache on the southeastern plains, and Governor Ralph Carr, who supported the rights of citizens interned at Amache. Inside the capitol Phyllis Woodard and the tour guide staff brought schoolchildren to the statehouse in 1985 to help decorate the building for Christmas, starting an annual tradition of recognizing Colorado youth during the holiday season. Artwork also helped increase public interest in the building, with a portrait of Dr. Martin Luther King Jr. on the first floor and five landscape paintings of various Colorado scenes in the House of Representatives chamber, which helped relieve some of the room's austerity. In 1988 the state's handicrafts went on display with the first Capitol Quilt Show, which displayed 176 quilts hung from rods suspended over the Corinthian pillars and pilasters throughout the atriums and hallways. This popular, unique display became a biennial tradition. Through the dedicated efforts of many Coloradoans, the capitol regained some of its tarnished reputation after the recent difficult decades.[27]

Centennial celebrations for the capitol provided another way to restore the building's public image. Aside from demonstrating the difficulty of determining the statehouse's exact age, 100th anniversaries in 1986 and 1990 offered an opportunity to return the capitol to a position of prominence in the hearts and minds of Coloradoans. The first honored the centennial of construction of the building in July 1986 with a ceremony presided over by well-known Denverites "Daddy" Bruce Randolph and Helen Johnson Tyler. The small crowd at the capitol released 100 balloons bearing a picture of the building while a military band from Fort Carson played patriotic tunes. Four years later a much larger event commemorated the 100th anniversary of the cornerstone ceremony. The legislature authorized a Centennial Cornerstone Committee to collect materials for a time capsule buried near the cornerstone under a specially quarried piece of Aberdeen granite. Echoing the great celebration of 1890, a Masonic parade wound up Seventeenth Street to the capitol before the capsule was sealed. But although the 1990 ceremony attempted to recapture some of the glory of that exciting day a century earlier, it could not overcome the statehouse's decaying structural condition and the lack of concern about the building from citizens and state leaders alike in recent decades. In many ways, after forty years of abuse and neglect the fresh slab of Aberdeen granite planted in the ground represented a tombstone for the Colorado State Capitol.[28]

During the period 1952 to 1990 the statehouse suffered a great deal but maintained its proud, dignified public image. Years of apathy toward and ignorance of the building's dangers resulted in a structure that, thanks to custodial crews, shone brilliantly on the outside but groaned with the problems of age underneath. It weathered threats during the 1950s to demolish part or all of the granite behemoth on Brown's Bluff but still suffered "vandalism in the name of progress" throughout these years with relentless modernization that often dismissed the idea of protecting the edifice's original fabric. Promoted by the local press, the budding historic preservation movement offered hope for the capitol's future but lacked enough broad support to fully protect the building. Regardless of such concerns the statehouse retained its position as the preeminent stage for acting out the dramas of Colorado life, particularly during the social protests of the 1960s and 1970s. The building witnessed some bright times as the twentieth century continued, such as the increasing interest in multicultural history, but visitors generally stayed away. Stabbings in the basement and homosexual prostitution on the grounds resulted in a tarnished reputation for the capitol in the minds of the people who owned it, the citizens of Colorado. Law enforcement officials could deal with statutory problems, but repairing the building's position as the state's most important symbol of collective identity proved far more difficult. As 1990 dawned the most important task remaining to ensure the survival of the statehouse was to clearly identify the building's many problems and figure out how best to deal with them. These challenges dominated the most recent years at the capitol as a new generation of Coloradoans attempted to preserve the legacy of their predecessors for themselves and their descendants.

CHAPTER EIGHT

# Too Important to Neglect
## 1990–Present

I doubt whether even our public edifices—our capitols, statehouses, court-houses, city-halls, and churches—ought to be
built of such permanent materials as stone or brick. It were
better that they should crumble to ruin, once in twenty years,
or thereabouts, as a hint to the people to examine into and
reform the institutions which they symbolize.

—Thomas Holgrave, from Nathaniel Hawthorne's
*The House of the Seven Gables*

A S THE LAST DECADE OF THE TWENTIETH CENTURY BEGAN, the Colorado
State Capitol teetered on the edge of collapse anticipated here by
the daguerreotypist Holgrave in Hawthorne's work. After almost a
century of occupation the statehouse sagged from the ravages of age, infested
with structural problems against which maintenance crews struggled daily.
Meanwhile, state leaders and citizens in general remained either ignorant of
or apathetic to the building's condition regardless of the efforts of some concerned Coloradoans in government and the media, perhaps the most troublesome aspect of the capitol's decline. A democratic society expressed its common goals and principles through public architecture, and the statehouse's
decay indicated a threat to this most essential of Colorado structures and, as
Hawthorne suggested, to the social and political institutions it represented.
This physical embodiment of the disparate peoples and geography of the Centennial State, a public symbol "too important to neglect" that had weathered

countless challenges over the years, stood in desperate need of assistance. As the twentieth century passed into the twenty-first, capitol caretakers anxiously searched for ways to combat the structure's physical weaknesses and its waning position as the state's most important symbol of collective identity.[1]

In the final decade of the twentieth century, most concerns about the capitol focused on its structural integrity. A report in 1990 detailed the extent of the problems in the building and encouraged action to prevent a disastrous catastrophe. Five years later another study reemphasized the statehouse's numerous physical dangers, but the solutions it proposed proved too expensive to gain much support. Reactive rather than proactive construction took place in the capitol during this period, responding to minor problems while often dismissing the building's major concerns. When the legislative and executive branches finally approved life safety work in the early twenty-first century, the limited scope of those projects indicated the diverted priorities and relative disinterest of many state leaders and citizens. Meanwhile, those in state government most concerned with the capitol faced seemingly insurmountable political challenges in their efforts to save the building. A weakened state and national economy prevented many Colorado officials from pursuing repairs they considered extravagant or unwarranted for a structure whose hazards were belied by a polished outward appearance. Following terrorist attacks on the United States in 2001, the physical representation of Colorado's democratic society suffered ignominious damage as draconian security measures changed the building's atmosphere from one of welcoming charm to forbidding suspicion. In recent years a number of politicians and citizens have engaged in serious attempts to adequately respond to these difficulties but have so far experienced little success in preserving the representative symbol of all Coloradoans.

After almost a century of occupation, many employees and state leaders quietly supposed that the capitol's strength had worn down. But no one knew the extent of the structural decay until officials called for a full study of the building. In 1990 the Department of Administration produced the "Colorado State Capitol Life Safety Plan," the first official report on the statehouse's status. It confirmed rumors and opinions traded by state employees and published by the media in recent decades. More than any other potential hazard in the building the report devoted many pages to the capitol's fire danger, a concern since the structure's earliest days. The *Denver Post* had worriedly reported on this issue in 1900: "The Capitol is supposed to be a fireproof building, but the danger of conflagration inside the offices and vaults, which are filled with wood work and books, is very great. Even a slight fire would do serious damage in these places." Minor blazes, quickly extinguished by state employees, had flared in the statehouse in the twentieth century, but the potential danger of any fire increased as the years passed. The 1990 report pointed out that although most of the building's physical elements would not burn, heat from a fire would weaken iron floor beams, making the statehouse "in a life safety context, the most unsafe building in the Capitol complex." In a nightmarish scenario detailed in the report, the building would experience structural collapse within ten minutes from the start of a blaze, resulting in slabs of marble, brass balustrades, and other deadly objects raining down throughout the capitol. Never before had Colorado officials so graphically acknowledged the building's potentially fatal condition.[2]

The tenets of historic preservation received only slight attention in the "Life Safety Plan," which focused instead on protecting the building's structural survival. Although the 1990 report commented that "improvements will be designed with utmost historic sensitivity," the building's physical safety presupposed the desires of preservationists to undo some of the damage done to the capitol's historic fabric throughout the twentieth century. But some state leaders encouraged projects aimed at restoring the statehouse's public image. To provide a sense of organization in the statehouse lacking since the Board of Capitol Managers' demise, the legislature established the State Capitol Building Advisory Committee in 1991 "to ensure that the historic character and architectural integrity of the Capitol building and grounds be preserved and promoted." The General Assembly's research agency, the Legislative Council, also adopted a proactive approach to promote cultural development and tourist amenities at the capitol. The building's guide program offered the best way to increase public awareness and appreciation of the statehouse. Mary Louise MacRossi had coordinated the tour program since Phyllis Woodard's departure in 1988. In 1996 Edna Pelzmann succeeded MacRossi as the manager of visitor services, supervising a diverse group of architects, historians, teachers, students, and volunteers from all walks of life. Accommodations for tourists and schoolchildren in the late twentieth century compared favorably to much of the building's past, as guides passed on the capitol's story with enthusiasm and adoration to thousands of people a year. In 1991 the state also refurbished the building's most famous aspect, the gold dome, weathered by relentless summer hailstorms that battered the statehouse crown. An expenditure of $233,300 allowed for the job, which used gold from Florence, Italy, to restore the dome. Although the "Life Safety Plan" brought the capitol's problems to the attention of all state leaders, many expressed a desire to also protect the structure's symbolic role.[3]

As the stage upon which Coloradoans enacted the dramas of contemporary life, the capitol had hosted many vibrant gatherings, especially in recent decades. But events in early 1992 threatened to tarnish the statehouse's place as a backdrop to encourage positive action. As had many citizens for several

Crews regilding the capitol dome in late summer of 1991, after several seasons of severe weather had pounded flecks of gold off the building's crown. Courtesy, Colorado State Capitol Tour Desk

years, on January 20 thousands of people marched past the capitol during Denver's annual celebration of Dr. Martin Luther King Jr.'s birthday. Over 100 supporters of the Ku Klux Klan gathered on the steps of the people's building and shouted racial epithets at the larger crowd passing by. Some of the marchers threw bottles and snowballs at the Klan sympathizers, threatening to escalate the situation into a race riot. Providing a sanctuary for the group not seen since the days of Governor Clarence Morley, Colorado State Patrol troopers attempted to diffuse the situation by bringing as many Klan supporters inside the statehouse as they could. The troopers escorted the group through the subbasement tunnels to the capitol complex power plant, where they boarded a bus and drove off. In the meantime, marchers from the parade expressed displeasure at the Klan's presence by shouting at the statehouse's massive, shut bronze doors. Police officers fired tear gas at the group, resulting in a melee as protestors and counterprotestors escaped by running through the capitol's neighborhood. Unfortunately, the day ended angrily as a positive gathering turned into a violent scene directly conflicting with the spirit of King's birthday celebration.[4]

Tensions of another sort plagued the building in the early 1990s, as some Coloradoans felt physically isolated from their representatives. With the passage of the federal government's Americans With Disabilities Act of 1990, caretakers of public buildings needed to ensure accessibility for handicapped persons, and many elements of the statehouse did not comply with this new directive. The executive branch responded quickly to the law by removing carpet too thick for wheelchairs to navigate from the governor's office. But the legislature's sluggishness resulted in threats of legal battles to make the chambers more accessible. In July 1992 a group of Coloradoans asked the U.S. Department of Justice to force action at the statehouse, arguing that "[t]he damage caused by the immoral and illegal exclusion of persons with disabilities from this critical focal point in the democratic process is enormous in scope." When the General Assembly failed to act in the 1993 regular session, disabled citizens went on the offensive. Several protested by leaving their wheelchairs behind and pulling themselves up the marble stairs to the House of Representatives anteroom. Although the "stair crawl" brought the problem to public light, legislators found themselves trapped between the demands for accessibility and the loss of historical integrity in the building, with little common ground between the two concerns. Partisan differences exacerbated the problem, as Democrats wanted to work with labor unions that offered to build the ramps for free while Republicans focused on the threat to the building's historical integrity. After a great deal of debate, in late 1993 crews installed a brass lift to the Senate anteroom, and outside the House of Representatives they built a large wooden ramp painted pink to blend with the rose

North atrium in the summer of 1999 during the biennial Capitol Quilt Show, with the wooden wheelchair ramp to the House of Representatives on the second floor at lower right. Author's collection

onyx. Although few architects or state employees approved of the sizable construction, by the time the General Assembly met in 1994 all Coloradoans could physically reach their elected officials.[5]

With the accessibility issue settled, some state leaders returned to the life safety proposals made four years earlier and subsequently set aside. Senator Dottie Wham of Denver, chair of the capitol advisory committee, promoted $34 million in construction to eliminate fire hazards and other problems and $16 million more for historic restoration. Reactions to her proposal indicated changing trends in the debate over the capitol's fate in the 1990s. Democratic governor Roy Romer objected to any program that would close the capitol for repairs, something he considered a threat to the legitimacy of government. Conscious of the building's vital role as the symbolic seat of collective authority, Governor Romer and others worried that the state could not effectively govern from outside the granite walls. Senator Wham's Republican colleagues in the legislature also disagreed on the notion of leaving the capitol for any length of time. Speaker of the House Chuck Berry expressed shock at the idea, whereas Senate president Tom Norton supported it. Senator Dave Wattenberg of Walden declaimed the concept, expecting "the damnedest outcry" from the public and promising a legislative filibuster if the advisory committee recommended closing the building. Although the cost and inconvenience of such extensive work often provoked a negative reaction from lawmakers, the 1990s witnessed the rise of a truly personal debate over preserving the capitol. Individuals rather than political parties steered the battle, creating tension between senators and representatives across the aisle and within partisan ranks as well.[6]

Under Senator Wham's dedicated leadership the advisory committee and the Legislative Council prepared a new report to reemphasize the structural concerns first expressed in 1990. Architects showed politicians slides of public buildings nationwide damaged in recent fires to rally support for a life safety and preservation project, the cost of which had risen within a year to $62.5 million. Wham and the committee members struggled to convince their fellow legislators of the need for haste and suggested moving state government to recently abandoned buildings at Stapleton International Airport for the duration of major construction. After several months of investigation, the Legislative Council released the "State Capitol Building Health and Life Safety Project" in 1995, the most drastic warning yet about the statehouse's condition. Like the plan five years earlier, much of the 1995 report focused on the structural safety of the capitol and the need for modern services and technologies in the building. The report offered four renovation proposals ranging from minor repairs in an occupied statehouse to closing the structure for several years for major work, renovating the State Capitol Annex, and erecting a new office building nearby. But like the 1990 plan, the "Health and Life Safety" report concentrated on protecting the capitol's physical stability and supported historic restoration only if it did not require additional funding. The cost and time needed to preserve the capitol shocked many state leaders, but the report's length and detail reflected the unanswered problems lurking within the granite hulk on Brown's Bluff.[7]

The debate over renovating the Colorado State Capitol emerged at a time when many states were conducting similar projects. The late twentieth century saw a blossoming of the historic preservation movement, and many capitol buildings reaped the benefits of that popularity. Construction projects affected approximately half of the nation's statehouses in the late 1990s, and both supporters and opponents of the various plans in Colorado took note of developments elsewhere. As had been the goal of the Board of Capitol Managers' 1883 tour of Midwest statehouses, the State Capitol Building Advisory Committee hoped to learn how to win legislative and executive support from other states' successes and failures. Concerned Coloradoans paid special attention to preservation efforts involving the other existing Elijah Myers statehouses. Indeed, perhaps the most widely acclaimed capitol restoration took place in the early 1990s in Lansing, Michigan. The project began in 1982 with executive support that six years later had grown into what Governor James Blanchard called "the Year of the Capitol." By 1992, in spite of an economic downturn that had threatened to stall the work several times, laborers finished the $58.1 million job. Once the work was completed, Michigan citizens gazed in admiration upon the most accurately and completely restored Gilded Age statehouse in the nation. The preservation of Myers's second statehouse, in Austin, Texas, cost $187 million and closed the building for five years. After several devastating fires in the 1980s, Texas legislators created the State Preservation Board to oversee renovation. Designers balanced historical integrity and the needs of modern government to turn the nation's largest statehouse into a beautiful, functional center of state authority. By the mid-1990s the capitols of Michigan and Texas represented the best in modern historic preservation, combining a respect for the past with the needs of the present and leaving a secure architectural legacy for the future.[8]

Beyond the Myers statehouses, proposals to renovate and restore capitols in the 1990s proved successful in several dozen states across the nation. As Charles Goodsell observed, "[G]overnments, to save money, often defer maintenance on their office buildings, but seldom on their capitols. As symbols, they are simply too important to neglect." But in Colorado, various personalities waged acrimonious battles over preserving the capitol. Opposition stemming from the anticipated cost of the work proved difficult to overcome. Several legislators wrote a resolution in 1996 that ensured the General

Assembly's direct participation in any capitol planning, stripping a great deal of influence from the advisory committee. By demanding the legislature's right to approve any "decisions regarding significant, multi-phase construction . . . affecting executive and legislative spaces in the Capitol Building," lawmakers threw stumbling blocks into the path of a project of the size needed to solve the structure's problems. Statutory spending limits approved by voters in 1992 exacerbated the challenge of paying for a large construction project. By adding Article X, Section 20, nicknamed the "Taxpayer's Bill of Rights," to the state constitution, citizens prevented the General Assembly from spending more than leaders budgeted, forbade legislative tax increases, forced an annual reduction in state taxes, and demanded a refund of excess revenue. This well-intentioned but controversial statute, perfectly described as a "constitutional noose" by John Straayer, meant that to spend excess revenue or raise more money for a statehouse renovation, the people's representatives would have to secure approval from voters instead of endorsing the job themselves. Should the state suffer a period of economic decline, few individuals would want to increase their financial burdens, no matter how vital the reason. The citizens of Colorado, as the people ultimately responsible for the condition of the symbol of their collective identity, unknowingly imposed upon themselves and their elected officials the greatest obstacle of all to protecting their decaying edifice.[9]

As the media had for several decades, newspapers returned the capitol debate to the public's attention in 1997. In the *Rocky Mountain News*, Mary Chandler called for "some combination of public and private money to keep the grand old lady on her toes." Chandler outlined Senate president Norton's arguments, whose engineering background allowed him to recognize the many structural problems in the building. He supported a proposal to move the Department of Revenue out of the State Capitol Annex and house statehouse employees there during construction. Fellow Republican, State Treasurer Bill Owens, however, opposed even the less expensive life safety projects. Contesting such opinions, capitol caretakers promoted the need for action to protect the building. Betty Chronic, vice chair of the advisory committee, called the statehouse "a disaster waiting to happen," and Senator Wham worried that "the motivation to fix it [will] be a tragedy." Paul Schauer, a supporter of preservation and former state representative, commented that "it's not going to get any cheaper, and the problems are not going away by themselves. Unfortunately, it will probably take a real disaster . . . to get us moving on this project." Support for preservation grew steadily in the legislature, culminating in 1998 when both houses passed a resolution calling the structure "the most important historic public building in the state." With high hopes and increasing interest in the project, the advisory committee submitted plans for a $120 million project for life safety and historic preservation, almost doubling the cost in the space of a year. Owens remained unconvinced: "I see scores of tourists each week walk by my office. Almost without exception, they're marveling at the wonderful state of preservation of this Capitol." Unfortunately, visitors and politicians alike often confused the statehouse's polished appearance with structural stability. As several reports had clearly shown, underneath the marble, brass, and rose onyx lay a catastrophe waiting to happen.[10]

Even as the General Assembly expressed its support for preservation, a more contentious situation developed at the capitol in 1998. Having stood in front of the statehouse for almost ninety years, the Civil War memorial reminded citizens of the violent territorial era. Listed last among the all but forgotten engagements in which Colorado troops fought was "Sand Creek, Colo.," a reference to the infamous 1864 massacre of Cheyenne and Arapaho Indians. Senator Bob Martinez of Commerce City railed against the inclusion of what most scholars considered a massacre among the minor conflicts that marked Colorado's participation in the war. A resolution cosponsored by four-fifths of the General Assembly called for the reference to Sand Creek to be removed from the monument, igniting a political, cultural, and historical storm. Although few citizens defended the soldiers for the horrific acts they perpetrated on the Colorado plains, some worried about fiddling with the interpretation of history. Tom Noel wrote an article for the *Denver Post* entitled "Don't Erase 'Sand Creek,'" pleading for the preservation of the monument: "Each generation must learn and revise the lesson for itself. . . . 'Sand Creek' should not be erased from Colorado history in the well-intentioned but misguided pursuit of political correctness." Following a proposal by the *Rocky Mountain News*, legislators eventually decided to leave the monument alone and to memorialize Sand Creek separately. In a ceremony on the 138th anniversary of the massacre in 2002, representatives from Cheyenne and Arapaho tribes joined Colorado lawmakers to dedicate a plaque clarifying Sand Creek's position in the state's history. Bolted to a flower bed at the base of the Civil War monument, the plaque represented changing interpretations of Colorado's past and the need to present all opinions at the capitol, reflecting its role as the symbol of all citizens.[11]

As the controversy over the Civil War monument indicated, the statehouse retained its purpose as a stage for great and small moments in Colorado life even as it suffered physical decline. At the end of the twentieth and beginning of the twenty-first centuries, the building hosted several events reminiscent of dignified moments earlier in its existence. During the economic Summit of the Eight, held at the Denver Public Library in late June 1997, the political talk show *This Week* broadcast from the capitol's south atrium, brightly

One hundred thirty-eight years after the Sand Creek Massacre, members of the Cheyenne and Arapaho tribes unveiled a plaque near the Civil War monument in front of
a crowd of several hundred Coloradoans and American Indians on November 29, 2002.
Author's collection

decorated with quilts from the biennial show. The show's guests included
U.S. secretary of state Madeline Albright and British prime minister Tony
Blair, appearing in what the show called the capitol's "tapestry room." Unfortunately, in preparation for the show some quilts were hastily pulled down,
damaging the Corinthian plasterwork and requiring repairs later in the year.

One of the capitol's most memorable guests arrived in 2002, when ten-
year-old King Oyo of Toro, a kingdom in Uganda, received a standing ova-
tion during a visit to the House of Representatives. In 1999, for the first time
in many years, the statehouse also fulfilled its most solemn duty by honoring
a fallen leader with a state memorial service. The flag-draped casket of Secretary of State Vicki Buckley lay in state on July 20 at the foot of the grand
staircase, surrounded by flowers and guarded by Colorado State Patrol troopers. The solemnity of the ceremony was broken only by the echoing noise of
statehouse elevators calling out floor numbers. A similar although more sub-
dued memorial service on October 2, 2003, honored former state representative Arie Taylor, whose open casket sat in the first floor's west wing for several

hours while mourners paid their respects. But fear, as well as joy and dignity, pervaded some moments in the capitol. During a normal morning of legislative debate on April 20, 1999, rumors started to spread about a shooting in a Denver metropolitan-area school. The work of the General Assembly ground to a halt as members rushed to televisions to watch the terrifying violence at Columbine High School play out before their eyes. As always, the behavior of state leaders in the structure that represented the citizenry echoed the emotions felt by Coloradoans as a whole.[12]

As legislative support for preservation increased steadily during the last years of the twentieth century, statehouse caretakers redoubled their efforts to protect the building in 1999. The advisory committee issued a report to the General Assembly with several recommendations, including undertaking a total renovation and restoration of the building, closing the structure for the duration of the work, and retaining its use as the seat of government after the project's conclusion. To circumvent the funding chokehold created by the "Taxpayer's Bill of Rights," Senator Dorothy Rupert of Boulder authored a bill to ask voters for $140 million of the state's revenue surplus for capitol work, but she encountered stiff opposition from some colleagues. Senator Doug Lamborn of Colorado Springs, who considered tax cuts "more important than Capitol restoration," helped defeat the bill in committee debate. Desperate to maintain momentum, the advisory committee returned to the 1995 life safety report to make proposals for less expensive life safety repairs. The committee members requested and received appropriations to extend four staircases on the upper floors for emergency egress and to install smoke detectors, fire sprinklers, and a public address system. The plan also suggested changes to the building's security after an independent study revealed weaknesses in the Colorado State Patrol's procedures. With the support of Governor Bill Owens, by January 2000 dispatchers were monitoring the capitol and grounds with dozens of security cameras. Gates limited access to the statehouse circle to elected officials and those with permission to pass from the state patrol. Although the capitol still boasted open doors, the adoption of new security measures indicated a changing atmosphere in which the dual requirements of protecting the statehouse and ensuring unfettered access to the people's government did not always coincide.[13]

In the last year of the twentieth century, hoping to capitalize on the approved life safety and security improvements, senators Rupert and Wham resumed their tireless efforts in support of historic preservation in the capitol. They introduced a resolution to put the proposal on a statewide ballot, and the proposal passed the upper house with bipartisan support in late April 2000. Rupert and Wham also secured media backing, evidenced by an editorial in the *Denver Post* on April 9 that called the senators' attempt "[t]he only hope for change" at the statehouse. Pleased with their success thus far, the senators introduced their resolution to the House of Representatives appropriations committee, which quickly killed it along party lines, with Democrats voting for and Republicans against. The measure's political and public supporters reeled at the unexpected loss. But after overcoming so many obstacles, Rupert, Wham, and others refused to let this partisan defeat stop their efforts to protect the statehouse. At the end of the legislative session they launched an initiative petition to put capitol renovation on the November 2000 state ballot.[14]

Once again the media came to the capitol's aid. The *Denver Post* printed an emotional appeal by James E. Hartmann, an advisory committee member and former state historic preservation officer, to rescue the proud but tattered structure. He argued for the necessity of spending a substantial sum to protect the legacy of previous generations: "In building the Capitol we have today, the General Assembly and the people of Colorado in the late 19th century set a standard for us to match. We should not fail them. We cannot fail ourselves. We must not fail our children." Hartmann went on:

> Why is the future of our Capitol being risked year after year? Why is the very symbol of our state in danger of being outmoded, damaged by fire or lost altogether? How could this happen to such an important building, the very symbol of our state? Is it because there is no constituency for our Capitol around the state? Because no one believes the reports, studies and recommendations on concerns with our Capitol? Because the building seems too solid and incombustible ever to ignite? Because the structure functions fine for the time being? Because our legislators want to make laws in the Capitol and not in some temporary space while the major repairs are done? Because prisons, roads and office buildings are more important? Because the Capitol has lasted 105 years without damage, so it should last 105 more? Possibly it is for all these reasons, but the need to do something—and soon—is very compelling.

But supporters failed to collect the requisite number of signatures for the 2000 initiative, and the preservation movement stalled. To make matters worse, Rupert and Wham no longer held seats in the legislature, victims of term limits imposed by voters in 1990. With the departure of the two individuals most dedicated to protecting the statehouse, no such vocal supporter of the proposal remained in the state legislature. Term limits and revenue laws approved by well-intentioned voters, along with partisan and personal opposition among legislative and executive officials, neutered the effort to preserve the capitol.[15]

The General Assembly did not consider any proposals for renovation or restoration in its first session of the twenty-first century. When historically minded volunteers gathered in the capitol to celebrate the 125th anniversary of statehood on August 1, 2001, they reflected on the woeful neglect of the building's many structural problems. But only weeks later a much more immediate danger supplanted the issue of historic preservation at the statehouse. As many Coloradoans headed to work or school on September 11, terrorists commandeered four airplanes and crashed them into New York City's World Trade Center, the Pentagon near Washington, D.C., and a field in Pennsylvania. The bloodiest foreign attack on the continental United States since the War of 1812 stunned people across the world. Concerned about an assault on the state's most important building, Colorado officials reacted immediately to the destruction. Governor Owens ordered all state buildings locked down, including the capitol. State patrol officers removed tourists from the building while employees remained inside, clustered around radios and portable television sets. As the most visible symbol of Colorado, the statehouse represented to some a potential target, whereas others found comfort at the base of the massive structure. Four days after the terrorist attacks, thousands of citizens marched through Denver in a display of solidarity, resolve, and patriotism. They did not congregate at the Civic Center, where Colorado sports teams had recently attracted great numbers of people to victory parties. The marchers did not turn to a church or a school or a shopping mall. Publicly experiencing uncertainty and hope, the people of Colorado returned to the capitol, the physical representation of their collective identity. In the shadow of the granite walls and golden dome, citizens rallied to find comfort in togetherness and strength in the continuity represented by their weary but dignified capitol.[16]

As the United States responded to the attacks with an assault on terrorists in Afghanistan in the weeks and months that followed, the worries of many Coloradoans echoed throughout the capitol's marble corridors. Visitors avoided the statehouse, and school groups canceled scheduled appointments with the tour staff and legislators. Heavy-handed security measures intended to protect the structure frightened many citizens away from their building. Within weeks of the attacks the welcoming atmosphere of the people's building had changed to one of tense suspicion. In early October 2001 the Department of Public Safety declared the observation deck, a perennial security concern, closed until further notice. Sue Mencer, the department's director, ordered the installation of metal detectors to scan everyone entering the capitol. When the General Assembly returned in January 2002, some legislators worried that the treatment of the capitol tarnished the representative nature of state government. Senator Dave Owen of Greeley referred to the building as "Fortress Colorado," and Senator Ed Perlmutter of Jefferson County remarked, "I don't blame the State Patrol for taking extra precautions, but this

is the people's building, and I want every citizen, every visitor to have access."
*Rocky Mountain News* reporter Peter Blake summed up the changes:

> Before, you were assumed to be harmless when you went to the Statehouse,
> interested only in observing or participating in the process. There was
> security, but it kept a low profile and was responsive rather than proactive.
> Now the assumption is you're a terrorist who wants to blow the place up.
> And patrol officers are all over the place. Perhaps we're lucky the Capitol's
> age of innocence lasted as long as it did.

Regardless of such criticism, the Department of Public Safety remained convinced that its actions would prevent any disaster from befalling the state's
most important building. In the meantime, Coloradoans lost to "supersecurity"
the one free, open symbol that united them all.[17]

Inspired by the need to protect the capitol from any possible threat, executive branch officials considered their efforts well worth any expense in the
months after the terrorist attacks. But shortly after the 2002 legislative session began, the carefully orchestrated system to shield the capitol and state
employees suffered an embarrassing failure. With state patrol officers relegated
to staffing metal detectors, they no longer wandered the statehouse grounds
to watch for illegal activities. One brazen individual took advantage of the
situation and stole Senator Ken Chlouber's brightly painted truck from the
capitol circle in plain view of surveillance cameras. An article in the *Denver
Post* chided, "So much for Capitol security." Although Denver police recovered Chlouber's truck later that same day, he and other legislators started
questioning the state's new security measures. A bipartisan resolution declared
that "the security measures that were adopted in the aftermath of September
11, 2001, should be abandoned entirely and the Colorado State Capitol should
be reopened." Colorado media took up the cause as well. The *Rocky Mountain
News* urged state leaders to reopen the doors of the building without metal
detectors. The *News* quoted Chlouber on the issue: "When we treat everybody like terrorists, the terrorists have won. We've got to quit hiding behind
those walls as though we were fairy princesses." Although Governor Owens
remained publicly silent, Mencer defended the changes. But in the end the
demands of the people's representatives won out over executive authority. In
early July 2002 the doors reopened, and state troopers returned to their regular patrols. The balance between protection and the rights of a democratic
society tipped toward the latter, rejecting oppressive security that contradicted
the structure's role as the symbol of collective identity.[18]

Although protecting the statehouse from attack dominated life in the
building in the first months of the twenty-first century, the need for preserving the crumbling structure remained. Three days after the terrorist attacks,

Fred Brown wrote in the *Denver Post* about the need to support the long-awaited life safety repairs. He commented on the building's "diplomatic immunity" regarding Denver safety codes, which if enforced would allow no more than nine people above the first floor at one time. Brown argued that "those horrific pictures of the collapsing World Trade Center towers only reinforced the need to protect the century-old symbol of Colorado. . . . The Colorado Capitol could burn. And collapse. Capitol preservationists, historians and engineers have known this for years." But the situation grew more problematic after several years of a nationwide economic slump, as the state's coffers suffered under "anemic" budgetary constraints. In an attempt to preserve revenue Governor Owens froze all state building projects less than 25 percent complete in 2002. The capitol life safety project, a victory achieved after so many challenges, stood at 22 percent. As he made tough choices about projects across Colorado, Owens deemed life safety construction in the statehouse expendable. But a deal struck with the Colorado Historical Fund, a historic preservation account created by revenues from legalized gambling in three mountain towns, promised to get the life safety project moving again. The fund pledged annual payments to provide $30 million for life safety repairs, the largest bequest ever made by the group.[19]

In the summer of 2003 work resumed on new staircases in the statehouse, using Italian red marble to blend with rose onyx. A year later, instigating perhaps the largest construction project in the building since its completion, life safety work closed the third floor and filled the legislative chambers and former supreme court room with scaffolding. Installation of fire suppression systems commenced immediately after the end of the 2004 legislative session. Marble hallways were paved with cardboard to prevent damage to the white tiles, and crews placed protective buffers on pilasters and rose onyx slabs. Tourists at the statehouse expressed dismay at the conditions but acknowledged the need to protect the structure. As one guide observed, "Our Capitol building is a mess . . . and visitors are somewhat upset." In 2005, work is scheduled to begin on the northwest quadrant and continue in sections around the building, extending staircases and installing fire sprinklers while, it is hoped, disturbing the work of government as little as possible.[20]

Yet the project, as vital as it is, remains somewhat unsatisfactory. Even with the financial support of the historical fund, the focus is—understandably—on immediate life safety improvements over historic preservation. The purpose of the work is to slow down a disaster, not to prevent it. Some individuals have privately compared the life safety project to placing a bandage on a patient in intensive care—it addresses the symptoms of the building's structural problems but not the root cause. Aging cast-iron beams and other weaknesses lurk in the building's shadows, invisible but nonetheless danger-

Ornamental ceiling plaster work disassembled to study possible fire sprinkler systems, part of the life safety construction in the spring of 2001. Author's collection

ous. Until enough support develops for an extensive and complete project, such as those undertaken in Michigan and Texas—perhaps as costly as $250 million and climbing every year—that embraces not only life safety but also modernization, preservation, and restoration, the capitol's limitations cannot and will not be fully addressed. Unfortunately, for several years the legislative and executive branches have not shown the courage necessary to fully recognize and respond to the building's desperate needs, and, as some have argued, they may not do so until the building comes crashing down around them.

With other priorities, legislators could provide little help from the state's meager coffers for the life safety project, making the assistance of the Colorado Historical Fund that much more important. The poor state and national economies had depleted revenue to a crisis point. Colorado officials searched for any way to combat the problems exacerbated by a number of constitutional spending requirements voters had approved in better times. Jared Polis, a member of the State Board of Education, suggested selling state buildings—including the capitol—to a public education fund. State treasurer Mike Coffman and House speaker Lola Spradley of Beulah opposed Polis's plan, citing their duty to citizens to care for the capitol. But the idea, tempting in such a difficult economy, intrigued more than one state politician. Senator

Dave Owen, chair of the Joint Budget Committee, wryly suggested that he might accept an offer of a billion dollars for the statehouse. But the always outspoken Senator Ken Chlouber of Leadville decried the proposal: "This can't be in the foggiest corner of anybody's mind a good idea. It's indigestible to me. It can't go down digestible to the general public. They're going to think, 'What kind of a funny farm are we running up here?'" Eventually, Governor Owens signed the hotly contested legislation, even though most state leaders considered the indignity of a "For Sale" sign on the carefully tended grounds a last resort. Still, the notion that Colorado officials would even propose selling the state's symbol of collective identity ranks as one of the most irresponsible judgments ever made within the granite walls.[21]

While lawmakers groped to resolve fiscal problems in Colorado and historically minded groups aided the life safety project, the executive branch continued to promote security improvements in the capitol. The governor's office received a telephone with a direct connection to the federal Department of Homeland Security to ensure prompt reaction to a threat against Colorado. But events on the other side of the world dictated more sweeping changes at the capitol. In the spring of 2003 the United States and a coalition of international forces invaded Iraq as part of a broader war against terrorism inspired by the attacks of September 11, 2001. The new conflict encouraged Colorado officials to reinstate draconian security measures abandoned several months earlier. Senate Majority Leader Norma Anderson of Lakewood suggested closing the building during extreme periods of danger "to anyone who does not have official business in the building." This suggestion demonstrated the popularity of contemporary reactionist policies that directly threatened the legitimacy of a representative government. State media again opposed the security changes, as evidenced by an article in the *Rocky Mountain News* written by Tom Noel:

> I noticed that the [Colorado Office of Homeland Security] has rigged up our stately Colorado Capitol with sinister-looking cameras and surveillance domes hanging from the coffered ceiling, arched openings, and doorway pediments. Steps that used to welcome visitors have been barricaded with tank-resistant unplanted planters. And I thought the gold-domed Capitol with flag-waving super patriotic politicos was the last place we had to worry about.[22]

A heightened national terror alert during the 2003 holiday season also resulted in the return of metal detectors and locked entrances at the statehouse, but troopers resumed their traditional patrols when the alert level dropped several weeks later. A serious flaw in the new security measures developed in April 2004 when an elevator motor overheated in the attic and began smoking, setting off the newly installed fire alarm. Fire engines were dispatched from Denver stations, but they could not enter the capitol's circle drive because the security gates remained closed as a result of miscommunication among various public safety agencies. The fire engines entered the statehouse driveway only after a disturbingly extended period of time, but, thankfully, the problem in the attic had already been solved. Numerous tests of the alarm system began to fray statehouse employees' nerves, resulting in confusion and at times opposition to leaving the building during an alarm. To avoid such challenges in the future, the Colorado State Patrol and other agencies worked diligently to resolve the communication problems and attempted to enforce evacuations of the building. In the meantime, Senator Sue Windels of Arvada continued her ongoing and as yet unsuccessful struggle to ban smoking from the areas of the capitol controlled by the Senate, the only remaining part of the building (or of any state building) that has yet to extinguish this dangerous practice. But between the new life safety system and the security procedures, the tenor of the statehouse changed perceptibly and dramatically. As often happened at the capitol during a period of potential danger, security and suspicion overshadowed the intended atmosphere of congeniality in the people's building.[23]

The capitol still suffered from structural decay, the frustration of the preservation movement, and oppressive security in the first years of the twenty-first century. But the edifice witnessed some bright moments interspersed among these challenges. The statehouse's neighborhood experienced revitalization as community groups rallied to polish the tarnished image of Colfax Avenue and actively sought to rid the area of prostitution and other vices. In 2003 the Denver Metro Visitors Bureau identified the capitol as the fourth-most-popular free tourist attraction that year in the metropolitan area. Also, although state budget cuts often limited the scope of festivities, volunteers dressed in historic costumes and welcomed tourists and Coloradoans alike to the capitol every year on Colorado Day, August 1. In 2003, for example, the celebration included guides portraying Clara Brown, Herman Lueders, Chipeta, David Moffat, Emily Griffith, and many other figures from the state's history, as well as featuring ecological tours of the trees on the grounds directed by the Colorado State University Cooperative Extension Service. Visitors applauded the volunteers who gave of themselves to help mark Colorado's birthday.[24]

Even so, many statehouse tourists expressed regret that they still could not visit the dome. The capitol's shuttered top prevented visitors from seeing the world-famous panorama from the observation deck, enjoyed by countless people for over a century. Ted Polito Jr., a friendly young man with Down syndrome, lost his job as dome attendant when the area closed to visitors in 2001. During the General Assembly's meeting in 2003, however, Representative

Lew Hopkins as David Moffat, speaking to visitors in the third-floor rotunda Gallery of Presidents on Colorado Day, August 1, 2003. Author's collection

Paul Weissmann of Louisville gave up his lunch hour to watch over the dome and provide visitors with a rare opportunity to enjoy the breathtaking view. Security and life safety concerns often outweighed the desires of tourists and the intended historical use of the dome's observation deck, keeping it off limits to the people Elijah Myers had rightly expected would marvel at the scene. Proposals to reopen the most popular aspect of the statehouse, although controversial, offered hope that Colorado officials had not forgotten the building's role as a symbol deserving of free access and appreciation.[25]

The Colorado State Capitol represents the citizens of the Centennial State better than anything else does, better than anything else can. In a disparate state with little geographical cohesion, the capitol unites Coloradoans through their common needs and interests, binding them as a civil society with a shared past and future. As the home of the democratically elected representative government, it provides the symbol of collective identity. Citizens gather there to make laws, to agitate for reform, to protest against injustice, and to celebrate their common heritage. It serves as a center for culture and history, using sculpture, paintings, and stained glass to portray the state's colorful past. The statehouse is the stage of the people of Colorado, upon which they enact the drama of their political community. Changes within the structure inevitably reflect the evolutionary nature of the society as a whole, corresponding to contemporary principles of people across the state. Decisions reached under the golden dome affect all citizens, as their chosen officials perform socially reflective public service. Many Coloradoans, particularly those living far from the architectural expression of their collective achievement, may not think of the building as often as those who pass through its shadow every day, but nevertheless the capitol belongs to them all on an equal basis. Simply by living in the Centennial State and participating in the political, economic, and social life of Colorado, the building erected as the representation of the people's goals and ideals becomes their own.

The capitol's construction in the late nineteenth century reflected the desire of a new state to prove itself worthy to stand equally alongside the older members of the Union. Although the building's design demonstrated Coloradoans' eagerness to show off their state's wealth, it also harkened back to classical traditions of architecture, placing the capitol comfortably among other accepted symbols of republican authority in the United States. As elected officials and civil servants moved into the building, it became the active and vibrant home of state government. Throughout the twentieth century the growing bureaucracy placed increased demands on the edifice and required a cornucopia of new structures surrounding the capitol to house the state's expanding authority. With age came wear, but rarely did responses to the statehouse's deteriorating condition fully address the substantial problems. Indeed, at times changes to the capitol amounted to outright threats to the building's historical and structural integrity. The lack of a successful historic preservation project, even with the necessary but limited life safety repairs, and the implementation of security that isolated the people from their building further weakened the edifice's position as the representation of collective identity for all Coloradoans. Yet as the twenty-first century commenced the capitol stood as proud as ever on Brown's Bluff, belying the largely unanswered problems of physical decay and general apathy concerning the survival of this essential symbol "too important to neglect."

Public edifices that dominate a cultural landscape convey hope for the immortality of society, as Thomas Holgrave eventually discovered in *The House of the Seven Gables*. He observed that in such buildings "the lapse of years might have been adding venerableness to [their] original beauty, and thus giving that impression of permanence, which I consider essential to the happiness of any one moment." Holgrave's enlightenment affords the people of Colorado an important insight into the purpose and needs of their statehouse. As Elijah Myers prophesized in 1886, "In our advanced American civilization there need be no apprehension that the Capitol building of Colorado will not stand, a handsome and stately structure, the admiration of future ages."[26] The statehouse is the people's building, an expression of their principles and a stage for their opinions. It remains the principal symbol of the authority of representative government and collective identity. As the twenty-first century progresses, the need to preserve and restore the structure both physically and emotionally, ensuring an existence as bright as the shine of the gold dome, dominates any interpretation of the statehouse's story. With proper care the Colorado State Capitol, the legacy of all the people of the Centennial State, will forever be the admiration of future ages.

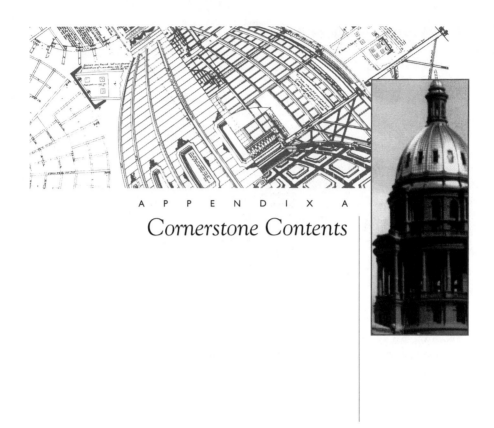

APPENDIX A

# Cornerstone Contents

The cornerstone for the Colorado State Capitol, laid on July 4, 1890, by the Grand Lodge of Colorado, contains a number of artifacts that describe the state in the late nineteenth century. Here is a list of the documents and objects placed in the copper box sealed in the cornerstone:

1811 edition of the journal of Capt. Zebulon Pike's 1806–1807 expedition

Artist's rendering of how the completed capitol would appear

Autographs of members of the Board of Capitol Managers

Business card of Edward S. Day, who built and donated the copper box for the cornerstone

Cane made from part of the keel of the USS *Constitution* ("Old Ironsides"), donated by Mark A. Richenbach

Copies of the 1889 annual reports for the Horticultural and Forestry Association, Insurance Department, Veterinary Sanitation Board, State Veterinary Surgeon, State

Historical and Natural History Society, State Agricultural College, Chamber of Commerce, and Board of Trade

Copies of the 1889 biennial reports for the Secretary of State, State Auditor, State Treasurer, Superintendent of Public Instruction, Attorney General, State Engineer, Adjutant General, Inspector of Coal Mines, and Forest Commission

Copies of the biennial reports of the Board of Capitol Managers for 1884, 1886, and 1888

Copies of the Declaration of Independence and United States Constitution

Copy of a report on state natural resources

Copy of Governor Job A. Cooper's 1889 Thanksgiving proclamation

Copy of Governor Cooper's inaugural address, January 8, 1889

Copy of the 1876 statehood Enabling Act

Copy of the 1885 state census

Copy of the 1890 Geddes and Seerie construction contract

Copy of the Colorado State Constitution

Copy of the most recent map of Colorado

Copy of the rules and rosters of standing committees of the Seventh General Assembly

Denver city directory for 1890

Editions of the *Rocky Mountain News*, *Denver Times*, *Denver Republican*, *Weekly Commonwealth*, and other Colorado newspapers for July 4, 1890

Gold and silver coins in various denominations

Holy Bible, donated by Charles Johnson, Governor Cooper's personal secretary

Impression of the state seal

Information on Masonic bodies in Denver and Colorado

List of 1890 executive and judicial officers

List of donors of land for the capitol

List of the cornerstone contents

List of members of the Seventh General Assembly (served 1889–1890)

Roster of executive staff and members of the Colorado National Guard

Schedule of capitol construction and copies of the instructions for contractors

Transcript of the cornerstone ceremony, July 3, 1890, for the Denver Masonic temple

Transcript of the Masonic cornerstone ceremony ritual

Transcripts of the cornerstone ceremony addresses of Governor Cooper, former governor Alva Adams, and Judge James B. Belford

United States flag, donated by Governor Cooper

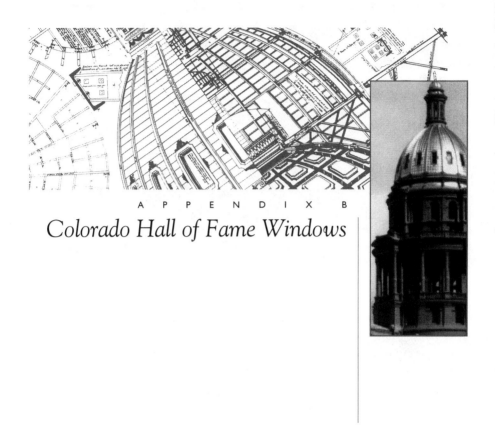

A P P E N D I X  B

# Colorado Hall of Fame Windows

A T THE END OF THE NINETEENTH CENTURY, the Board of Capitol Managers honored sixteen Colorado pioneers with stained glass windows in the dome. This list includes some of the better-known potential honorees considered by the board, culled from the substantial roster of possible choices. The managers chose Hughes, Ouray, Carson, Denver, Baker, Eaton, and Byers, in that order, on August 11, 1899. Gilpin and Evans were selected next, on November 24, 1899. Completing the Colorado Hall of Fame, on July 13, 1900, the managers picked Hill, Barela, Palmer, Majors, Buckingham, Dyer, and Jacobs, in that order. A star (*) denotes persons chosen by the managers for the honor. A cross (†) denotes suggested persons later honored with a stained glass window elsewhere in the Colorado State Capitol.

James Archer
James Baker*
Casimiro Barela*
Jim Beckwourth

Mary Bent
William Bent
Benjamin Bonneville
Albert G. Boone

Jim Bridger
Clara Brown†
Richard G. Buckingham*
Elizabeth Byers
William N. Byers*
Kit Carson*
Edwin Carter
Jerome B. Chaffee
George M. Chilcott
John M. Chivington
D. C. Collier
Alexander Cummings
James W. Denver*
John L. Dyer*
Benjamin Eaton*
Samuel Elbert
Joel Estes
John Evans*
Eugene Field
John C. Frémont
William Gilpin*
Owen J. Goldrick
John H. Gregory
John W. Gunnison
Horace M. Hale
Frank Hall
Moses Hallett
Bret Harte
Ferdinand V. Hayden
Lafayette Head
Nathaniel P. Hill*
Charles F. Holly
Sam Houston
John D. Howland
Bela M. Hughes*
Alexander C. Hunt†
Andrew Jackson
Helen H. Jackson
William H. Jackson
Frances Jacobs*

Thomas Jefferson
George Johnson
Matilda K. Kelly
William H. Larimer
Stephen H. Long
William A.H. Loveland
Joseph P. Machebeuf
Alexander Majors*
Randolph B. Marcy
Lucien Maxwell
Cyrus McLaughlin
J. A. McMurtrie
Otto Mears†
Arvilla D. Meeker
Josephine Meeker
Nathan C. Meeker
Katrina W. Murat
Edward S. Nettleton
Ouray*
William J. Palmer*
Zebulon Pike
Frederick J. Pitkin
James H. Platt
James Pursley
Sylvester Richardson
John Routt†
William G. Russell
Mary F. Shields
John P. Slough
Richard Sopris
Ceran St. Vrain
Robert W. Steele
Augusta Tabor
Horace A.W. Tabor
Samuel F. Tappan
David K. Wall
Lewis L. Weld
Beverly D. Williams
Ezekiel Williams

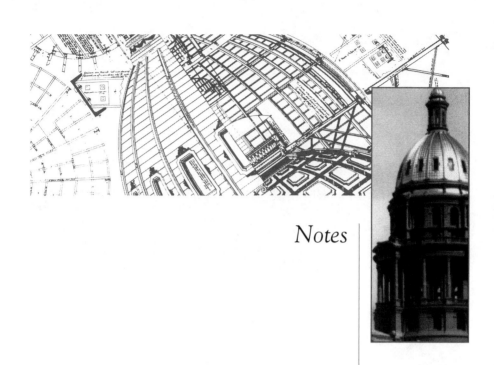

Notes

## ABBREVIATIONS

| | |
|---|---|
| CSA | Colorado State Archives, Denver |
| DWM | David W. Mullins Library, University of Arkansas, Fayetteville |
| ISC | Indiana Supreme Court Law Library, Indiana State House, Indianapolis |
| LJS | Leslie J. Savage Library, Western State College, Gunnison, Colorado (Aberdeen box) |
| LL | Legislative Library, Colorado State Capitol, Denver |
| SCL | Colorado State Supreme Court Library, Denver |

## INTRODUCTION: THE HEART OF COLORADO

1. See Malcolm L. Comeaux, "Attempts to Establish and Change a Western Boundary," *Annals of the Association of American Geographers* 72: 2 (June 1982), 254–271; Thomas J. Noel, Paul F. Mahoney, and Richard E. Stevens, *Historical Atlas of Colorado* (Norman: University of Oklahoma Press, 1994), 1, 3, 5, 7; William Wyckoff, *Creating*

*Colorado: The Making of a Western American Landscape, 1860–1940* (New Haven: Yale University Press, 1999), 1–23.

2. "State Dedicates New Gold Dome," *Denver Post*, October 11, 1950, 1.

3. Jay M. Price, "Capitol Improvements: Style and Image in Arizona's and New Mexico's Public Architecture," *Journal of Arizona History* 41: 4 (Winter 2000), 353; John A. Straayer, *The Colorado General Assembly* (Niwot: University Press of Colorado, 2000), 337.

4. Henry-Russell Hitchcock and William Seale, *Temples of Democracy: The State Capitols of the U.S.A.* (New York: Harcourt Brace Jovanovich, 1976); Charles T. Goodsell, *The American Statehouse: Interpreting Democracy's Temples* (Lawrence: University Press of Kansas, 2001); Charles T. Goodsell, "The Architecture of Parliaments: Legislative Houses and Political Culture," *British Journal of Political Science* 18: 3 (July 1988), 287–302.

5. Don Severin, *The Encyclopedia of State Capitols and Capitals: A Detailed Look at the 50 Capitol Buildings and the Capital Cities* (Cove, OR: Mt. Fanny, 1999); Thomas G. Aylesworth, *State Capitals* (New York: Gallery, 1990); Eldon Hauck, *American Capitols: An Encyclopedia of the State, National, and Territorial Capital Edifices of the United States* (Jefferson, NC: McFarland, 1991); Clarice Eleanore Moffett, "History of Colorado's Capitals and Capitols" (M.A. thesis, University of Denver, 1936); William R. Pyle, "History of the Colorado State Capitol Complex" (M.A. thesis, University of Denver, 1962); Margaret Coel, Gladys Doty, and Karen Gilleland, *Under the Golden Dome: Colorado's State Capitol* (Boulder: Colorado and West, 1985); Margaret Coel, *The Pride of Our People: The Colorado State Capitol* (Denver: Colorado General Assembly, 1992).

## CHAPTER 1: SOMETHING SOLEMNLY FUNNY, SETTLEMENT–1886

1. Carl Ubbelohde, Maxine Benson, and Duane A. Smith, *A Colorado History* (Boulder: Pruett, 1995 [1965]), 94; extract in James H. Baker (ed.), *History of Colorado*, V. 2 (Denver: Linderman, 1927), 485–486.

2. Baker, *History of Colorado*, V. 2, 486; Constitution of the Provisional Government of Jefferson Territory, Article V, Section 5, printed in *Rocky Mountain News*, October 20, 1859, 2; *Rocky Mountain News*, November 10, 1859; Wilbur Fisk Stone (ed.), *History of Colorado*, V. 1 (Chicago: S. J. Clarke, 1918), 171.

3. U.S. Serial Set, vol. 1027, Thirty-sixth Congress, First Session, Senate executive document 15, February 20, 1860, 1–23; Baker, *History of Colorado*, V. 2, 489–490.

4. Jerome C. Smiley (ed.), *History of Denver With Outlines of the Earlier History of the Rocky Mountain Country* (Denver: Times-Sun, 1901), 318, 490; Howard R. Lamar, *The Far Southwest, 1846–1912: A Territorial History* (Albuquerque: University of New Mexico Press, 2000 [1966]), 190.

5. Baker, *History of Colorado*, V. 2, 490; Mark Twain [Samuel L. Clemens], *Roughing It* (New York: Penguin, 1985 [1872]), 205.

6. "Local Matters," *Rocky Mountain News*, September 7, 1861, 3; Stone, *History of Colorado*, V. 1, 172; Lamar, *The Far Southwest*, 204.

7. *Rocky Mountain News*, October 14, 1861, 2.

8. Harry E. Kelsey Jr., *Frontier Capitalist: The Life of John Evans* (Boulder: Pruett, 1969) 121; Irving Howbert, *Memories of a Lifetime in the Pike's Peak Region* (Glorieta, NM: Rio Grande, 1925), 72–74; Territorial Laws of Colorado, 1861, 63; William C. Prochaska, "Colorado City, Colorado, 1859–1870" (M.A. thesis, Western State College of Colorado, 1980), 38.

9. Howbert, *Memories of a Lifetime*, 74–75.

10. Territorial Laws of Colorado, 1862, 99; Smiley, *History of Denver*, 493; John D.W. Guice, *The Rocky Mountain Bench: The Territorial Supreme Courts of Colorado, Montana, and Wyoming, 1861–1890* (New Haven: Yale University Press, 1972), 22.

11. Quoted in Georgina Brown, *The Shining Mountains* (Gunnison, CO: B&B, 1976), 29, 31; "Local Matters," *Rocky Mountain News*, February 5, 1864, 3.

12. Kelsey, *Frontier Capitalist*, 156. The historiography of the Sand Creek Massacre is extensive. For a good overview see Kelly Barlow, "A Legacy of Controversy: Public Opinion and the Sand Creek Massacre," HY 511 historiographical essay, Colorado State University, December 2002.

13. Brown, *Shining Mountains*, 30.

14. George W. Collins, "Colorado's Territorial Secretaries," *Colorado Magazine* 43: 3 (Summer 1966), 197–198; Richard J. Broad Jr., *When Golden Was the Capital* (Golden, CO: Mt. Lookout Chapter DAR, 1922), 3; Lamar, *The Far Southwest*, 224–228; Richard Gardner, "Territorial Executive's Mansion Is 130," *Golden Transcript*, May 17, 1994.

15. Ubbelohde, Benson, and Smith, *A Colorado History*, 139; Elbert quoted in Baker, *History of Colorado*, V. 2, 505.

16. *Rocky Mountain News*, December 7, 1866, 4.

17. Territorial Laws of Colorado, 1867, 90–91; quote about Golden in Smiley, *History of Denver*, 493; Lorraine Wagenbach and Jo Ann Thistlewood, *Golden: The 19th Century* (Littleton, CO: Harbinger House, 1987), 15; Broad, *When Golden Was the Capital*, 3; Robert G. Athearn, *The Coloradans* (Albuquerque: University of New Mexico Press, 1976), 66.

18. Ubbelohde, Benson, and Smith, *A Colorado History*, 115.

19. "Men Who Are Building Up Colorado," *Denver Times*, November 17, 1901, 3; William J. Barker, "Brown's Bluff," *Denver Post Empire Magazine*, December 28, 1958, 10; Smiley, *History of Denver*, 956–958; Thomas J. Noel, *Denver's Larimer Street: Main Street, Skid Row and Urban Renaissance* (Denver: Historic Denver, Inc., 1981), 75.

20. Samuel Bowles, *The Parks and Mountains of Colorado: A Summer Vacation in the Switzerland of America, 1868*, ed. James H. Pickering (Norman: University of Oklahoma Press, 1991 [1869]), 60; Charlotte A. Barbour, "Vanished Neighborhood on Capitol Hill, Denver," *Colorado Magazine* 37: 4 (October 1960), 254–264; Smiley, *History of Denver*, 374; Phil Goodstein, *The Ghosts of Denver: Capitol Hill* (Denver: New Social Publications, 1996), 11, 15–19; Wyckoff, *Creating Colorado*, 112–114.

21. U.S. Serial Set, vol. 1436, Forty-first Congress, Second Session, House of Representatives report 27, February 16, 1870, 1–3; Territorial Laws of Colorado, 1872, 66–67, 235–236; U.S. Serial Set, vol. 1526, Forty-second Congress, Second Session,

House of Representatives miscellaneous document 123, March 11, 1872, 1–2. See also Earl S. Pomeroy, *The Territories and the United States, 1861–1890: Studies in Colonial Administration* (Seattle: University of Washington Press, 1969 [1947]), 41–42.

22. "The Capital Question," *Rocky Mountain News*, February 3, 1874, 2; Smiley, *History of Denver*, 460; Territorial Laws of Colorado, 1874, 63–65.

23. Frank Hall, *History of the State of Colorado*, V. 2 (Chicago: Blakely, 1890), 485–487.

24. "The Legislature," *Rocky Mountain News*, February 10, 1874, 4; Smiley, *History of Denver*, 90–91, 506–507.

25. Byers quote in "Capitol Buildings," *Denver Tribune*, May 6, 1875; Baker, *History of Colorado*, V. 2, 520–521.

26. Enabling Act of Colorado, 1875, Section 8; Colorado State Constitution, 1876, Article VIII, Section 4, and Schedule, Section 3.

27. Extract in "Lot Jumping," *Denver Tribune*, May 10, 1879; "Mr. Brown's Trespass," *Denver Tribune*, May 15, 1879; Smiley, *History of Denver*, 866; Martin A. Wenger, "Raising the Gold-Plated Dome," in *1952 Brand Book of the Denver Posse of the Westerners*, ed. Elvon L. Howe (Denver: Arthur Zeuch, 1953), 110.

28. "Mr. Brown's Trespass," *Denver Tribune*, May 15, 1879; "Mr. Brown Gets the Bounce," *Rocky Mountain News*, October 16, 1879, 8; Frank Hall, *History of the State of Colorado*, V. 3 (Chicago: Blakely, 1891), 92.

29. Colorado Reports, April 1881 Term, 496–497, 501, 505.

30. Session Laws of Colorado, 1881, 41–43; *Denver Tribune* quoted in *Rocky Mountain News*, October 25, 1881.

31. Moffett, "History of Colorado's Capitals and Capitols," 44–46; Smiley, *History of Denver*, 508; Juan Espinosa, "Looking for a Fair Trade?" *Pueblo Chieftain*, January 11, 2004.

32. "The Capitol Building," *Denver Tribune*, November 10, 1881; Session Laws of Colorado, 1881, 43–44.

33. United States Reports, October 1882 Term, 95, 98; "Colorado's Capitol," *Denver Tribune*, November 21, 1882, 1.

34. "The Site Suit," *Rocky Mountain News*, January 12, 1884, 9; "Will Go Higher," *Rocky Mountain News*, February 9, 1884, 5.

35. Board of Capitol Managers, Records Book A, April 15, 1885; United States Reports, October 1885 Term, 598–600.

36. Letter from Theodore H. Thomas to the Board of Capitol Managers, February 10, 1886, CSA box 32199.

## CHAPTER 2: DIGNITY OF APPEARANCE, 1883–1886

1. Thomas Paine, *Common Sense* (London: Penguin, 1986 [1776]), 67.

2. Charles Lummis, *Letters From the Southwest: September 20, 1884, to March 14, 1885*, ed. James W. Byrkit (Tucson: University of Arizona Press, 1989), 51; Wyckoff, *Creating Colorado*, 113. See also William Willard Howard, "The City of Denver," *Harper's Weekly*, April 23, 1887, 299; Edwards Roberts, "The City of Denver," *Harper's Monthly* 76: 456 (1888), 944–957.

3. "His Last Words," *Rocky Mountain News*, January 5, 1883, 3; Session Laws of Colorado, 1883, 44–50.

4. "The Capitol Commissioners," *Rocky Mountain News*, February 26, 1883, 6; Session Laws of Colorado, 1883, 45, 48.

5. Records Book A, March 1, March 8, April 23, 1883; Hall, *History of the State of Colorado*, V. 3, 95; First Biennial Report of the Board of Capitol Managers, 1884, 9–12. The Nettleton plans for erecting the "Tuebor" design were found in CSA box 32209.

6. First Biennial Report, 1884, 12–13; "Capitol Commissioners," *Rocky Mountain News*, June 5, 1883, 8.

7. Hitchcock and Seale, *Temples of Democracy*, 148, 157–158.

8. "Capitol Commissioners," *Rocky Mountain News*, June 5, 1883, 8; First Biennial Report, 1884, 13, 17–19; Records Book A, June 9, 1883.

9. First quote in "The Capitol Question," *Rocky Mountain News*, June 10, 1883, 1; First Biennial Report, 1884, 19–21, 23–50; Records Book A, June 20, October 8, December 4, 1883; second quote in "The Extra Session," *Rocky Mountain News*, June 19, 1883, 1; "The Capitol Question," *Rocky Mountain News*, June 21, 1883, 2; Hall, *History of the State of Colorado*, V. 3, 96; Smiley, *History of Denver*, 508.

10. Records Book A, December 1, 1884; Report of the Committee on Building Stone to the Board of Capitol Managers, July 3, 1884; Smiley, *History of Denver*, 509.

11. Session Laws of Colorado, 1885, 53–59; Records Book A, April 15, 1885; Second Biennial Report of the Board of Capitol Managers, 1886, 6–9.

12. Letter from Elijah E. Myers to the Board of Capitol Managers, April 24, 1885, CSA box 32199; "Capitol Commissioners," *Rocky Mountain News*, June 5, 1883, 8.

13. William Elton Green, "'A Question of Great Delicacy': The Texas Capitol Competition, 1881," *Southwestern Historical Quarterly* 92: 2 (October 1988), 264; "The State Capitol: A Grand Old Dame Reaches One Hundred," *Michigan History* 62: 4 (November-December 1978), 17–18; quote in Paul Goeldner, "The Designing Architect: Elijah E. Myers," *Southwestern Historical Quarterly* 92: 2 (October 1988), 273–274; Hitchcock and Seale, *Temples of Democracy*, 174–177. See also "'Tuebor': The Capitol Craftstmanship of Elijah E. Myers," *Michigan History* 62: 4 (November-December 1978), 22–28.

14. William Seale, *Michigan's Capitol: Construction and Restoration* (Ann Arbor: University of Michigan Press, 1995), 13; Smiley, *History of Denver*, 543–547; Goeldner, "Designing Architect," 275–277; Green, "A Question of Great Delicacy," 270; Hitchcock and Seale, *Temples of Democracy*, 160, 178, 180–188, 196; Willard B. Robinson, "Pride of Texas: The State Capitol," *Southwestern Historical Quarterly* 92: 2 (October 1988), 236.

15. Hitchcock and Seale, *Temples of Democracy*, 178, 193; Goeldner, "Designing Architect," 287.

16. Second Biennial Report, 1886, 9–10, 15–16; Records Book A, July 13, July 14, July 15, August 31, 1886.

17. "Colorado's Capitol," *Rocky Mountain News*, September 1, 1885, 8.

18. Damie Stillman, "From the Ancient Roman Republic to the New American One: Architecture for a New Nation," in *A Republic for the Ages: The United States Capitol and the Political Culture of the Early Republic*, ed. Donald R. Kennon

(Charlottesville: University Press of Virginia, 1999), 275, 281, 293, 315; Goodsell, "Architecture of Parliaments," 290; Second Biennial Report, 1886, 61–62.

19. Quote in Goodsell, *American Statehouse*, 15, 186–187; Goodsell, "Architecture of Parliaments," 287.

20. Straayer, *Colorado General Assembly*, 1, 4, 7, 127, 256, 335.

21. Second Biennial Report, 1886, quote on 62, 64. In another example of governmental symbolism, the color scheme of the legislative chambers in the early twentieth century matches that of Great Britain's Parliament. The House of Representatives is predominantly green, like the House of Commons, whereas the Senate's red carpet echoes the design of the House of Lords.

22. Hanno-Walter Kruft, *A History of Architectural Theory From Vitruvius to the Present*, trans. Ronald Taylor, Elsie Callander, and Anthony Wood (New York: Princeton Architectural Press, 1994), 360–361; Goodsell, "Architecture of Parliaments," 288; Goodsell, *American Statehouse*, 113, 131. Myers designed the height of each floor to correspond with its perceived importance in the governmental process. The subbasement stands twelve feet six inches high, the basement fourteen feet one inch, the first floor twenty feet, the second floor twenty feet three inches, and the third floor nineteen feet eleven inches.

23. Second Biennial Report, 1886, 63–70, 72.

24. Ibid., 74; Goodsell, "Architecture of Parliaments," 295–296.

25. Quote in Fred J. Maroon and Suzy Maroon, *The United States Capitol* (New York: Stewart, Tabori and Chang, 1993), 43.

26. Second Biennial Report, 1886, 65, 75; Ross King, *Brunelleschi's Dome: How a Renaissance Genius Reinvented Architecture* (New York: Penguin, 2000), 10.

27. Hitchcock and Seale, *Temples of Democracy*, 192–193.

28. Robert L. Chase, "Sure, It's Real Gold on Capitol," *Rocky Mountain News*, October 5, 1950, 27.

29. Wenger, "Raising the Gold-Plated Dome," 127; Paul D. Harrison, "Building Colorado's Capitol," in *1959 Brand Book of the Denver Posse of the Westerners*, ed. Raymond G. Colwell (Boulder: Johnson, 1960), 217, 223.

30. Pyle, "History of the Colorado State Capitol Complex," 40, 82–83; Moffett, "History of Colorado's Capitals and Capitols," 76–77.

31. Coel, *Pride of Our People*, 3; Coel, Doty, and Gilleland, *Under the Golden Dome*, 6–7; "Legislative and State House Blue Book of Colorado" (Denver: Carson-Harper and W. H. Lawrence, 1899), 7, 10; Colorado Writers' and Art Programs, *Colorado Capitol Buildings* (Denver: Colorado Advertising and Publicity Committee, 1939), 3.

32. Bill Handley, "Why We Like the Capitol: A New Theory," *Colorado State Capitol Tour Guide Newsletter* (October 1997).

33. "The Colorado Capitol," *Harper's Weekly*, May 1, 1886, 283; Records Book A, January 2, January 4, 1886; Second Biennial Report, 1886, 66.

### CHAPTER 3: FROM HER OWN ETERNAL HILLS, 1886–1893

1. Second Biennial Report, 1886, 16, 29–30; Records Book A February 20, March 1, 1886; "The Contract Let," *Fort Collins Express*, April 3, 1886, 1.

2. "Fort Collins Sandstone," *Larimer County Express*, April 2, 1880, 3; quote in "Stout Stone Favored," *Fort Collins Express*, March 27, 1886, 1; Records Book A, March 29, 1886; "Colorado Stone Industries," *Silver Standard*, August 13, 1887, 4; "Stout and Stone," *Fort Collins Express Columbian Industrial Edition*, 1894, 10; Kenneth Jessen, *Railroads of Northern Colorado* (Boulder: Pruett, 1982), 46–60.

3. Records Book A, April 1, 1886; Second Biennial Report, 1886, 22–29.

4. Second Biennial Report, 1886, 55; Letter from William D. Richardson to the Board of Capitol Managers, June 17, 1886, CSA box 32199; quote in *Fort Collins Express*, July 24, 1886, 1; Board of Capitol Managers, Records Book B, April 15, 1887; "Arkins," *Fort Collins Express Columbian Industrial Edition*, 1894, 36; Hall, *History of the State of Colorado*, V. 3, 98.

5. "Capitol Hill People Furious," *Denver Republican*, June 25, 1887; *Silver Standard*, July 2, 1887, 1; "The State Capitol," *Silver Standard*, November 12, 1887, 1.

6. "Granite for the Capitol," *Silver Standard*, August 11, 1887, 2; quote in "Our Coming Boom," *Silver Standard*, August 20, 1887, 2; "The Granite Quarries of Silver Plume and Brownville," *Silver Standard*, August 27, 1887, 3; *Silver Standard*, September 3, 1887, 1; *Silver Standard*, October 15, 1887, 3; Christine Bradley, *William A. Hamill: The Gentleman From Clear Creek* (Fort Collins: Colorado State University Cooperative Extension Service, 1977), 36; "Prosperity Demands It," *Silver Standard*, September 17, 1887, 2.

7. Records Book B, October 24, 1887; Letter from William D. Richardson to the Board of Capitol Managers, October 25, 1887, CSA box 32199; "Trouble at the Capitol," *Silver Standard*, November 5, 1887, 1; Third Biennial Report of the Board of Capitol Managers, 1888, 9–10.

8. "The State Capitol," *Silver Standard*, November 12, 1887, 1; *Silver Standard*, November 26, 1887, 2; quote in *Silver Standard*, December 31, 1887, 2; *Georgetown Courier*, January 5, 1888, 2; "The State Capitol," *Silver Standard*, February 4, 1888, 3; Records Book B, February 9, 1888; Board of Capitol Managers, Records Book C, December 6, 1891; Session Laws of Colorado, 1891, 54–55; Hall, *History of the State of Colorado*, V. 3, 99.

9. Records Book B, March 27, 1888; Third Biennial Report, 1888, 24–25.

10. Quote in Third Biennial Report, 1888, 28; "Gunnison Will Get It," *Gunnison Review-Press*, June 2, 1888, 1; "Brownville Quarry Started to Work," *Silver Standard*, July 21, 1888, 2; Rex Myers, "Railroads, Stone Quarries, and the Colorado State Capitol," *Journal of the West* 39: 2 (Spring 2000), 41.

11. Records Book B, May 7, November 7, 1888, June 14, 1889; Records Book C, August 21, 1889; "State Capitol," *Silver Standard*, July 14, 1888, 2; "A Granite Capitol," *Gunnison Review-Press*, January 31, 1889, 2; Session Laws of Colorado, 1889, 360–367; "Blue Book," 1899, 16; E. F. Tucker, *Otto Mears and the San Juans* (Montrose, CO: Western Reflections, 2003), 55.

12. *Silver Standard*, April 6, 1889, 2; "The Largest Stone Ever Quarried in Colorado," *Silver Standard*, April 13, 1889, 2; Records Book B, April 20, 1889; "Granite for the Capitol," *Silver Standard*, April 20, 1889, 2; Ann D. Zugelder, ed., "Frederick G. ZugelderCThe Man and His Role in the Quarrying Process," in *The Aberdeen Quarry*, by Ann D. Zugelder (Gunnison, CO: Publisher unknown, 1989), 22–23.

13. "Gunnison Granite Against the World," *Gunnison Review-Press*, April 23, 1889, 1; "The Capitol Commissioners' Visit," *Gunnison Review-Press*, April 27, 1889, 1; "Granite! Granite! Granite!" *Gunnison Review-Press*, May 9, 1889, 1; *Denver Republican* quote in "An Expert in Granite," *Silver Standard*, May 11, 1889, 2; "A Comparison of Granite," *Silver Standard*, May 11, 1889, 2; Records Book B, May 22, May 24, 1889; *Silver Standard*, May 25, 1889, 2.

14. Letter from James C. Pilling to the Board of Capitol Managers, June 19, 1889, CSA box 32199; Fourth Biennial Report of the Board of Capitol Managers, 1890, 18; Records Book B, June 26, 1889; "The State Capitol," *Silver Standard*, June 29, 1889, 1; *Silver Standard*, June 29, 1889, 2; "We 'Got There!'" *Gunnison Review-Press*, June 22, 1889, 1.

15. Session Laws of Colorado, 1889, 355–359, 362; Records Book B, June 1, 1889; "Mr. Myers Is Discharged," *Denver Republican*, June 4, 1889, 9.

16. "Mr. Myers Is Discharged," *Denver Republican*, June 4, 1889, 9; "The State Capitol Muddle," *Rocky Mountain News*, June 5, 1889, 4; Letter from Elijah E. Myers to the Board of Capitol Managers, September 26, 1889, CSA box 32199.

17. Green, "A Question of Great Delicacy," 270; Hitchcock and Seale, *Temples of Democracy*, 194; Goeldner, "Designing Architect," 279, 287.

18. "The Granite Quarry," *Gunnison Review-Press*, June 25, 1889, 1; "Gunnison Granite," *Gunnison Review-Press*, June 29, 1889, 1; "Rising State Capitol," *Denver Republican*, October 22, 1890, 7; Fourth Biennial Report, 1890, 16–17; Wallace Moore, "Aberdeen, Thriving Town of 150 Inhabitants, Supplied Granite for Colorado State Capitol," in *The Aberdeen Quarry*, ed. Zugelder, 30–31.

19. Records Book C, July 3, 1889, January 21, November 5, 1890; William Cronon, *Nature's Metropolis: Chicago and the Great West* (New York: W. W. Norton, 1991), 312.

20. "The Granite Quarries," *Gunnison Review-Press*, September 17, 1889, 1; Seerie quote in "Aberdeen Granite Quarries," *Gunnison Review-Press*, March 8, 1890, 1; *Gunnison Review-Press*, May 17, 1890, 4; "Instantly Killed," *Gunnison Review-Press*, May 24, 1890, 4.

21. "The People," *Rocky Mountain News*, July 5, 1890, 1. The managers did not approve the inscriptions on the north and east faces of the cornerstone until November 30, 1896. This description of the cornerstone ceremony comes primarily from the lengthy *News* article.

22. Maroon and Maroon, *The United States Capitol*, 27–29; Allison S. Cartwright, "A Capitol Investment," *Michigan History* 72: 6 (November-December 1988), 26, 30; Wayne C. Temple, "Reminders of Lincoln in a Cornerstone," *Lincoln Herald* 68: 3 (1966), 149–159; Rick Ewig, Linda G. Rollins, and Betty Griffin, *Wyoming's Capitol* (Cheyenne: Wyoming State Press, 1987), 3–4.

23. "Rising State Capitol," *Denver Republican*, 7; Records Book C, April 14, May 14, 1891; Session Laws of Colorado, 1889, 47; Fourth Biennial Report, 1890, 18; Don Etter and Carolyn Etter, *Forgotten Dreamer: Reinhard Schuetze, Denver's Landscape Architect* (Denver: Denver Public Library Western History Collection, 2001), 13.

24. "Welcomed," *Rocky Mountain News*, May 13, 1891, 1–3.

25. Quarrymen's National Union Branch 46 Records Book April 4, 1891, 3–5; Quarrymen's National Union Constitution, Article I, Section 2; Letter from William

Morgan to William Thompson, May 3, 1891, LJS; Letter from William Morgan to William Thompson, May 14, 1891, LJS; Gary M. Fink (ed.), *Labor Unions* (Westport, CT: Greenwood, 1977), 11, 136, 359; Marjory Harper, "Emigrant Strikebreakers: Scottish Granite Cutters and the Texas Capitol Boycott," *Southwestern Historical Quarterly* 95: 4 (April 1992), 465–486.

26. Letter from Walter E. Brooks to William Thompson, May 14, 1891; Branch 46 Records Book, May 30, 1891; Letter from John J. Byron to Peter Olsen, June 2, 1891, LJS.

27. Branch 46 Records Book, May 30, 1891; "The Men Struck," *Gunnison Tribune*, June 6, 1891, 3; Letter from John J. Byron to Peter C. Olsen, June 8, 1891, LJS; Wallace Moore and Lois Borland, "Quarrying the Granite for the State Capitol," *Colorado Magazine* 24: 2 (March 1947), 52.

28. *Gunnison Tribune*, June 13, 1891, 4; Moore, "Aberdeen," 32; Aberdeen box (strike settlement document), LJS.

29. Branch 46 Records Book, April 1, 1892; "Granite for Chicago," *Gunnison Tribune*, June 25, 1897, 1; "Gunnison Granite Quarry at Aberdeen," *Gunnison News-Champion*, February 12, 1909, 1; United States Geological Survey Bulletin 540 (Washington, DC: General Printing Office, 1914), 359–362; Hall, *History of the State of Colorado*, V. 3, 102; "Aberdeen Granite Quarries at Gunnison," *Gunnison News-Champion*, December 12, 1929, 1; Moore, "Aberdeen," 33; Moore and Borland, "Quarrying the Granite for the State Capitol," 45.

30. Records Book C, March 25, May 4, August 3, September 10, October 5, November 11, 1892, January 4, May 3, 1893; Fifth Biennial Report of the Board of Capitol Managers, 1892, 13.

### CHAPTER 4: WORKING IN GOOD FAITH, 1893–1901

1. *Silver Standard*, January 14, 1888, 2.

2. Ubbelohde, Benson, and Smith, *A Colorado History*, 225.

3. Records Book C, February 1, 1893; Session Laws of Colorado, 1893, 72. See Alfrieda Gabiou, "The Burning of the First Capitol," *Gopher Historian* 23: 1 (1968), 5–8; Robinson, "Pride of Texas," 230–231; Ralph Emerson Twitchell, *The Leading Facts of New Mexican History*, V. 2 (Cedar Rapids, IA: Torch, 1912), 515. See also Sara E. Wermiel, *The Fireproof Building: Technology and Public Safety in the Nineteenth-Century American City* (Baltimore: Johns Hopkins University Press, 2000), 187–188.

4. Records Book C, April 12, August 2, November 1, November 10, December 6, 1893, February 7, July 24, August 27, October 3, 1894; Board of Capitol Managers, Records Book D, August 27, 1894; Smiley, *History of Denver*, 648; Wermiel, *Fireproof Building*, 164, 167–168.

5. Records Book C, February 1, February 15, April 10, 1894.

6. *Marble City Times*, February 16, 1894, 4; Duane Vandenbusche, *The Gunnison Country* (Gunnison, CO: B&B, Gunnison, Inc., 1980), 234–235.

7. Records Book C, April 10, 1894; E-mail from Jim Cappa to Derek Everett, July 17, 2002; Beulah Historical Society, *From Mace's Hole, the Way It Was, to Beulah, the Way It Is: A Comprehensive History of Beulah, Colorado* (Colorado Springs: Century, 1979), 115–117.

8. *Gunnison Review-Press*, May 4, 1889, 1; *Gunnison Tribune*, April 4, 1891, 2; *Marble City Times*, February 16, 1894, 4; *Marble City Times*, February 23, 1894, 1; *Marble City Times*, March 9, 1894, 4.

9. Records Book D, August 27, September 15, October 8, October 16, October 31, November 7, November 28, December 5, 1894, February 6, 1895; Sixth Biennial Report of the Board of Capitol Managers, 1894, 26. The Brunswick Balke Collender Company was most famous for building elaborately carved bars for saloons all over the American West in the late nineteenth century.

10. "In the New Capitol," *Rocky Mountain News*, November 10, 1894, 6; "Court Dedication," *Rocky Mountain News*, November 18, 1894, 9; "Blue Book," 1899, 73; Smiley, *History of Denver*, 768.

11. *Denver Times* quote in Moffett, "History of Colorado's Capitals and Capitols," 70–72; Uzzell quote in "Organized," *Rocky Mountain News*, January 3, 1895, 1. See also Elizabeth M. Cox, *Women State and Territorial Legislators, 1895–1995: A State-by-State Analysis, With Rosters of 6,000 Women* (Jefferson, NC: McFarland, 1996), 12–21; Quintard Taylor, *In Search of the Racial Frontier: African Americans in the American West, 1528–1990* (New York: W. W. Norton, 1998), 130.

12. Records Book D, January 2, 1895, June 1, 1896; "Blue Book," 1899, 8, 75–80; Smiley, *History of Denver*, 330, 372, 385, 768–769, 815.

13. Board of Capitol Managers, Records Book E, February 27, November 30, 1897; Eighth Biennial Report of the Board of Capitol Managers, 1898, 12; "Gossip From Denver and the State Capitol," *Gunnison News*, July 21, 1899, 3; "Blue Book," 1899, 8, 81–83.

14. *Gunnison Tribune*, April 4, 1891, 2.

15. "Capitol Grounds Plans," *Rocky Mountain News*, May 17, 1895, 8; Records Book D, May 16, June 20, July 3, August 5, 1895; Etter and Etter, *Forgotten Dreamer*, 14.

16. Records Book D, April 16, August 16, 1895.

17. "Terrible Explosion," *Denver Post*, August 19, 1895, 1; quote in "Twenty Bodies Found," *Denver Post*, August 21, 1895, 1; Dick Kreck, *Denver in Flames: Forging a New Mile High City* (Golden, CO: Fulcrum, 2000), 73–89.

18. Records Book D, August 30, November 1, 1895 (quote); "Gunnison Marble," *Gunnison Tribune*, November 8, 1895, 3; Duane Vandenbusche and Rex Myers, *Marble, Colorado: City of Stone* (Denver: Golden Bell, 1970), 25.

19. Records Book D, November 13, November 26, 1895, January 18, February 4, April 1, April 9, May 1, June 30, July 31, August 9, 1896; Records Book E, October 19, 1896, October 30, 1897, July 30, November 15, 1898; Seventh Biennial Report of the Board of Capitol Managers, 1896, 18; *Gunnison Tribune*, October 9, 1896, 2; Smiley, *History of Denver*, 974.

20. Records Book E, October 19, October 31, December 31, 1896.

21. Session Laws of Colorado, 1897, 132–134; Eighth Biennial Report, 1898, 36.

22. Fifth Biennial Report, 1892, 19; Records Book E, June 30, July 31, September 30, October 30, 1897, July 27, 1899; Board of Capitol Managers, Records Book F, May 28, June 1, June 6, 1900; Smiley, *History of Denver*, 884.

23. Much of the information about *The Closing Era* comes from a short composition in the capitol box of the Colorado Historical Society, written by the women's

group to chronicle the story of the statue. See also John R. Henderson, "The Indian and Buffalo Statue on the State Capitol Grounds," *Colorado Magazine* 13: 5 (September 1936), 183–186; Frederick Jackson Turner, "The Significance of the Frontier in American History," in Turner, ed., *The Frontier in American History* (New York: Dover, 1996 [1920]), 1.

24. Records Book D, May 1, 1896, June 1, June 30, 1897; Records Book E, September 30, November 30, 1896, April 30, June 1, August 31, 1897.

25. "Mourners at the Capitol," *Rocky Mountain News*, July 7, 1897, 2.

26. Records Book E, December 31, 1896, April 1, June 30 (first quote), July 30, September 2, in October 3, 1898 (second quote); Records Book F, February 25, 1901; Denver City Directory, 1899, 1189; Thomas J. Noel and Barbara S. Norgren, *Denver: The City Beautiful* (Denver: Historic Denver, 1987), 196; Ubbelohde, Benson, and Smith, *A Colorado History*, 234. See also James Whiteside, "It Was a Terror to the Horses: Bicycling in Gilded-Age Denver," *Colorado Heritage* (Spring 1991), 2–16.

27. "Imported Marble for State Capitol," *Denver Post*, August 27, 1898, 8; Editorial cartoon, *Denver Post*, August 31, 1898, 1.

28. Records Book E, November 15, November 30, 1898, April 19, June 3, 1899 (quote); "Change the Capitol Dome," *Denver Times*, December 1, 1898, 8; "What the Colorado Legislature Is Doing," *Gunnison News*, February 10, 1899, 2; "The Crystal River Mining District," *Marble City Times*, April 7, 1899, 4; "May Use Foreign Marble in the New Statehouse," *Denver Times*, April 16, 1899, 6; "Gossip From the Capital," *Gunnison News*, April 28, 1899, 2.

29. "An Explosion at the Capitol," *Rocky Mountain News*, January 3, 1899, 1, 5.

30. "Bryan on the Duties of Legislators," *Rocky Mountain News*, January 18, 1899, 1, 5. Bryan returned to address a joint session of the General Assembly in the House of Representatives chamber in February 1909.

31. "Gov. Cooper Buried at Riverside," *Rocky Mountain News*, January 24, 1899, 10; "In State at the Capitol," *Rocky Mountain News*, April 14, 1899, 2; "Homage of Hundreds," *Rocky Mountain News*, December 4, 1899, 2.

32. "Finish Capitol Within a Year," *Rocky Mountain News*, May 31, 1899, 4; Records Book E, July 26, 1899; Records Book F, November 30 (Thomas quote), December 26, 1899, January 31, 1900.

33. Records Book E, June 30, 1898, August 11, 1899; Records Book F, November 11, December 27, 1899, July 13, 1900; "Two Probable Pictures for the Dome," *Denver Post*, November 12, 1899, 8; "Their Faces May Appear in the Capitol Dome," *Denver Republican*, December 25, 1899, 10; Levette J. Davidson, "Colorado's Hall of Fame," *Colorado Magazine* 35: 3 (July 1958), 208–218; Mears quote in Mary Martin and Gene Martin, *Colorado's Hall of Fame: A Quick Picture History* (Colorado Springs: Little London, 1974), 1, 64.

34. Smiley, *History of Denver*, 950. For information on the capitol's cannon, see Derek R. Everett, "The Admiration of Future Ages: Colorado's State Capitol" (M.A. thesis, Colorado State University, 2003), 177n–178n.

35. Records Book F, September 13, October 5, 1900.

36. Deborah Frazier, "Eternal Marble," *Rocky Mountain News*, May 29, 2000, 7A, 9A; David Frey and Ed Kosmicki, "Marble," *Denver Post Empire Magazine*, August 10,

1997, 13–19; Linda Walker Sadler, "Marble Quarry Back in Business," *Rocky Mountain News*, August 8, 1990, 43; Vandenbusche and Myers, *Marble*, 37, 49, 132, 176–178.

37. See Beulah Historical Society, *From Mace's Hole*, 117.

38. "Capitol Building at Last Finished," *Denver Times*, June 11, 1903, 2; "Colorado's Capitol Almost Free of Debt," *Rocky Mountain News*, December 26, 1903, 7; Smiley, *History of Denver*, 513.

39. "Completion of Colorado's Capitol to Close Century," *Rocky Mountain News*, October 14, 1900, 14; Adams quote in David A. Shannon (ed.), *Beatrice Webb's American Diary, 1898* (Madison: University of Wisconsin Press, 1963), 111–115.

40. "Capitol Is Complete," *Denver Times*, October 7, 1900, 24; "Mile High Marker on Statehouse Steps to Stay," *Denver Post*, July 14, 1947, 24; "Geological Study Proves Capitol Step Is Mile High," *Rocky Mountain News*, February 4, 1952, 27; Smiley, *History of Denver*, 513. Improved technology in later decades led to new measurements of the mile-high marker, once by Colorado State University students in 1969 and the most recent study in 2003, resulting in three different altitude identifications on the west steps. See "New Mile-High Marker Placed by CSU Students at Capitol," *Denver Post*, May 12, 1969; Steve Lipsher, "No Tall Tale: State Higher Than Thought," *Denver Post*, July 7, 2002, 1A, 14A; John J. Sanko, "Mile High Step Is Lowered at Capitol," *Rocky Mountain News*, September 29, 2003, 6A; Dave Curtin, "13 Steps to Mile High," *Denver Post*, September 29, 2003; Mindy Sink, "Hoping Third Try Is Right, Mile High City Marks the Spot," *New York Times*, October 5, 2003, 18; E-mail from Lew Hopkins to Derek Everett, December 3, 2003.

## CHAPTER 5: THE WEIGHT PILED UPON IT, 1901–1921

1. Records Book F, December 20, 1900, February 7, February 25, March 20, 1901; Session Laws of Colorado, 1944, 35.

2. Session Laws of Colorado, 1901, 407–408; Board of Capitol Managers, Records Book G, November 29, 1902.

3. Tenth Biennial Report of the Board of Capitol Managers, 1902, 9–10; "Capitol Dome to Be Gilded," *Denver Times*, September 16, 1902, 2.

4. "Capitol Is Complete," *Denver Times*, October 7, 1900, 24; quote in "Globe for Dome," *Denver Times*, June 11, 1901; Smiley, *History of Denver*, 513.

5. "Married High in the Air, Where the Birds Fly," *Denver Times*, December 25, 1902, 1, 5; Smiley, *History of Denver*, 544. The capitol has hosted other weddings over the years, including one on the observation deck in 1937, officiated by a state representative with the attorney general as best man, and one on the west balcony off the House of Representatives chamber in the summer of 2002. See "Couple Select Capitol Dome as Spot for Sunset Wedding," *Denver Post*, May 9, 1937, 4.

6. Records Book F, April 30, October 10, November 7, 1901; William C. Jones and Kenton Forrest, *Denver: A Pictorial History* (Boulder: Pruett, 1973), 156.

7. "Thousands of Guests Unable to Enter the Capitol," *Rocky Mountain News*, January 14, 1903, 1, 5; Records Book G, April 2, 1903; "40,000 People Gather at the State Capitol," *Denver Post*, May 4, 1903, 5; "Denver Did Herself Proud With President Roosevelt," *Rocky Mountain News*, May 5, 1903, 1; Jones and Forrest, *Denver*, 157.

8. Eleventh Biennial Report of the Board of Capitol Managers, 1904, 8–9; Records Book G, March 17, 1905.

9. Records Book G, April 10, May 12, May 13, 1905; Board of Capitol Managers, Records Book H, March 7, 1906; Tucker, *Otto Mears*, 80–81; Colorado Legislative Council, "Memorials and Art in and Around the Colorado State Capitol: History of Memorials and Art in and Around the Capitol, in the Legislative Services Building, and in Lincoln Park," June 1992; Session Laws of Colorado, 1911, 693.

10. Session Laws of Colorado, 1905, 78–79; Twelfth Biennial Report of the Board of Capitol Managers, 1906, 11; Records Book H, October 11, 1907; Session Laws of Colorado, 1921, 736–737; "Civil War Work of State Told in Soldier Monument Tablets," *Denver Post*, July 27, 1923, 5; Irving W. Stanton, *Sixty Years in Colorado: Reminiscences and Reflections of a Pioneer of 1860* (Denver: Publisher unknown, 1922), 223–228.

11. Records Book H, August 3, 1905, February 7, 1906; Twelfth Biennial Report, 1906, 8.

12. "People From All Walks of Life Attend Funeral of Benefactor H. C. Brown," *Rocky Mountain News*, March 12, 1906, 7; "Portrait of Henry C. Brown, Donator of Capitol Site, Given State by Son," *Denver Republican*, July 2, 1910, 5; "Hundreds Pay Last Tribute to J. L. Routt," *Denver Post*, August 15, 1907, 1, 3; Joyce B. Lohse, *First Governor, First Lady: John and Eliza Routt of Colorado* (Palmer Lake, CO: Filter, 2002), 138–139. Contrary to James Brown's wishes, the portrait of his father now hangs in the west wing near the governor's office.

13. Charles A. Johnson, *Denver's Mayor Speer* (Denver: Green Mountain, 1969), 42–43, 59, 195; Edgar C. MacMechen (ed.), *Robert W. Speer: A City Builder* (Denver: Smith-Brooks, 1919), 46.

14. Records Book H, November 5, 1907; Thirteenth Biennial Report of the Board of Capitol Managers, 1908, 9–10, 46, 52.

15. "William C. Ferril," *Denver Post*, December 31, 1903, 4; extract from "DenverCThe City Beautiful," *Denver Post*, July 5, 1908; "Where Is Espinoza's Head?" *Denver Post*, November 12, 1899, 8; Smiley, *History of Denver*, 155; Ralph C. Taylor, *Colorado: South of the Border* (Denver: Sage, 1963), 210–216; Kelsey, *Frontier Capitalist*, 133, 289; Maxine Benson, "A Centennial Legacy," *Colorado Magazine* 57 (1981), 10, 12; Phil Goodstein, *The Seamy Side of Denver* (Denver: New Social Publications, 1993), 18–21; James E. Perkins, *Tom Tobin: Frontiersman* (Pueblo West, CO: Herodotus, 1999), 127–176.

16. Ubbelohde, Benson, and Smith, *A Colorado History*, 269–270; Tucker, *Otto Mears*, 83; quote in Thirteenth Biennial Report, 1908, 6–7.

17. Records Book H, November 11, December 10, 1908, January 7, 1909; "Plans Are Made for Sixty Room Capitol Addition," *Denver Post*, January 10, 1909, 2; "Gunnison Granite Quarry at Aberdeen," *Gunnison News-Champion*, February 12, 1909, 1; "New Wing to Capitol Favored by Governor," *Denver Post*, December 12, 1908, 4; Stephen J. Leonard, Thomas J. Noel, and Donald L. Walker Jr., *Honest John Shafroth: A Colorado Reformer* (Denver: Colorado Historical Society, 2003), 50.

18. Twelfth Biennial Report, 1906, 9; Records Book H, December 12, December 19, 1906, December 9, 1907, October 2, 1909; "State Museum Plans Have Been

Approved," *Denver Republican*, October 3, 1909, 6; Smiley, *History of Denver*, 646; Leonard, Noel, and Walker, *Honest John Shafroth*, 58; Henry S. Fellerman, "Will C. Ferril, Newspaperman and Historian," in *The 1961 Brand Book of the Denver Posse of the Westerners*, ed. Don L. Griswold (Boulder: Johnson, 1962), 256–257.

19. "Taft Is Substitute for Colorado's Sun," *Denver Republican*, September 22, 1909, 1; "Teddy Flays Solons Who Place Party Above People," *Rocky Mountain News*, August 30, 1910, 3; Leonard, Noel, and Walker, *Honest John Shafroth*, 63.

20. "To Determine the Status of the Capitol Board," *Denver Republican*, July 1, 1910, 12; "Small Prospect of Capitol Board Losing Out Now," *Denver Post*, July 2, 1910, 4.

21. Fourteenth Biennial Report of the Board of Capitol Managers, 1910, 7–10; "Big Statehouse Blast Imminent, Says Engineer: Cut Off the Gas," *Denver Times*, April 10, 1912, 3; Frank E. Edbrooke, "A Descriptive Report on the Finished Colorado State Museum Bldg.," submitted to the Board of Capitol Managers on March 30, 1912, CSA box 32200; Richard R. Brettell, *Historic Denver: The Architects and the Architecture, 1858–1893* (Denver: Historic Denver, 1973), 63.

22. "Federal Probe of Coal Strike to Open Today," *Rocky Mountain News*, February 9, 1914, 1, 3; "Juries Fixed, Officials Corrupt, Laws Blocked in Colorado Declares State Labor Chief Brake," *Denver Post*, February 10, 1914, 11; "Troops Sent to Strike Zone Never Needed, Asserts Lawson," *Rocky Mountain News*, February 12, 1914, 5; Carl Abbott, Stephen J. Leonard, and David McComb, *Colorado: A History of the Centennial State* (Niwot: University Press of Colorado, 1994), 153–154; Ubbelohde, Benson, and Smith, *A Colorado History*, 247–249.

23. "Denver Women in Mass Meeting Shout Protest Against the Massacre of Innocents at Ludlow," *Rocky Mountain News*, April 24, 1914, 7; "Thousands of Denver Women to March to Capitol and Demand of Ammons Withdrawal of Militia," *Denver Post*, April 24, 1914, 20; "500 Women Storm Capitol, Corner Squirming Governor, and Demand Strike War End," *Denver Post*, April 25, 1914, 1, 3; "Army of 1,000 Women Storm State Capitol and Force Gov. Ammons to Ask Wilson for Aid of Federal Troops," *Rocky Mountain News*, April 26, 1914, 4; "Army of Women Camps All Day at State House and Compels Writhing Governor to Do Bidding," *Denver Post*, April 26, 1914, 6; "Capitol Grounds Scene of Demonstration in Which Speakers Assail State Officials and Demand Action," *Rocky Mountain News*, April 27, 1914, 3; "Women Again Besiege Governor 8 Hours to Force Action Ending Coal Field War," *Rocky Mountain News*, April 28, 1914, 2.

24. "Capitol Board Spurns Law and Refuses to Buy Coal Supply of Lowest Bidders," *Denver Post*, December 19, 1914, 1, 3; "Threat of Grand Jury Investigation Hangs Over Capitol Managers' Heads," *Denver Post*, December 23, 1914, 1, 8; Session Laws of Colorado, 1917, 114–115; Eighteenth Biennial Report of the Board of Capitol Managers, 1918, 5.

25. "18,000 View Cody's Body, Doors Close Upon 12,000," *Rocky Mountain News*, January 15, 1917, 1; Louisa Ward Arps, *Denver in Slices: A Historical Guide to the City* (Athens: Swallow Press, Ohio University Press, 1959), 205.

26. "People of All Walks of Life Pay Their Tribute at Bier," *Rocky Mountain News*, January 14, 1911, 3; "10,000 at Bier Pay Tribute to Moffat," *Rocky Mountain*

*News*, March 24, 1911, 1, 5; "Colorado Pays Last Honor to Late ex-Governor Grant," *Rocky Mountain News*, November 5, 1911, 9; "Silent Thousands Pay Their Final Tribute as Body of Henry M. Teller Rests in Capitol," *Rocky Mountain News*, February 26, 1914, 4; "Honor to Peabody Is Paid by Denver," *Rocky Mountain News*, November 26, 1917, 5.

27. Eighteenth Biennial Report, 1918, 8.

28. Ibid.; "Colorado War Conference at the Capitol Building, Denver, May 7th and 8th, 1918," CSA box 32200; "Dome of State Capitol Will Be Opened Soon," *Rocky Mountain News*, March 6, 1920, 14.

29. "30,000 School Children and Parents Welcome President at Capitol," *Rocky Mountain News*, September 26, 1919, 3.

30. Session Laws of Colorado, 1919, 138–139; "Masons Laying Corner Stone for State Building," *Denver Post*, June 5, 1920, 4; Twentieth Biennial Report of the Board of Capitol Managers, 1922, 11, 16; Pyle, "History of the Colorado State Capitol Complex," 60.

31. Noel and Norgren, *Denver*, 24; Virginia McConnell, "For These High Purposes," *Colorado Magazine* 44: 3 (Summer 1967), 216–217; Johnson, *Denver's Mayor Speer*, 200, 216.

32. "Soldier Guards Pacing Statehouse Corridors," *Rocky Mountain News*, November 15, 1919, 4; "Lurid I.W.W. Stickers Plastered Thru Capitol," *Rocky Mountain News*, January 1, 1920, 1; Fink, *Labor Unions*, 151–154; Ubbelohde, Benson, and Smith, *A Colorado History*, 285; Abbott, Leonard, and McComb, *Colorado*, 279.

## CHAPTER 6: BEYOND THE SUNDOWN, 1921–1952

1. "Thousands Pay Final Tribute to Memory of John Shafroth," *Denver Post*, February 23, 1922, 9; "Friends of Senator Nicholson Gather Reverently at Bier to Pay Final Tribute of Respect," *Rocky Mountain News*, January 30, 1923, 1, 5.

2. "Carlson's Body to Lie in State," *Rocky Mountain News*, December 7, 1926, 5; Harvey T. Sethman, "Hundreds of Lads in Khaki File Past Queen of Rumania," *Rocky Mountain News*, November 11, 1926, 3.

3. Session Laws of Colorado, 1921, 865; Twentieth Biennial Report, 1922, 14; Session Laws of Colorado, 1923, 778–779; Twenty-first Biennial Report of the Board of Capitol Managers, 1924, 9; Twenty-second Biennial Report of the Board of Capitol Managers, 1926, 9; Session Laws of Colorado, 1927, 128–129, 763–764; Session Laws of Colorado, 1931, 872–873.

4. Quote in David M. Chalmers, *Hooded Americanism: The History of the Ku Klux Klan* (New York: New Viewpoints, 1981 [1965]), 126; James H. Davis, "Colorado Under the Klan," *Colorado Magazine* 42: 2 (Spring 1965), 94, 95, 104; Abbott, Leonard, and McComb, *Colorado*, 285; Stephen J. Leonard and Thomas J. Noel, *Denver: Mining Camp to Metropolis* (Niwot: University Press of Colorado, 1990), 199; David Sarasohn, "The Election of 1916: Realigning the Rockies," *Western Historical Quarterly* 11: 3 (July 1980), 298.

5. Davis, "Colorado Under the Klan," 96, 100–101, 106–107; Chalmers, *Hooded Americanism*, 133.

6. Ubbelohde, Benson, and Smith, *A Colorado History*, 298–309; Abbott, Leonard, and McComb, *Colorado*, 289–300.

7. Twenty-second Biennial Report, 1926, 7; first quote in "Colorado Runs Out of Rooms for Government," *Denver Post*, October 24, 1926, 9; "Crowded Capitol Shifts Offices to Make More Room," *Denver Post*, July 19, 1931, 5; Ubbelohde, Benson, and Smith, *A Colorado History*, 301; Harlean James, "Seven Southern State Capitols," *Social Forces* 4: 2 (December 1925), 394.

8. McConnell, "For These High Purposes," 218–219; Etter and Etter, *Forgotten Dreamer*, 15; Hitchcock and Seale, *Temples of Democracy*, 256; "Razing of Old Courthouse Is Under Way," *Denver Post*, November 29, 1933, 3.

9. Richard D. Lamm and Duane A. Smith, *Pioneers and Politicians: 10 Colorado Governors in Profile* (Boulder: Pruett, 1984), 128; quotes in Session Laws of Colorado, 1933, 210; Pyle, "History of the Colorado State Capitol Complex," 62; Letter from James Merrick to Governor John C. Vivian, October 1, 1945, CSA box 32227.

10. Frank Clay Cross, "Revolution in Colorado," *The Nation* 138: 3579 (February 7, 1934), 152–153; Johnson quote in Edgar M. Wahlberg, *Voices in the Darkness: A Memoir* (Boulder: Roberts Rinehart, 1983), 73–75; Lamm and Smith, *Pioneers and Politicians*, 130; Stephen J. Leonard, *Trials and Triumphs: A Colorado Portrait of the Great Depression, With FSA Photographs* (Niwot: University Press of Colorado, 1993), 54.

11. Session Laws of Colorado, 1931, 15; First Biennial Report of the Superintendent of Public Buildings, 1934, 6; "State Capitol Will Have New Elevators," *Denver Post*, September 13, 1935, 28; "Spirit of Colorado Depicted on Brass Elevator Doors," *Rocky Mountain News*, April 29, 1936, 2; "State Bureaus Must Pay Rent," *Rocky Mountain News*, November 28, 1934, 2; "State Departments Ordered to Pay Rent," *Denver Post*, November 28, 1934, 22.

12. "55,000 Roar City's Enthusiasm at Roosevelt's Visit to Denver," *Denver Post*, October 12, 1936, 1; "Secret Service Men Guard the President From Handshakers," *Denver Post*, October 12, 1936, 5.

13. "Statehouse Spy Plot Bared," *Rocky Mountain News*, March 19, 1937, 1, 7.

14. "Dictograph Jury Indicts Nine; Four Legislators Named," *Rocky Mountain News*, August 29, 1937, 1, 2; "News Reveals First Inkling of Scandal," *Rocky Mountain News*, August 29, 1937, 3; *News* quote in "That's That," *Denver Post*, August 29, 1937, 2.

15. "Realtors Join in Protesting State Building," *Denver Post*, December 12, 1937, 12; "All-State Committee Will Back up Tax Revolters' Demands on Governor," *Denver Post*, December 16, 1937, 1, 3; "State Offices Are Outgrown Before Built," *Denver Post*, December 26, 1937, 1, 2.

16. Second Biennial Report of the Superintendent of Public Buildings, 1936, 3; "Legislature to Be Asked for New Office Building," *Denver Post*, December 13, 1936, 10; "Ammons Tries to Buy 4 Lots for Building," *Rocky Mountain News*, October 7, 1937, 16; "$700,000 Plant for Capitol's Power Asked," *Denver Post*, June 8, 1938, 3; "Colorado Stone Wanted," *Rocky Mountain News*, October 14, 1937, 16; "Capitol Annex to Have Minnesota Granite Base," *Denver Post*, April 27, 1938, 12; "State Settles Building Row," *Rocky Mountain News*, May 15, 1938, 5; "Capitol Marble Ready to Ship," *Rocky Mountain News*, August 31, 1938, 7; Vandenbusch and Myers, *Marble*, 129–138; Pyle, "History of the Colorado State Capitol Complex," 69.

17. "Council Considers Offer of Paintings for State Capitol," *Denver Post,* September 29, 1938, 18; Fourth Biennial Report of the Superintendent of Public Buildings, 1940, 4; John C. Buechner, "Ferril and the West," in *Thomas Hornsby Ferril and the American West,* ed. Robert C. Baron, Stephen J. Leonard, and Thomas J. Noel (Golden, CO: Fulcrum, 1996), ix–x; Francis Wayne, "Murals in the State Capitol DomeCHonor to Charles Boettcher," *Denver Post,* June 30, 1940, 15; Jean W. Smith and Elaine C. Walsh, *Queen of the Hill: The Private Life of the Colorado Governor's Mansion* (Denver: A. B. Hirschfeld, 1979), 55; Alisa Zahller, "Allen Tupper True's State Capitol Mural Studies," *Colorado History Now* (February 2002), 8. Governor Richard D. Lamm appointed Ferril the state's fifth poet laureate in 1979, a position Ferril held until his death in 1988.

18. Ubbelohde, Benson, and Smith, *A Colorado History,* 321; Abbott, Leonard, and McComb, *Colorado,* 303–304.

19. Letter from James Merrick to Lieutenant Governor John C. Vivian, June 23, 1942, CSA box 32223; Letter from James Merrick to Governor Ralph Carr, September 15, 1942, CSA box 32223; Letter from James Merrick to Colorado State Capitol telephone operators, January 15, 1942, CSA box 32223; Letter from James Merrick to Governor Ralph Carr, December 15, 1942, CSA box 32223; Letter from Governor John Vivian to executive department heads, January 20, 1943, CSA box 32223.

20. Letter from Governor Ralph Carr to James Merrick, September 28,1942, CSA box 32223; Colorado War Bond Committee, "Colorado Defense Bond News," February 26, 1942.

21. Letter from Governor John Vivian to executive department heads, October 5, 1943, CSA box 32223; "Vivian Approves Pay Raise for Building Help Over Protests," *Denver Post,* October 13, 1943; Letter from James Merrick to Governor John Vivian, April 27, 1944, CSA box 32225; Herbert O. Brayer, "Status of Our State Archives Work," *Colorado Magazine* 21: 3 (May 1944), 118–119; "Plans Made to Use Less Space for State Offices," *Rocky Mountain News,* July 2, 1944, 15; Letter from James Merrick to Governor John Vivian, November 14, 1944, CSA box 32225; Herbert O. Brayer and Virgil V. Peterson, "Annual Report of the State Archivist of Colorado," *Colorado Magazine* 22: 1 (January 1945), 40–47; "Report of the Housing of Colorado Boards, Bureaus and Departments," CSA box 32228.

22. "Denver Roars Greeting to Truman; 65,000 Turn Out for Welcome," *Denver Post,* September 20, 1948, 3; quote in "25,000 Hear Truman in Front of Capitol," *Denver Post,* September 20, 1948, 3; "GOP 'Hypocrisy' Hit," *New York Times,* September 21, 1948, 1, 22.

23. Bert Hanna, "State Pays Respects to Ralph Carr," *Denver Post,* September 26, 1950, 1.

24. "Price-Pegging Doubles Value of Gold on State Capitol Dome," *Rocky Mountain News,* February 28, 1940, 8; "Somebody Really Ought to 'Gold Up' That Capitol Dome," *Denver Post,* September 6, 1942, 5; "Lackluster Statehouse Dome May Get Coat of Colorado Gold," *Denver Post,* March 2, 1948, 1; "State Senator to Ask Funds to Releaf Dome of Capitol With Gold," *Denver Post,* March 5, 1948, 16; Dan Cronin, "Statehouse Gets No Gold, No Guide, No Cash for Frills," *Rocky Mountain News,* April 28, 1949, 5; "Capitol Dome Gilders up in Air Over Pay," *Rocky Mountain News,*

August 16, 1950, 5; quote in "State Dedicates New Gold Dome," *Denver Post*, October 11, 1950, 1, 3.

25. "Governor Urges Building of State Office Space," *Denver Post*, November 15, 1950, 20; "Four Buildings Asked for State Agencies," *Rocky Mountain News*, November 16, 1950, 32; Tom Gavin, "State Office Building Proposed on Grant St. Side of Capitol Lawn," *Rocky Mountain News*, November 20, 1951, 5; Session Laws of Colorado, 1952, 187; Pyle, "History of the Colorado State Capitol Complex," 72–73.

26. Quote in "Lack of Guides at Statehouse Is Deplored," *Rocky Mountain News*, June 18, 1948, 12; "Governor Wants Guides at Statehouse," *Rocky Mountain News*, April 28, 1951, 14; "Western-Clad College Girls to Guide Statehouse Visitors," *Rocky Mountain News*, June 13, 1951, 5; Tom Gavin, "Paid Guides at Capitol OK'd, But No Volunteers," *Rocky Mountain News*, May 3, 1951, 32; Letter from F. Ross Brown to James Merrick, June 19, 1951, CSA box 32234; Letter from James Merrick to Governor Dan Thornton, August 16, 1951, CSA box 32234; Letter from Governor Edwin Johnson to James Merrick, May 9, 1955, CSA box 35501.

### CHAPTER 7: VANDALISM IN THE NAME OF PROGRESS, 1952–1990

1. Harry Gessing and Bert Hanna, "Thornton Threatened," *Denver Post*, March 11, 1952, 1; Al Nakkula and Tom Gavin, "Man Leaps to Death in Statehouse Here," *Rocky Mountain News*, March 19, 1952, 1, 6; "Statehouse Suicide First One in History," *Denver Post*, March 19, 1952, 19; "Capitol Employees Alerted to Prevent New Suicides," *Rocky Mountain News*, March 19, 1952, 6; Letter from James Merrick to Governor Thornton, March 4, 1953, CSA box 35500.

2. Letter from O. J. Wiemann to Frank L. Humphrey, November 24, 1950, CSA box 32232; "Statehouse Restaurant Faced With Closing," *Denver Post*, November 26, 1950, 2A; Tom Gavin, "Big Chandeliers Appear Doomed," *Rocky Mountain News*, February 21, 1954, 12; "State Capitol Building Renovating Bids Asked," *Denver Post*, May 13, 1954, 28; "Capitol Chandeliers Won't Be Scrapped," *Rocky Mountain News*, February 27, 1954; Session Laws of Colorado, 1955, 968; quotes in "Capitol Eatery Must Clean up or Close," *Rocky Mountain News*, April 29, 1955, 17; "Lunchroom Closed at State Capitol," *Denver Post*, May 10, 1955, 10; "End of a Legislative Era," *Rocky Mountain News*, December 30, 1958, 8.

3. "Facts From the State Planning Division," August 1958, 7; "Governor's Suite to Be Remodeled," *Rocky Mountain News*, April 30, 1957; "Steve's New Office Wins Feminine OK," *Rocky Mountain News*, January 22, 1958; "Committee Favors Capitol Remodeling," *Denver Post*, December 18, 1959, 50; "Capitol Bldg. Remodeling OKd," *Rocky Mountain News*, February 14, 1960, 39; Jim Ritchie, "Museum Bldg. Projected for E. Colfax Site," *Denver Post*, June 8, 1960, 3; "Capitol's $200,000 Remodel Job Starts," *Denver Post*, September 21, 1960, 34.

4. Session Laws of Colorado, 1955, 36–37; Bob Whearley, "Johnson to Get Baker's Quarters," *Rocky Mountain News*, August 4, 1955, 5; " 'Tallest Tower in the West' Highlights New Capitol Plan," *Denver Post*, April 14, 1957, 2A; "State Services Building Final Plans Approved," *Rocky Mountain News*, August 17, 1957, 28; "Facts From the State Planning Division," August 1958, 7; "Steve Dedicates 7-Story Building,"

*Denver Post*, June 14, 1960, 21; Pyle, "History of the Colorado State Capitol Complex," 74–79.

5. Insurance company quote in "Skyscraper a Blot on Capitol Landscape?" *Denver Post*, June 21, 1959, 3A; Michael Shay, "Denver's Capitol Hill: Reflections of a Neighborhood," *Colorado Heritage* 4 (1983), 25; Abbott, Leonard, and McComb, *Colorado*, 312; Leonard and Noel, *Denver*, 409–410; Pyle, "History of the Colorado State Capitol Complex," 93, 100–101.

6. "Rush to the Rockies Centennial, 1959," *Colorado Magazine* 36: 2 (April 1959), 125; "Territory's Famed 1st Capitol to Nestle Near Big Dome," *Rocky Mountain News*, June 27, 1958, 46; "State Acquires Old Log Cabin, Prized Historical Memento," *Rocky Mountain News*, July 1, 1958, 12; Alex Murphree, "Historians' Views Varied on Cabin Capitol," *Denver Post*, December 21, 1958, 3A; "First Capitol or Not, Old Log Cabin Sits It Out," *Denver Post*, April 21, 1960, 24.

7. "Finishing Touches on a Shroud," *Rocky Mountain News*, July 4, 1959, 22; Gene Lindberg, "Robot in Capitol Can Answer 1,500 Queries About Colorado," *Denver Post*, July 26, 1959, 22A.

8. "Love Expresses Shock, Sorrow, Horror," *Rocky Mountain Collegian*, November 22, 1963, 1; "JFK Assassination Shocks Gov. Love," *Denver Post*, November 22, 1963, 3.

9. Charles Roos, "Statehouse Showing Signs of Wear," *Rocky Mountain News*, July 16, 1965, 26; Robert L. Chase, "Take a Good Look Where We're Going," *Rocky Mountain News*, May 30, 1966, 41; Fred Brown, "Capitol Well Flooring Studied," *Denver Post*, January 29, 1967, 34.

10. "Statehouse Plan Contract Awarded," *Rocky Mountain News*, January 7, 1967, 5; Richard O'Reilly, "$60 Million Capitol Master Plan Shown," *Rocky Mountain News*, July 15, 1967, 5, 6; Fred Brown, "$60 Million Capitol 'Campus' Idea Urged," *Denver Post*, July 16, 1967, 25; "State Land Buying Urged," *Denver Post*, November 22, 1968, 4.

11. Letter from Governor Edwin Johnson to James Merrick, March 11, 1955, CSA box 35501; "Filming to Close Public Snack Bar," *Rocky Mountain News*, November 8, 1968, 30; Love quote in "Colo. House Refuses to Skirt Mini Issue," *Rocky Mountain News*, January 15, 1969, 5; "Mini-Minis Overruled at Colo. House," *Denver Post*, January 15, 1969, 28.

12. Ubbelohde, Benson, and Smith, *A Colorado History*, 348, 354; Shay, "Denver's Capitol Hill," 33; John Kokish, "McKevitt Denounced in Black Panther's Talk," *Denver Post*, November 3, 1968, 3.

13. "Quiet Marchers File Into State Capitol," *Denver Post*, March 26, 1969, 1; Vickie Porter, "Prominent 'System' Adversaries Speak at Saturday's Anti-War Demonstration," *Rocky Mountain Collegian*, April 26, 1969; Gonzales quote in "Hispano March Aims at School Needs," *Denver Post*, September 16, 1969, 3; George Lane, "2,000 Join in Mexican Independence Parade," *Denver Post*, September 18, 1972; Ubbelohde, Benson, and Smith, *A Colorado History*, 355; Abbott, Leonard, and McComb, *Colorado*, 324–334; Shay, "Denver's Capitol Hill," 34; Leonard and Noel, *Denver*, 383; David G. Gutiérrez, *Walls and Mirrors: Mexican Americans, Mexican Immigrants, and the Politics of Ethnicity* (Berkeley: University of California Press, 1995), 184–186.

14. Cindy Kish, "Love Commends Student Non-violence, Will Propose 40 Per Cent Fund Increase," *Rocky Mountain Collegian*, April 18, 1969, 1, 3; Gill quote in "14 Arrested for Halting State Senate," *Denver Post*, May 7, 1969, 1, 48.

15. "Students Protest Four Campus Deaths, War," *Rocky Mountain News*, May 8, 1970, 8; "Protestors March on Capitol," *Denver Post*, May 8, 1970, 3; Richard Tucker, "12,000 Gather at Capitol for Peaceful Protest," *Rocky Mountain News*, May 10, 1970, 28; Todd Phipers, "Capital Protest Peaceful," *Denver Post*, May 10, 1970, 1, 3, 7.

16. "Rededication of the State Social Services Building," pamphlet, December 9, 1987; Session Laws of Colorado, 1968, 262; "Coloradoans Pay Last Respects to Big Ed," *Denver Post*, June 1, 1970, 17; "Gov. Love Pays Last Respects to Big Ed," *Denver Post*, June 2, 1970, 1; "Johnson Eulogized as Man of the People," *Denver Post*, June 2, 1970, 3; Session Laws of Colorado, 1972, 652; "Legislators Feel Capitol Air-Conditioning Ban 'Uncool,'" *Denver Post*, November 8, 1973, 27.

17. Joan McCoy, "Enthusiastic Guide at State Capitol," *Rocky Mountain News*, March 10, 1972, 62; Charles Roos, "Fowler's Plans for New Café Includes [sic] Exclusivity," *Rocky Mountain News*, July 22, 1975, 5, 22; Fred Brown, "Fowler Keeper of Capitol," *Denver Post*, August 17, 1975, 35; "Capitol Care Bill Advanced," *Denver Post*, January 20, 1976, 2; Bessie Boyd, "Tour Guide Program," *From the Tour DeskY* 5: 3 (March 2002), 2; Joanne Ditmer, "Holiday Spirit Proves Elusive," *Denver Post*, December 23, 1973, 32.

18. Session Laws of Colorado, 1974, 480; Session Laws of Colorado, 1975, 1587; "Senate Windows Finished," *Denver Post*, December 28, 1975, 3; "3 Windows Dedicated in State Senate," *Denver Post*, January 7, 1976, 2; "Love to Be Repaired; Faceless Ed to Stay," *Denver Post*, January 11, 1976, 37; Frances Melrose, "Tapestry to Honor Role of Women in State's History," *Rocky Mountain News*, July 13, 1976, 8, 12; Session Laws of Colorado, 1977, 1989; Abbott, Leonard, and McComb, *Colorado*, 340; Marshall Sprague, *Colorado: A History* (New York: W. W. Norton, 1976), 193. In 1986 a portrait of state senator Ruth Stockton replaced the Griffith window, which moved to a spot in the north wing of the second floor. The nineteen women honored on "Women's Gold" are Chipeta, Francis Cabrini, Betty Pellet, Olga Schaarf Little, Clara Brown, Ellen Jack, Antonia Brico, Doña Salazar y Gallegos, Florence Rena Sabin, Agnes Reid Tammen, Emily Griffith, Mary Coyle Chase, Helen Bonfils, Mary Elitch Long, Frances Jacobs, Diana Goldberg, Margaret Crawford, "Silver Heels," and Patricia Mackintosh.

19. Session Laws of Colorado, 1975, 860; "Stained Glass Honor," *Rocky Mountain News*, April 28, 1976, 8. Eugene H. Berwanger persuasively suggested that some sources excessively emphasize the roles of Barney Ford and "Aunt" Clara Brown over perhaps more influential African Americans in Colorado history. See Berwanger, *The West and Reconstruction* (Urbana: University of Illinois Press, 1981), 8–9, 144–147.

20. Session Laws of Colorado, 1973, 1669–1670; Abbott, Leonard, and McComb, *Colorado*, 348.

21. Kathy Gosliner, "Chandelier Move Meets Opposition," *Rocky Mountain News*, August 7, 1976, 1; Session Laws of Colorado, 1976, 841; Bob Ewegen, "Chandelier's Heat Output Exceeds Light," *Denver Post*, August 7, 1976, 3; "Chandelier Battle Ended," *Rocky Mountain News*, February 3, 1977, 8.

22. Ted Carey, "Colorado Legislators to Open '77 Session," *Rocky Mountain News,* January 5, 1977, 6; "Newest Honorary Windows in State Capitol," *Denver Post,* January 29, 1977, 1; "Indians Honored," *Rocky Mountain News,* February 19, 1977, 1; Todd Engdahl, "Lawmakers to Find Capitol Still Lacking," *Denver Post,* November 26, 1978, 40; Sharon Sherman, "A Portent of 'Elegant' Laws?" *Denver Post,* February 20, 1979, 52.

23. Bill Logan, "Patrol, Watchmen Statehouse Use Debated," *Rocky Mountain News,* December 11, 1970, 16; Glenn Troelstrup, "Boy Streetwalkers Fact of Denver Life," *Denver Post,* June 12, 1977, 35, 38; Louis Kilzer, "Capitol Hill Area's Male Prostitution Soars," *Rocky Mountain News,* September 27, 1978, 6; Jay Pfieiffer, "Legislative Official Stabbed in Capitol," *Rocky Mountain News,* January 5, 1979, 1, 38; Sharon Sherman and Todd Engdahl, "Denver Police May Guard Statehouse," *Denver Post,* January 5, 1979, 1, 16; Brad Martisius, "Capitol Security a Chronic Problem," *Denver Post,* January 5, 1979, 16; Session Laws of Colorado, 1979, 981–982; "City Police Role at Capitol OK'd," *Denver Post,* March 9, 1979, 31; "Police Given Capitol Jurisdiction," *Out Front,* June 22, 1979, 1; "Police to Join State Patrol In Guarding Colo. Capitol," *Denver Post,* October 2, 1979, 8; John Sanko, "Dick Seeks Beefed-up Capitol Security," *Rocky Mountain News,* February 13, 1986, 8; Jeffrey A. Roberts, "Security Force Urged for Capitol," *Denver Post,* July 11, 1986, 1B.

24. Session Laws of Colorado, 1975, 819–820; "State Capitol History Handbook," *Rocky Mountain News "Now,"* July 16, 1978, 2; Joanne Ditmer, "Preserving Our Past: Our State Capitol," *Denver Post Empire Magazine,* October 28, 1979, 15; Leonard and Noel, *Denver,* 411, 448–454.

25. Fred Brown, "Capitol Needs Rewiring Badly," *Denver Post,* March 14, 1976, 26; "Capitol Dome to Get New Coat of Gold," *Rocky Mountain News,* July 17, 1978, 5; John J. Sanko, "State Capitol Roof Leaks Into Barrels and Barrels," *Rocky Mountain News,* May 7, 1979, 147; "State Capitol's Dome Is Due to Take on a Brighter Hue," *Rocky Mountain News,* September 11, 1979, 30; "Almost Ready," *Rocky Mountain News,* October 29, 1980, 5; Frances Melrose, "Capitol Dome Sporting New Gilding," *Rocky Mountain News,* December 9, 1980, 8; "State Capitol's Wiring Poses Fire Threat," *Rocky Mountain News,* May 11, 1981, 14; John G. White, "How Denver's Dome Got Gilded," *Americana Magazine* 9: 4 (September-October 1981), 75–77.

26. Cindy Parmenter, "State Office Building to Close as Hazard," *Denver Post,* September 10, 1983, 1A, 5A; Peter Blake, "Lamm Shuts 'Dangerous' Old Offices," *Rocky Mountain News,* September 10, 1983, 1, 14; John Sanko, "Renovation of State Building Praised," *Rocky Mountain News,* July 15, 1985, 8; "State Workers to Move to Safer Office Friday," *Rocky Mountain News,* September 16, 1983, 72; Peter Blake, "Panel Will Study How to Upgrade Eight State Buildings," *Rocky Mountain News,* November 23, 1983, 9; Turner quote in Peter Blake, "State Office Revamping Urged," *Rocky Mountain News,* September 24, 1984, 1, 11; Dodge quote in John Sanko, "State Revenue Building a Fire Hazard, Romer Told," *Rocky Mountain News,* November 13, 1986, 34; "Rededication of the Legislative Services Building," pamphlet, November 21, 1986; "Rededication of the State Social Services Building," pamphlet, December 9, 1987.

27. Al Nakkula, "Group Plans Memorial to Colorado Veterans," *Rocky Mountain News,* November 6, 1983, 174; Session Laws of Colorado, 1984, 1154; "Monument

Site to Be Dedicated," *Rocky Mountain News*, November 9, 1984, 10; Carl Hilliard, "Christmas Finally Comes to the Capitol," *Denver Post*, December 15, 1985, 9C; Kathy O'Dell, "Tribute to King Draws Thousands in Denver to March, Remember," *Rocky Mountain News*, January 21, 1986, 8; John Sanko, "Capitol Show," *Rocky Mountain News*, June 17, 1988, 14; "Art of the House: Paintings in the House of Representatives, State Capitol, Denver, Colorado," pamphlet, November 1990.

28. Session Laws of Colorado, 1986, 83; "State Capitol Celebrating a Birthday, Too," *Denver Post*, July 5, 1986, 3C; Session Laws of Colorado, 1990, 1482–1483; Frances Melrose, "The Old Lady of Sherman Street Hits 100," *Rocky Mountain News*, July 1, 1990, 12M–13M; "Capitol Building Cornerstone Rededication Set," *Rocky Mountain News*, July 1, 1990, 14M; "Colorado State Capitol Cornerstone Centennial Celebration," pamphlet, August 4, 1990.

### CHAPTER 8: TOO IMPORTANT TO NEGLECT, 1990–PRESENT

1. Nathaniel Hawthorne, *The House of the Seven Gables* (New York: Penguin, 1986 [1851]), 183–184.

2. "Colorado State Capitol Life Safety Plan," Department of Administration, Capitol Complex Division, September 1990, 1, 3–5; "The Capitol Fire Companies," *Denver Post*, March 28, 1900, 2.

3. "Life Safety Plan," 1990, 4; Session Laws of Colorado, 1991, 858–862; John Sanko, "Regilding to Restore Capitol's Shine," *Rocky Mountain News*, August 15, 1991; Session Laws of Colorado, 1992, 1058–1059; "Souvenir Book Recounts Proud History of State's Capitol," *Denver Post*, November 17, 1992, 1E; Session Laws of Colorado, 1993, 288–289; Boyd, "Tour Guide Program," 3.

4. Patrick O'Driscoll, "Thousands Honor King; Klan Exit Sparks Violence," *Denver Post*, January 21, 1992, 1A, 2A.

5. John Sanko, "Suit Aims to Make Capitol Accessible to Disabled," *Rocky Mountain News*, July 7, 1992, 9; Fawn Germer, "Activists Want Accessible Capitol," *Rocky Mountain News*, May 24, 1993, 5A; Fawn Germer, "Free Ramps at Capitol Snubbed," *Rocky Mountain News*, July 15, 1993, 15A; "State of Colorado House and Senate Antechamber Accessibility Conceptual Design Report," Department of Administration, Capitol Complex Division, September 23, 1993; John Sanko, "Access Plan for Capitol Draws Praise," *Rocky Mountain News*, December 11, 1993, 18A; "Wheelchair Users Laud Ramps at Capitol," *Rocky Mountain News*, January 13, 1994, 16A. The wooden ramp was replaced with an obtrusive wheelchair lift in 2001.

6. Jennifer Gavin, "Work Could Close Capitol," *Denver Post*, April 13, 1994, 1A, 17A; John Sanko, "Capitol Idea: Shut Down for Repairs," *Rocky Mountain News*, April 14, 1994, 18A.

7. John Sanko, "Fire Could Devastate Capitol, Architect Warns," *Rocky Mountain News*, December 3, 1994, 14A; Margaret Clarke, "House Treated to Slide Show; Capitol Needs FaceliftCSoon," *Capitol Reporter*, January 30, 1995, 2; Geraldine Haldner, "Capitol Gamble," *Capitol Reporter*, March 6, 1995, 1; Geraldine Haldner, "Capitol Fix-up Delayed; Plans to Be Fine-tuned," *Capitol Reporter*, Apri. 10, 1995, 2; "State Capitol Building Health and Life Safety Project: Report to the Colorado General As-

sembly," Colorado Legislative Council, Research Publication 410, December 1995, 3–5, 7–15, 151–156.

8. "Every Building Needs a Friend," *Michigan History* 71: 5 (September-October 1987), 34; Kathryn B. Eckert, "Elijah Would Be Proud! The Restoration of the Michigan State Capitol," *Michigan History* 74: 4 (July-August 1990), 16, 18–19; Kerry Chartkoff, "Unveiling a Masterpiece: A Walking Tour Through the Restoration Process," *Michigan History* 74: 4 (July-August 1990), 25; Dave McNeely, "Texas' Capitol Grows Bigger, Better and More Beautiful," *State Legislatures* 18: 8 (August 1992), 18–21; Jacquelynn Boyle, "Michigan Recaptures Capitol's Glory," *State Legislatures* 18: 8 (August 1992), 23–24; Allen Freeman, "Thinking Big," *Historic Preservation* 47: 1 (January-February 1995), 56, 97–98.

9. Goodsell, *American Statehouse*, 82; Session Laws of Colorado, 1996, 1925–1926; Straayer, *Colorado General Assembly*, 216–217.

10. Mary Chandler, "At 93, Capitol Needs Facelift, Shot of Money," *Rocky Mountain News*, March 2, 1997, 4D; Chronic and Wham quote in Sean M. Miller, "Capitol Renovation in the Works," *Capitol Reporter*, April 14, 1997; Schauer quote in Laura Loyacono, "The Cost and Benefits of a Facelift," *State Legislatures* 23: 7 (July-August 1997), 67–68; Owens quote in John Sanko, "A Capitol Idea," *Rocky Mountain News*, November 30, 1997, 32A–33A; Session Laws of Colorado, 1998, 2252–2253; Letter from George Delaney to Secretary of State Victoria Buckley, March 25, 1998.

11. "Change the Statue?" *Denver Post*, April 14, 1998; "Sand Creek Was 'Massacre,'" *Rocky Mountain News*, April 14, 1998; Tom Noel, "Don't Erase 'Sand Creek,'" *Denver Post*, July 5, 1998, 1G, 4G; "State Capitol Building Advisory Committee: Report to the Colorado General Assembly," Colorado Legislative Council, Research Publication 454, August 1999, 3–4; "Editing a War Memorial," *Rocky Mountain News*, August 8, 1998; Session Laws of Colorado, 1999, 2283–2284; John Sanko, "Sand Creek Might Stay on Marker After All," *Rocky Mountain News*, March 20, 1999; "Statue Decision Is Reconsidered," *Denver Post*, March 20, 1999; John J. Sanko, "Sand Creek Plaque to Set Record Straight," *Rocky Mountain News*, October 3, 2002; Steven K. Paulson, "Correcting Tragic Record," *Rocky Mountain News*, November 23, 2002; Kit Miniclier, "Sand Creek Will Get Its Historical Due," *Denver Post*, November 27, 2002; "Anniversary of a Massacre," *Denver Post*, November 29, 2002; Robert Weller, "History Is Corrected at State Capitol," *Pueblo Chieftain*, November 30, 2002.

12. Dusty Saunders, "'This Week' Sets up Shop in Capitol Hallway," *Rocky Mountain News*, June 21, 1997, 125; "Lawmakers Applaud Young King," *Denver Post*, April 26, 2002, 13A; Mike Soraghan, "Colorado Leaders Honor Buckley," *Denver Post*, July 21, 1999, 1B, 4B; Bill Scanlon, "Owens, Rogers Eulogize Buckley," *Rocky Mountain News*, July 21, 1999; Mike Soraghan, "Colorado After Columbine: The Gun Debate," *State Legislatures* 26: 6 (June 2000), 15; Virginia Culver, "Taylor's Body to Lie in State," *Denver Post*, October 1, 2003; E-mail from Edna Pelzmann to Derek Everett, October 3, 2003; E-mail from Lew Hopkins to Derek Everett, November 3, 2003.

13. "State Capitol Building Advisory Committee, 1991–1998: Statutory Authority, Guidelines and Recommendations," Colorado Legislative Council, Research Publication 453, March 1999, 41–43; Mike Soraghan, "Capitol Renovation Bill Dies," *Denver Post*, April 30, 1999; Fred Brown, "Capitol Security Under Scrutiny," *Denver*

*Post*, June 26, 1999, 1B, 8B; John Sanko, "Panel Requests $7 Million to Repair Capitol," *Rocky Mountain News*, August 21, 1999; Fred Brown, "Capitol Renovation a 'Life-Safety' Issue," *Denver Post*, August 22, 1999; Julia C. Martinez, "Troopers Seek More Security at Capitol," *Denver Post*, November 23, 1999, 1A, 21A; John Sanko, "Security a Concern at Capitol," *Rocky Mountain News*, November 29, 1999, 4A, 16A; "New Security at Capitol," *Denver Post*, December 4, 1999; Mark Obmascik, "At Capitol, Security Not up for Debate," *Denver Post*, March 26, 2000, 1A, 23A; "Long Arm of Law Dropping on Capitol," *Denver Post*, April 11, 2000.

14. "Capitol Renovation Amendment Announced," *Denver Post*, March 29, 2000; "Hope Renewed for Capitol Fix-up," *Denver Post*, April 4, 2000; Fred Brown, "Senate Endorses Plan to Renovate State Capitol," *Denver Post*, April 28, 2000; "Prevention First at Capitol," *Denver Post*, April 9, 2000; Sandra Fish, "Sen. Rupert's Capitol Renovation Bill Dies," *Boulder Daily Camera*, May 2, 2000; "Capitol-fix Resolution Defeated," *Denver Post*, May 2, 2000.

15. John Sanko, "Senator Launches Drive to Fix Statehouse," *Rocky Mountain News*, May 27, 2000; James E. Hartmann, "More Than Safety at Stake in Fixing Colorado's 'Pride,'" *Denver Post*, May 28, 2000, 1G, 6G; Straayer, *Colorado General Assembly*, 54–56.

16. "Owens Orders State Building 'Lock-down,'" *Denver Post*, September 11, 2001, extra edition, 10A; Fred Brown, Julia C. Martinez, and Trent Seibert, "State Closed to Tourists," *Denver Post*, September 12, 2001; Sheba R. Wheeler, "'United We Stand' Rally, March Draw Thousands," *Denver Post*, September 16, 2002, 1B, 3B.

17. John Sanko, "Resolution Calls for Formation of State Security Task Force," *Rocky Mountain News*, October 3, 2001; David Olinger and Julia Martinez, "Security Tightened Throughout Colorado," *Denver Post*, October 9, 2001; Julia C. Martinez, "Further Security Upgrades Considered at State Capitol," *Denver Post*, October 10, 2001; John Sanko, "Committee Supports Request to Help Tighten Capitol Security," *Rocky Mountain News*, November 16, 2001; Michele Ames, "Capitol Dome Now Off-limits," *Rocky Mountain News*, January 5, 2002, 3B; "Lawmakers Warned Capitol Possible Target," *Rocky Mountain News*, January 15, 2002; "Capitol to Get New Weapons Detector," *Fort Collins Coloradoan*, January 17, 2002, B4; Owen and Perlmutter quotes in Peter Blake, "Fortress Colorado," *Rocky Mountain News*, January 5, 2002, 4B, 5B.

18. "Bandits Outside Capitol Make off With Chlouber's Flaming Coach," *Denver Post*, February 15, 2002, 14A; John Sanko, "Security Changes Proposed," *Rocky Mountain News*, February 16, 2002, 22A; John Sanko, "Senators: Reopen Capitol," *Rocky Mountain News*, April 10, 2002; Session Laws of Colorado, 2002, 3134–3135; "Open Doors: Let's Reopen Doors at State Capitol," *Rocky Mountain News* editorial printed in *Denver Post*, April 14, 2002, 7E; Sue Mencer, "Speakout: Security Measures at Capitol Are Prudent," *Rocky Mountain News*, May 6, 2002, 36A; "Statehouse Security Eases," *Rocky Mountain News*, June 15, 2002, 2B; "Reopening the Capitol," *Rocky Mountain News* editorial printed in *Denver Post*, July 7, 2002, 7E.

19. Fred Brown, "Keeping Our Capitol Safe," *Denver Post*, September 14, 2001; John Sanko, "Betting on Capitol Safety," *Rocky Mountain News*, October 4, 2002; Peggy Lowe, "Budget Cuts Continue," *Rocky Mountain News*, December 21, 2002, 4A; Joanne Ditmer, "It's Time to Protect Funds for Open Space," *Denver Post*, January 19,

2003; Troy A. Eid, "Capitol Safety Project Rolls Ahead Thanks to Colorado Historical Society," *Stateline* (February-March 2003), 3; Jennifer Cook, "A Capitol Idea: Improving Safety Features in Colorado's Statehouse," *Colorado History Now* (March 2003), 5; Trent Seibert, "Capitol Renovation Takes Step Forward," *Denver Post,* March 3, 2003, 1B; "Cost to Fix Capitol Rises to $30 Million," *Denver Post,* April 25, 2003, 3B.

20. "How to Repair the State Capitol," *Rocky Mountain News,* December 14, 2003, 7E; John Sanko, "A Working Tour of Capitol for Lawmakers," *Rocky Mountain News,* January 13, 2004; "Roll Call," *Rocky Mountain News,* January 14, 2004; John Sanko, "Capitol Gets Another $6.8 Million for Construction," *Rocky Mountain News,* May 13, 2004, 24A; John Sanko, "Hard Hat Area Forces Capitol Visitors on Detour," *Rocky Mountain News,* May 14, 2004, 28A; E-mail from Lew Hopkins to Derek Everett, August 5, 2004.

21. Steven K. Paulson, "For Sale or Rent: One Capitol, Gold Dome Included?" *Boulder Daily Camera,* January 30, 2003; Julia C. Martinez, "Joint Session to Discuss Cash Crisis," *Denver Post,* February 13, 2003; Chlouber quote in John Sanko, "Just Listed! Statehouse With Dome; Call Dave," *Rocky Mountain News,* April 19, 2003, 17A; Sandra Fish, "State Considers Building Sales for Fast Cash," *Boulder Daily Camera,* April 22, 2003; Julia C. Martinez, "State Might Sell, Lease Back Buildings," *Denver Post,* April 22, 2003; John Sanko, "Here's a Capitol Idea," *Rocky Mountain News,* April 30, 2003; John Sanko, "Colorado Likely to Avoid Sale of Buildings, Tobacco Funds," *Rocky Mountain News,* May 21, 2003; John Sanko, "Owens OKs Sale of Tobacco Funds, State Buildings," *Rocky Mountain News,* June 7, 2003, 10A.

22. Michael C. Bender, "Owens Urges Calm Among Coloradans," *Grand Junction Daily Sentinel,* February 7, 2003; Kieran Nicholson and Art Kane, "Colorado on Alert," *Denver Post,* February 8, 2003; Anderson quote in "New Metal Detector Unveiled," *Denver Post,* March 18, 2003; Tom Noel, "Terrorists in Tuxedoes Threaten Homefront," *Rocky Mountain News,* June 7, 2003, 16D.

23. Dick Foster, "'Orange' Alert Casts Shadow Across State," *Rocky Mountain News,* December 23, 2003, 25A, 27A; "Security Precautions Ease at Statehouse," *Rocky Mountain News,* January 15, 2004; E-mail from Lew Hopkins to Derek Everett, April 12, 2004. See also Julia C. Martinez, "Capitol on Record as Smoker's Haven," *Denver Post,* January 22, 2000, 1B–3B; Fred Brown, "Where There's Smoke, There's Ire," *Denver Post,* January 26, 2000; "Effort Would Snuff Statehouse Smoking," *Denver Post,* April 11, 2000; Julia C. Martinez, "Smoking Extinguished in Capitol Basement," *Denver Post,* January 27, 2001, 9A; "Three Lawmakers Shun Fire Drill," *Denver Post,* May 4, 2002.

24. Joanne Kelley, "Travel Travails for Metro Area," *Rocky Mountain News,* June 10, 2004. See also "State Unwraps Birthday Plans, But Budget Cuts Take the Cake," *Rocky Mountain News,* July 25, 2003; John Sanko, "Capitol Party to Proceed," *Rocky Mountain News,* July 29, 2004.

25. Trent Seibert, "Dome to Close for Project," *Denver Post,* January 16, 2002, 10A; Trent Seibert, "Capitol Dome May Reopen," *Denver Post,* May 21, 2002; Sandra Fish, "Senator to Play Security Guard," *Boulder Daily Camera,* January 27, 2003; Allyson Reedy, "Weissmann Helps Keep Dome Open," *Boulder Daily Camera,* February 4, 2003.

26. Hawthorne, *House of the Seven Gables,* 314–315; Second Biennial Report, 1886, 61.

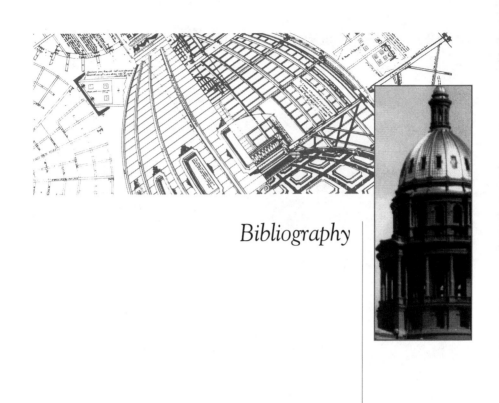

# Bibliography

## ABBREVIATIONS

CSA       Colorado State Archives, Denver
DWM    David W. Mullins Library, University of Arkansas, Fayetteville
ISC        Indiana Supreme Court Law Library, Indiana State House, Indianapolis
LJS        Leslie J. Savage Library, Western State College, Gunnison, Colorado
              (Aberdeen box)
LL         Legislative Library, Colorado State Capitol, Denver
SCL      Colorado State Supreme Court Library, Denver

## ARTICLES

Barbour, Charlotte A. "Vanished Neighborhood on Capitol Hill, Denver." *Colorado Magazine* 37: 4 (October 1960), 254–264.
Benson, Maxine. "A Centennial Legacy." *Colorado Magazine* 57 (1981), 1–70.
Boyd, Bessie. "Tour Guide Program." *From the Tour Desk...* 5: 3 (March 2002), 2.

Boyle, Jacquelynn. "Michigan Recaptures Capitol's Glory." *State Legislatures* 18: 8 (August 1992), 23–24.

Brayer, Herbert O. "Status of Our State Archives Work." *Colorado Magazine* 21: 3 (May 1944), 118–119.

Brayer, Herbert O., and Virgil V. Peterson. "Annual Report of the State Archivist of Colorado." *Colorado Magazine* 22: 1 (January 1945), 40–47.

Bucco, Edith E. "Founded on Rock: Colorado's Stout Stone Industry." *Colorado Magazine* 51: 4 (October 1974), 313–335.

Buechner, John C. "Ferril and the West." In *Thomas Hornsby Ferril and the American West,* ed. Robert C. Baron, Stephen J. Leonard, and Thomas J. Noel. Golden, CO: Fulcrum, 1996, ix–x.

Cartwright, Allison S. "A Capitol Investment." *Michigan History* 72: 6 (November-December 1988), 24–31.

Chartkoff, Kerry. "Unveiling a Masterpiece: A Walking Tour Through the Restoration Process." *Michigan History* 74: 4 (July-August 1990), 20–27.

Collins, George W. "Colorado's Territorial Secretaries." *Colorado Magazine* 43: 3 (Summer 1966), 185–208.

Comeaux, Malcolm L. "Attempts to Establish and Change a Western Boundary." *Annals of the Association of American Geographers* 72: 2 (June 1982), 254–271.

Cross, Frank Clay. "Revolution in Colorado." *The Nation* 138: 3579 (February 7, 1934), 152–153.

Davidson, Levette J. "Colorado's Hall of Fame." *Colorado Magazine* 35: 3 (July 1958), 208–218.

Davis, James H. "Colorado Under the Klan." *Colorado Magazine* 42: 2 (Spring 1965), 93–108.

Drutchas, Geoffrey G., and Kerry K. Chartkoff. "As Lasting as Time Itself." *Michigan History* 83: 1 (January-February 1999), 9–17.

Eckert, Kathryn B. "Elijah Would Be Proud! The Restoration of the Michigan State Capitol." *Michigan History* 74: 4 (July-August 1990), 16–19.

"Every Building Needs a Friend." *Michigan History* 71: 5 (September-October 1987), 34–35.

Fellerman, Henry S. "Will C. Ferril, Newspaperman and Historian." In *1961 Brand Book of the Denver Posse of the Westerners,* ed. Don L. Griswold. Boulder: Johnson, 1962, 247–270.

Freeman, Allen. "Thinking Big." *Historic Preservation* 47: 1 (January-February 1995), 52–59, 96–98.

Gabiou, Alfrieda. "The Burning of the First Capitol." *Gopher Historian* 23: 1 (1968), 5–8.

Goeldner, Paul. "The Designing Architect: Elijah E. Myers." *Southwestern Historical Quarterly* 92: 2 (October 1988), 271–287.

Goodsell, Charles T. "The Architecture of Parliaments: Legislative Houses and Political Culture." *British Journal of Political Science* 18: 3 (July 1988), 287–302.

Green, William Elton. "'A Question of Great Delicacy': The Texas Capitol Competition, 1881." *Southwestern Historical Quarterly* 92: 2 (October 1988), 247–270.

Handley, Bill. "Why We Like the Capitol: A New Theory." *Colorado State Capitol Tour Guide Newsletter* (October 1997).

Harper, Marjory. "Emigrant Strikebreakers: Scottish Granite Cutters and the Texas Capitol Boycott." *Southwestern Historical Quarterly* 95: 4 (April 1992), 465–486.

Harrison, Paul D. "Building Colorado's Capitol." In *1959 Brand Book of the Denver Posse of the Westerners*, ed. Raymond G. Colwell. Boulder: Johnson, 1960, 215–231.

Henderson, John R. "The Indian and Buffalo Statue on the State Capitol Grounds." *Colorado Magazine* 13: 5 (September 1936), 183–186.

James, Harlean. "Seven Southern State Capitols." *Social Forces* 4: 2 (December 1925), 386–394.

"The John D. Howland Collection." *Colorado Magazine* 8: 2 (March 1931), 60–63.

Loyacono, Laura. "The Cost and Benefits of a Facelift." *State Legislatures* 23: 7 (July-August 1997), 67–70.

McConnell, Virginia. "For These High Purposes," *Colorado Magazine* 44: 3 (Summer 1967), 204–223.

McNeely, Dave. "Texas' Capitol Grows Bigger, Better and More Beautiful." *State Legislatures* 18: 8 (August 1992), 18–21.

Moore, Wallace. "Aberdeen, Thriving Town of 150 Inhabitants, Supplied Granite for Colorado State Capitol." In *The Aberdeen Quarry*, ed. Ann D. Zugelder. Gunnison, CO: Publisher unknown, 1989, 30–35.

Moore, Wallace, and Lois Borland. "Quarrying the Granite for the State Capitol." *Colorado Magazine* 24: 2 (March 1947), 49–58.

Myers, Rex. "Railroads, Stone Quarries, and the Colorado State Capitol." *Journal of the West* 39: 2 (Spring 2000), 37–45.

Peel, Sheila Sudquist. "The Wyoming State Capitol." *Annals of Wyoming* 57: 1 (1985), 35–39.

Price, Jay M. "Capitol Improvements: Style and Image in Arizona's and New Mexico's Public Architecture." *Journal of Arizona History* 41: 4 (Winter 2000), 353–384.

Putman, John J. "Denver, Colorado's Rocky Mountain High." *National Geographic* 115: 3 (March 1979), 383–411.

Roberts, Edwards. "The City of Denver." *Harper's Monthly* 76: 456 (1888), 944–957.

Robinson, Willard B. "Pride of Texas: The State Capitol." *Southwestern Historical Quarterly* 92: 2 (October 1988), 227–246.

"Rush to the Rockies Centennial, 1959." *Colorado Magazine* 36: 2 (April 1959), 123–125.

Sarasohn, David. "The Election of 1916: Realigning the Rockies." *Western Historical Quarterly* 11: 3 (July 1980), 285–305.

Shay, Michael. "Denver's Capitol Hill: Reflections of a Neighborhood." *Colorado Heritage* 4 (1983), 25–35.

Soraghan, Mike. "Colorado After Columbine: The Gun Debate." *State Legislatures* 26: 6 (June 2000), 14–21.

"The State Capitol: A Grand Old Dame Reaches One Hundred." *Michigan History* 62: 4 (November-December 1978), 14–21.

Stillman, Damie. "From the Ancient Roman Republic to the New American One: Architecture for a New Nation." In *A Republic for the Ages: The United States Capitol and the Political Culture of the Early Republic*, ed. Donald R. Kennon. Charlottesville: University Press of Virginia, 1999, 271–315.

Temple, Wayne C. "Reminders of Lincoln in a Cornerstone." *Lincoln Herald* 68: 3 (1966), 149–159.

"'Tuebor': The Capitol Craftsmanship of Elijah E. Myers." *Michigan History* 62: 4 (November-December 1978), 22–28.

Turner, Frederick Jackson. "The Significance of the Frontier in American History." In *The Frontier in American History*, ed. Turner. New York: Dover, 1996 [1920], 1–38.

Wenger, Martin A. "Raising the Gold-Plated Dome." In *1952 Brand Book of the Denver Posse of the Westerners*, ed. Elvon L. Howe. Denver: Arthur Zeuch, 1953, 107–132.

White, John G. "How Denver's Dome Got Gilded." *Americana Magazine* 9: 4 (September-October 1981), 75–77.

Whiteside, James. "It Was a Terror to the Horses: Bicycling in Gilded-Age Denver." *Colorado Heritage* (Spring 1991), 2–16.

Wilson, William H. "A Diadem for the City Beautiful: The Development of Denver's Civic Center," *Journal of the West* 22: 2 (Spring 1983), 73–83.

Zugelder, Ann D. "Frederick G. Zugelder—The Man and His Role in the Quarrying Process." In *The Aberdeen Quarry*, ed. Ann D. Zugelder. Gunnison, CO: Publisher unknown, 1989, 21–23.

## BOOKS

Abbott, Carl, Stephen J. Leonard, and David McComb. *Colorado: A History of the Centennial State*. Niwot: University Press of Colorado, 1994.

Arps, Louisa Ward. *Denver in Slices: A Historical Guide to the City*. Athens: Swallow/ Ohio University Press, 1959.

Athearn, Robert G. *The Coloradans*. Albuquerque: University of New Mexico Press, 1976.

Aylesworth, Thomas G. *State Capitals*. New York: Gallery, 1990.

Baker, James H., ed. *History of Colorado*, V. 2. Denver: Linderman, 1927.

———. *History of Colorado*, V. 3. Denver: Linderman, 1927.

Berwanger, Eugene H. *The West and Reconstruction*. Urbana: University of Illinois Press, 1981.

Beulah Historical Society. *From Mace's Hole, the Way It Was, to Beulah, the Way It Is: A Comprehensive History of Beulah, Colorado*. Colorado Springs: Century, 1979.

Bowles, Samuel. *The Parks and Mountains of Colorado: A Summer Vacation in the Switzerland of America, 1868*. Ed. James H. Pickering. Norman: University of Oklahoma Press, 1991 [1869].

Bradley, Christine. *William A. Hamill: The Gentleman From Clear Creek*. Fort Collins: Colorado State University Cooperative Extension Service, 1977.

Brettell, Richard R. *Historic Denver: The Architects and the Architecture, 1858–1893*. Denver: Historic Denver, 1973.

Broad, Richard J., Jr. *When Golden Was the Capital*. Golden, CO: Mt. Lookout Chapter DAR, 1922.

Brown, Georgina. *The Shining Mountains*. Gunnison, CO: B&B, 1976.

Cassells, E. Steve. *The Archaeology of Colorado*. Boulder: Johnson, 1983.

Chalmers, David M. *Hooded Americanism: The History of the Ku Klux Klan*. New York: New Viewpoints, 1981 [1965].

Clearfield, Elaine Abrams. *Our Colorado Immortals in Stained Glass*. Denver: Mountain Bell, 1986.

Coel, Margaret. *The Pride of Our People: The Colorado State Capitol*. Denver: Colorado General Assembly, 1992.

Coel, Margaret, Gladys Doty, and Karen Gilleland. *Under the Golden Dome: Colorado's State Capitol*. Boulder: Colorado and West, 1985.

Colorado Writers' and Art Programs. *Colorado Capitol Buildings*. Denver: Colorado Advertising and Publicity Committee, 1939.

Cox, Elizabeth M. *Women State and Territorial Legislators, 1895–1995: A State-by-State Analysis, With Rosters of 6,000 Women*. Jefferson, NC: McFarland, 1996.

Cronon, William. *Nature's Metropolis: Chicago and the Great West*. New York: W. W. Norton, 1991.

Dallas, Sandra. *Yesterday's Denver*. Miami: E. A. Seemann, 1974.

*Distinctive Denver: The Romance of an American Capital*. Denver: Denver Chamber of Commerce, 1926.

Ehlert, Willis J. *America's Heritage: Capitols of the United States*. Madison, WI: State House Publishing, 2000.

Ellis, Richard N., and Duane A. Smith. *Colorado: A History in Photographs*. Niwot: University Press of Colorado, 1991.

Etter, Don, and Carolyn Etter. *Forgotten Dreamer: Reinhard Schuetze, Denver's Landscape Architect*. Denver: Denver Public Library Western History Collection, 2001.

Ewig, Rick, Linda G. Rollins, and Betty Griffin. *Wyoming's Capitol*. Cheyenne: Wyoming State Press, 1987.

Fink, Gary M., ed. *Labor Unions*. Westport, CT: Greenwood, 1977.

Ford, Nancy J.I. *Stone Quarrying in Loveland's Foothills: Through the Centuries*. Loveland, CO: Loveland Museum/Gallery, 2002.

Fowler, Charles F. *Building a Landmark: The Capitol of Nebraska*. Lincoln: Nebraska State Building Division, 1981.

Goodsell, Charles T. *The American Statehouse: Interpreting Democracy's Temples*. Lawrence: University Press of Kansas, 2001.

Goodstein, Phil. *The Ghosts of Denver: Capitol Hill*. Denver: New Social Publications, 1996.

———. *The Seamy Side of Denver*. Denver: New Social Publications, 1993.

Guice, John D.W. *The Rocky Mountain Bench: The Territorial Supreme Courts of Colorado, Montana, and Wyoming, 1861–1890*. New Haven: Yale University Press, 1972.

Gutiérrez, David G. *Walls and Mirrors: Mexican Americans, Mexican Immigrants, and the Politics of Ethnicity*. Berkeley: University of California Press, 1995.

Hall, Frank. *History of Colorado*, V. 2. Chicago: Blakely, 1890.

———. *History of Colorado*, V. 3. Chicago: Blakely, 1891.

Hansen, James E., II. *Democracy's College in the Centennial State: A History of Colorado State University*. Fort Collins: Colorado State University, 1977.

Hauck, Eldon. *American Capitols: An Encyclopedia of the State, National, and Territorial Capital Edifices of the United States.* Jefferson, NC: McFarland, 1991.

Hawthorne, Nathaniel. *The House of the Seven Gables.* New York: Penguin, 1986 [1851].

Hayes, Augustus Allen, Jr. *New Colorado and the Santa Fe Trail.* New York: Harper and Brothers, 1880.

Hitchcock, Henry-Russell, and William Seale. *Temples of Democracy: The State Capitols of the U.S.A.* New York: Harcourt Brace Jovanovich, 1976.

Howbert, Irving. *Memories of a Lifetime in the Pike's Peak Region.* Glorieta, NM: Rio Grande, 1925.

Jessen, Kenneth. *Railroads of Northern Colorado.* Boulder: Pruett, 1982.

Johnson, Charles A. *Denver's Mayor Speer.* Denver: Green Mountain, 1969.

Jones, William C., and Kenton Forrest. *Denver: A Pictorial History.* Boulder: Pruett, 1973.

Kelsey, Harry E., Jr. *Frontier Capitalist: The Life of John Evans.* Boulder: Pruett, 1969.

King, Ross. *Brunelleschi's Dome: How a Renaissance Genius Reinvented Architecture.* New York: Penguin, 2000.

Kreck, Dick. *Denver in Flames: Forging a New Mile High City.* Golden, CO: Fulcrum, 2000.

Kruft, Hanno-Walter. *A History of Architectural Theory From Vitruvius to the Present.* Trans. Ronald Taylor, Elsie Callander, and Anthony Wood. New York: Princeton Architectural Press, 1994.

Lamar, Howard R. *The Far Southwest, 1846–1912: A Territorial History.* Albuquerque: University of New Mexico Press, 2000 [1966].

Lamm, Richard D., and Duane A. Smith. *Pioneers and Politicians: 10 Colorado Governors in Profile.* Boulder: Pruett, 1984.

Leonard, Stephen J. *Trials and Triumph: A Colorado Portrait of the Great Depression, With FSA Photographs.* Niwot: University Press of Colorado, 1993.

Leonard, Stephen J., and Thomas J. Noel. *Denver: Mining Camp to Metropolis.* Niwot: University Press of Colorado, 1990.

Leonard, Stephen J., Thomas J. Noel, and Donald J. Walker Jr. *Honest John Shafroth: A Colorado Reformer.* Denver: Colorado Historical Society, 2003.

Lohse, Joyce B. *First Governor, First Lady: John and Eliza Routt of Colorado.* Palmer Lake, CO: Filter Press, 2002.

Lummis, Charles. *Letters From the Southwest: September 20, 1884 to March 14, 1885.* Ed. James W. Byrkit. Tucson: University of Arizona Press, 1989.

MacMechen, Edgar C., ed. *Robert W. Speer: A City Builder.* Denver: Smith-Brooks, 1919.

Marín, Christine. *A Spokesman of the Mexican American Movement: Rodolfo "Corky" Gonzales and the Fight for Chicano Liberation, 1966–1972.* San Francisco: R and E Research Associates, 1977.

Maroon, Fred J., and Suzy Maroon. *The United States Capitol.* New York: Stewart, Tabori and Chang, 1993.

Martin, Mary, and Gene Martin. *Colorado's Hall of Fame: A Quick Picture History.* Colorado Springs: Little London, 1974.

McCollum, Oscar, Jr. *Marble: A Town Built on Dreams,* V. 2. Denver: Sundance, 1993.

McConnell, Stuart. *Glorious Contentment: The Grand Army of the Republic 1865–1900*. Chapel Hill: University of North Carolina Press, 1992.

Noel, Thomas J. *Buildings of Colorado*. New York: Oxford University Press, 1997.

———. *Denver's Larimer Street: Main Street, Skid Row and Urban Renaissance*. Denver: Historic Denver, 1981.

Noel, Thomas J., Paul F. Mahoney, and Richard E. Stevens. *Historical Atlas of Colorado*. Norman: University of Oklahoma Press, 1994.

Noel, Thomas J., and Barbara S. Norgren. *Denver: The City Beautiful*. Denver: Historic Denver, 1987.

Paine, Thomas. *Common Sense*. London: Penguin, 1986 [1776].

Perkins, James E. *Tom Tobin: Frontiersman*. Pueblo West, CO: Herodotus, 1999.

Pomeroy, Earl S. *The Territories and the United States, 1861–1890: Studies in Colonial Administration*. Seattle: University of Washington Press, 1969 [1947].

Prather, Thomas. *Geology of the Gunnison Country*. Gunnison, CO: B&B, 1982.

Ruland, Sylvia. *The Lion of Redstone*. Boulder: Johnson, 1981.

Seale, William. *Michigan's Capitol: Construction and Restoration*. Ann Arbor: University of Michigan Press, 1995.

Severin, Don. *The Encyclopedia of State Capitols and Capitals: A Detailed Look at the 50 Capitol Buildings and the Capital Cities*. Cove, OR: Mt. Fanny, 1999.

Shannon, David A., ed. *Beatrice Webb's American Diary, 1898*. Madison: University of Wisconsin Press, 1963.

Sloan, Samuel. *Sloan's Constructive Architecture: A Guide to the Practical Builder and Mechanic*. Philadelphia: J. B. Lippincott, 1859.

Smiley, Jerome C., ed. *History of Denver With Outlines of the Earlier History of the Rocky Mountain Country*. Denver: Times-Sun, 1901.

Smith, Jean W., and Elaine C. Walsh. *Queen of the Hill: The Private Life of the Colorado Governor's Mansion*. Denver: A. B. Hirschfeld, 1979.

Sprague, Marshall. *Colorado: A History*. New York: W. W. Norton, 1976.

Stanton, Irving W. *Sixty Years in Colorado: Reminiscences and Reflections of a Pioneer of 1860*. Denver: Publisher unknown, 1922.

Stone, Wilbur Fisk, ed. *History of Colorado*, V. 1. Chicago: S. J. Clarke, 1918.

Straayer, John A. *The Colorado General Assembly*. Niwot: University Press of Colorado, 2000.

Taylor, Quintard. *In Search of the Racial Frontier: African Americans in the American West, 1528–1990*. New York: W. W. Norton, 1998.

Taylor, Ralph C. *Colorado: South of the Border*. Denver: Sage, 1963.

Tucker, E. F. *Otto Mears and the San Juans*. Montrose, CO: Western Reflections, 2003.

Twain, Mark [Samuel L. Clemens]. *Roughing It*. New York: Penguin, 1985 [1872].

Twitchell, Ralph Emerson. *The Leading Facts of New Mexican History*. Cedar Rapids, IA: Torch, 1912.

Ubbelohde, Carl, Maxine Benson, and Duane A. Smith. *A Colorado History*. Boulder: Pruett, 1995 [1965].

Vandenbusche, Duane. *The Gunnison Country*. Gunnison, CO: B&B, Gunnison, 1980.

Vandenbusche, Duane, and Rex Myers. *Marble, Colorado: City of Stone*. Denver: Golden Bell, 1970.

Wagenbach, Lorraine, and Jo Ann Thistlewood. *Golden: The 19th Century*. Littleton, CO: Harbinger House, 1987.

Wahlberg, Edgar M. *Voices in the Darkness: A Memoir*. Boulder: Roberts Rinehart, 1983.

Wermiel, Sara E. *The Fireproof Building: Technology and Public Safety in the Nineteenth-Century American City*. Baltimore: Johns Hopkins University Press, 2000.

West, Elliott. *The Contested Plains: Indians, Goldseekers, and the Rush to Colorado*. Lawrence: University Press of Kansas, 1998.

Wyckoff, William. *Creating Colorado: The Making of a Western American Landscape, 1860–1940*. New Haven: Yale University Press, 1999.

## GOVERNMENT DOCUMENTS

Board of Capitol Managers. Biennial Reports, 1884, 1886, 1888, 1890, 1892, 1894, 1896, 1898, 1900, 1902, 1904, 1906, 1908, 1910, 1912, 1918, 1922, 1924, 1926, 1928 (CSA).

Board of Capitol Managers. Records Books A-H, February 24, 1883–November 11, 1911 (CSA box 32199).

Colorado Reports, April 1881 Term (SCL).

"Colorado State Capitol Life Safety Plan." Department of Administration, Capitol Complex Division, September 1990 (LL).

Colorado State Constitution, 1876 (CSA).

Enabling Act of Colorado, 1875 (CSA).

"Legislative and State House Blue Book of Colorado." Denver: Carson-Harper and W. H. Lawrence, 1899 (SCL).

"Memorials and Art in and Around the Colorado State Capitol: History of Memorials and Art in and Around the Capitol, in the Legislative Services Building, and in Lincoln Park." Colorado Legislative Council, June 1992 (LL).

"Presidents and Speakers of the Colorado General Assembly: A Biographical Portrait From 1876." Colorado Legislative Council. Denver: Eastwood, 1980 (LL).

Report of the Committee on Building Stone to the Board of Capitol Managers, July 3, 1884 (CSA box 32199).

Session Laws of Colorado. Colorado General Assembly, 1881, 1883, 1885, 1889, 1893, 1895, 1897, 1899, 1901, 1905, 1907, 1909, 1911, 1913, 1917, 1919, 1921, 1923, 1925, 1927, 1929, 1931, 1933, 1937, 1944, 1952, 1955, 1960–1961, 1966–1977, 1979, 1983–1986, 1990–2000, 2002 (LL).

"The Stained Glass Windows of the Colorado State Senate Chamber." State Capitol Building Advisory Committee, 2000 (LL).

"State Capitol Building Advisory Committee: Report to the Colorado General Assembly." Colorado Legislative Council, Research Publication 454, August 1999 (LL).

"State Capitol Building Advisory Committee, 1991–1998: Statutory Authority, Guidelines and Recommendations." Colorado Legislative Council, Research Publication 453, March 1999 (LL).

"State Capitol Building Health and Life Safety Project: Report to the Colorado General Assembly." Colorado Legislative Council, Research Publication 410, December 1995 (LL).

"State of Colorado House and Senate Antechamber Accessibility Conceptual Design Report." Department of Administration, Capitol Complex Division, September 23, 1993 (LL).

Superintendent of Public Buildings. Biennial Reports, 1934, 1936, 1940 (CSA boxes 32215, 32218, 32219).

Territorial Laws of Colorado. Colorado Territorial Assembly, 1861, 1862, 1867, 1872, 1874 (ISC).

United States Geological Survey Bulletin 540. Washington, DC: General Printing Office, 1914 (LJS).

United States Reports, October 1882 Term (SCL).

United States Reports, October 1885 Term (SCL).

U.S. Serial Set. U.S. Congress, 1860, 1870, 1872. Vols. 1027, 1436, 1526 (DWM).


## NEWSPAPERS AND PERIODICALS

*Boulder Daily Camera*
*Capitol Reporter* [Metropolitan State College of Colorado]
*Colorado History Now* [Colorado Historical Society]
*Denver Post*
*Denver Republican*
*Denver Times*
*Denver Tribune*
*Fort Collins Coloradoan*
*Fort Collins Express*
*Georgetown Courier*
*Golden Transcript*
*Grand Junction Daily Sentinel*
*Gunnison News*
*Gunnison News-Champion*
*Gunnison Review-Press*
*Gunnison Tribune*
*Harper's Weekly*
*Larimer County Express*
*Longmont Times*
*Marble City Times*
*New York Times*
*Out Front* [Denver]
*Pueblo Chieftain*
*Rocky Mountain Collegian* [Colorado State University]
*Rocky Mountain News* [Denver]
*Silver Standard* [Silver Plume]
*Stateline* [Colorado state government]
*Weekly Commonwealth* [Golden]
*Westword* [Denver]

## THESES AND UNPUBLISHED PAPERS

Barlow, Kelly. "A Legacy of Controversy: Public Opinion and the Sand Creek Massacre." HY 511 historiographical essay, Colorado State University, December 2002.

Everett, Derek R. "The Admiration of Future Ages: Colorado's State Capitol." M.A. thesis, Colorado State University, May 2003.

———. "The Admiration of Future Ages: The Story of the Colorado State Capitol." Western Honors Program thesis, Western State College of Colorado, May 2001.

Hopkins, Lew. "The Old Schoolhouse and Mount Yale: As Portrayed in Ralph Oberg's Painting in the House of Representatives." Denver: December 2001.

Moffett, Clarice Eleanore. "History of Colorado's Capitals and Capitols." M.A. thesis, University of Denver, 1936.

Prochaska, William C. "Colorado City, Colorado, 1859–1870." M.A. thesis, Western State College of Colorado, 1980.

Pyle, William R. "History of the Colorado State Capitol Complex." M.A. thesis, University of Denver, 1962.

Rand, Cynthia. "AIDS and the Denver Gay Community." HY 610 research paper, Colorado State University, May 2002.

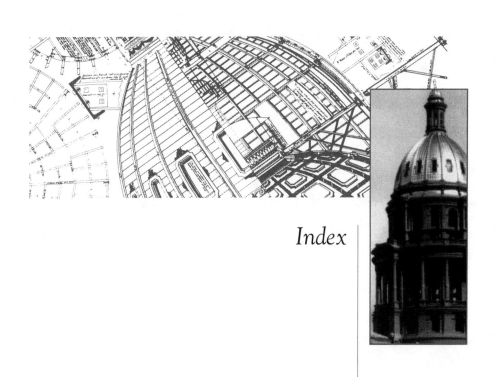

# Index

233